Contemporary Film Theory

LONGMAN CRITICAL READERS

General Editor:

STAN SMITH, Professor of English, University of Dundee

Published titles:

K.M. NEWTON, *George Eliot*

MARY EAGLETON, *Feminist Literary Criticism*

GARY WALLER, *Shakespeare's Comedies*

JOHN DRAKAKIS, *Shakespearean Tragedy*

RICHARD WILSON AND RICHARD DUTTON, *New Historicism and Renaissance Drama*

PETER BROOKER, *Modernism/Postmodernism*

PETER WIDDOWSON, *D. H. Lawrence*

RACHEL BOWLBY, *Virginia Woolf*

FRANCIS MULHERN, *Contemporary Marxist Literary Criticism*

ANNABEL PATTERSON, *John Milton*

CYNTHIA CHASE, *Romanticism*

MICHAEL O'NEILL, *Shelley*

STEPHANIE TRIGG, *Medieval English Poetry*

ANTONY EASTHOPE, *Contemporary Film Theory*

TERRY EAGLETON, *Ideology*

CONTEMPORARY FILM THEORY

Edited and Introduced by

ANTONY EASTHOPE

LONGMAN
LONDON AND NEW YORK

Addison Wesley Longman Limited,
Edinburgh Gate,
Harlow, Essex CM20 2JE, England
and Associated Companies throughout the world.

*Published in the United States of America
by Addison Wesley Longman Inc., New York*

© Longman Group UK Limited 1993

First published 1993
Fourth impression 1996

ISBN 0-582-09031-8 csd
ISBN 0-582-09032-6 ppr

British Library Cataloguing-in-Publication Data

A catalogue record for this book is
available from the British Library

Library of Congress Cataloging-in-Publication Data

Contemporary film theory/edited and introduced by Antony Easthope.
    p. cm.–(Longman critical readers)
  Includes bibliographical references and index.
  ISBN 0-582-09031-8. ISBN 0-582-09032-6 (pbk.)
  1. Motion pictures–Philosophy. I. Easthope, Antony.
  II. Series.
PN1995.C634 1993
791.43'01-dc20
                                                      93-22884
                                                      CIP

Set in 9/11.5 Palatino by 14K
Produced by Longman Singapore Publishers (Pte) Ltd.
Printed in Singapore

Contents

General Editors' Preface

The outlines of contemporary critical theory are now often taught as a standard feature of a degree in literary studies. The development of particular theories has seen a thorough transformation of literary criticism. For example, Marxist and Foucauldian theories have revolutionised Shakespeare studies, and 'deconstruction' has led to a complete reassessment of Romantic poetry. Feminist criticism has left scarcely any period of literature unaffected by its searching critiques. Teachers of literary studies can no longer fall back on a standardised, received, methodology.

Lecturers and teachers are now urgently looking for guidance in a rapidly changing critical environment. They need help in understanding the latest revisions in literary theory, and especially in grasping the practical effects of the new theories in the form of theoretically sensitised new readings. A number of volumes in the series anthologise important essays on particular theories. However, in order to grasp the full implications and possible uses of particular theories it is essential to see them put to work. This series provides substantial volumes of new readings, presented in an accessible form and with a significant amount of editorial guidance.

Each volume includes a substantial introduction which explores the theoretical issues and conflicts embodied in the essays selected and locates areas of disagreement between positions. The pluralism of theories has to be put on the agenda of literary studies. We can no longer pretend that we all tacitly accept the same practices in literary studies. Neither is a *laissez–faire* attitude any longer tenable. Literature departments need to go beyond the mere toleration of theoretical differences: it is not enough merely to agree to differ; they need actually to 'stage' the differences openly. The volumes in this series all attempt to dramatise the differences, not necessarily with a view to resolving them but in order to foreground the choices presented by different theories or to argue for a particular route through the impasses the differences present.

The theory 'revolution' has had real effects. It has loosened the grip of traditional empiricist and romantic assumptions about language and literature. It is not always clear what is being proposed as the new agenda for literary studies, and indeed the very notion of 'literature' is questioned by the post-structuralist strain in theory. However, the uncertainties and obscurities of contemporary theories appear much less worrying when we see what the best critics have been able to do with them in practice. This series aims to disseminate the best of recent criticism and to show that it is possible to re-read the canonical texts of literature in new and challenging ways.

RAMAN SELDEN AND STAN SMITH

The Publishers and fellow Series Editor regret to record that Raman Selden died after a short illness in May 1991 at the age of fifty-three. Ray Selden was a fine scholar and a lovely man. All those he has worked with will remember him with much affection and respect.

Acknowledgements

We are grateful to the following for permission to reproduce copyright material:

British Film Institute for the essay 'Double Indemnity' by Claire Johnston from *Women in Film Noir* edited by E. Ann Kaplan (BFI Publishing 1978, revised edition 1980); the author, Elizabeth Cowie for extracts from her article 'Fantasia' from the journal *m/f* no 9 (1984), reprinted in *The Woman in Question* edited by P. Adams and E. Cowie (MIT/Verso, 1990) and in *To Represent Woman* by Elizabeth Cowie (Macmillan Ltd); The Hogarth Press, an imprint of Random Century Group Ltd., The Institute of Psycho-Analysis and Basic Books, a division of HarperCollins Publishers, Inc., for the essay 'Fetishism' by Sigmund Freud from *The Standard Edition of the Complete Psychological Works of Sigmund Freud*, Volume 21, translated and edited by James Strachey (Hogarth Press Ltd), US title *The Collected Papers of Sigmund Freud*, Vol V, edited by James Strachey (Basic Books, Inc., by arrangement with the Hogarth Press Ltd and the Institute of Psycho-Analysis, London); Macmillan Education Ltd for an extract from the essay 'Narrative Space' from *Questions of Cinema* by Stephen Heath (1981); Macmillan Education Ltd and the author, Laura Mulvey, for the essays 'Visual Pleasure and Narrative Cinema' and 'Afterthoughts on "Visual Pleasure and Narrative Cinema" inspired by King Vidor's *Duel in the Sun* 1946' from *Visual and Other Pleasures* by Laura Mulvey (1989); Macmillan Press Ltd, Indiana University Press and the author, Mary Ann Doane for an extract from *Desire to Desire: The Woman's Film of the 1940's* (1988), © Mary Ann Doane 1988; Manchester University Press for extracts from the essay 'Realism and the cinema: Notes on some Brechtian Theses' from *Theoretical Essays: Film, Linguistics, Literature* by Colin MacCabe (1985); Routledge, a division of Routledge, Chapman and Hall Ltd, and W. W. Norton and Company, Inc., for the essay 'The Mirror Stage' from *Ecrits: A Selection* by Jacques Lacan, translated by Alan Sheridan (Tavistock Publications Ltd 1977), copyright © by Tavistock Publications Ltd; Routledge, a division of Routledge, Chapman and Hall, Inc., and the author, Fredric Jameson for extracts from the essay 'Class and Allegory in Contemporary Mass Culture: *Dog Day Afternoon* as a Political Film' from *Signatures of the Visible* (1990); the editors of the journal *Screen* and the authors, Michael Westlake and Rob Lapsley for the article 'From "Casablanca" to "Pretty Woman": The Politics of Romance' from *Screen* March 1991; the editors of the journal

Screen and Editions de L'Etoile for the article 'Cinema/Ideology/Criticism' by Jean-Louis Comolli and Jean Narboni, translated by Susan Bennett from *Screen Reader 1: Cinema/Ideology/Politics* (1977), originally published as 'Cinema/Ideologie/Critique' in the journal *Les Cahiers du Cinema* no **216**, October 1969.

Introduction

Every version of contemporary theory has begun by breaking with the naturalist attitude. Naturalism in this sense is the assumption, stretching back to Plato's belief that the real world was a copy of a world of ideal forms, that texts try to imitate reality and may be judged in terms of how well or badly they succeed in reproducing it. Though it is not surprising we should still be arguing about the relation between, say, scientific texts and reality,[1] it is – or should be – strange to find the naturalist attitude applied to artistic texts which are avowedly fictional and to that extent do not claim to give a picture of reality, either true or false.

Beginning with the publication in 1953 of *Writing Degree Zero*, the work of the French literary critic, Roland Barthes, is a sustained attempt to show that realism in literature is achieved not by copying something outside or prior to the literary text but rather by writing in a way which gives 'the effect of the real'.[2] But that same battle had to be fought in each different field – for example, in art history. The doctrine that painting was an 'Essential Copy' of reality extends as far back as the ancient writer Pliny, who said Zeuxis had painted grapes so life-like birds tried to eat them. In 1983 in *Vision and Painting* Norman Bryson was able to confute the traditional attitude by showing that even the most life-like visual representation in the Western Renaissance or **Quattrocento*** style (which tries to render three dimensions in two) could do no more than give 'the effect of the real'.[3] In the area of film theory the break with the naturalist fallacy was made in the 1970s.

Before then there was what we may call classic film theory. Theory and practice never advance independently but always hand in hand, and so it was with theoretical discussion of film. In the 1930s, writing by Rudolf Arnheim, Sergei Eisenstein and others theorised film very much in a way appropriate to the great classics of the silent cinema. A second wave, linked particularly to the work of André Bazin and Siegfried Kracauer, was produced by people who were thinking about 'talking

---

*Terms in **bold** type are explained in the glossary at the end of the book.

pictures' as they developed in Europe and America in the decades between 1930 and 1960. Correspondingly, the new theory came about in conjunction with work of the so-called 'New Wave' directors who began to make films in France from 1960. In Godard's film of 1967, *The Wind from the East*, a subtitle states 'CE N'EST PAS UNE JUSTE IMAGE' ('This is not a true image') followed by 'C'EST JUSTE UNE IMAGE' ('This is just an image'). Such filmic practice led to a breach with the naturalist fallacy at the level of theory. And, arguably, what defines classic film theory was its belief that cinema copies the world we perceive.

Classic film theory

After visiting the first photographic Exhibition in Paris in 1859 the poet Charles Baudelaire complained as follows:

> On the question of painting and sculpture the present *credo* of fashionable people, particularly in France (I don't believe anyone dare claim otherwise) is this: 'I believe in nature and I believe only in nature (there are good reasons for that). I believe art is and can only be the exact reproduction of nature (a timid dissenting sect wants certain disgusting natural objects such as the chamber pot and the skeleton excluded). So an industrial process which could give us a result identical to nature would be the perfect form of art.' A vengeful God has granted the wishes of this multitude. Daguerre was his Messiah.[4] And now they say: 'Since photography gives us every desirable guarantee of exactitude (the fools believe that!), then art *is* photography.'[5]

For all its cantankerous and exaggerated terms Baudelaire's assertion perfectly anticipates the difficulty film theory laboured under for so long, that film works by reproducing the real.

Support for this assumption can be found in the philosophic writings of C. S. Peirce (1839–1914).[6] Defining a sign as something that stands for something, Peirce discriminates three kinds of relation that may hold between a sign and the object it represents: **iconic, indexical, symbolic**. In an iconic relation the sign resembles what it stands for (a diagram is similar to or like what it shows); indexically the sign may have a causal relation to its object (smoke is the sign of a fire); and in a symbol the relation between sign and object is purely arbitrary (language in particular is symbolic – there is no natural connection between, say, the word 'tree' and a tree growing in someone's garden). As Peirce pointed out, a photograph has both an iconic and an indexical relation to what it represents. For it resembles its object but (unlike painting) it is also caused by its object since it is actually produced by the impact of light-rays reflected from the object striking light-sensitive film.

Since cinema originates in photography it also obviously counts as bearing an iconic and indexical relation to reality. This is the commonsense understanding classic film theory tried but failed to free itself from. Accordingly, such theory falls into two categories. There are the **creationists** or **formalists** (including Rudolf Arnheim, Sergei Eisenstein, V.I. Pudovkin, and Béla Balázs), who defend cinema as an art form which goes beyond realism; then there are the **realists**, especially André Bazin and Siegfried Kracauer, who celebrate cinema specifically because it sticks so close to the real.

Rudolf Arnheim's *Film*, first published in 1933, well typifies the formalist position, for its aim is 'to refute the assertion that film is nothing but the feeble mechanical reproduction of real life'.[7] This Arnheim does first by denial and then by assertion. Negatively, he advances a series of instances showing how film effects a different kind of experience from what we perceive empirically in the everyday. Such perception gives us a three-dimensional world. Cinema, in contrast, tends to reduce this into a two-dimensional effect: we see the world in colour, film is black and white (or was then); the edges of the screen delimit cinematic vision, everyday vision is potentially limitless; in everyday perception space–time is continuous, while in the cinema it is ordered through shots and editing; cinema is silent (at this date); and of course it gives no equivalent to the sense of smell.

In all these respects cinema fails to match perception, though by the same token it introduces a positive relation between camera and the world set before it (the **profilmic**) which can be used expressively and artistically to *make* film. Arnheim illustrates the multiple ways film can construct a signifying effect, including: the use of camera angles (level, low angle, high angle, etc.); depth of focus giving juxtapositions within the frame; all kinds of lighting effects; framing (e.g. close-up); camera mobility (towards, away from, alongside the profilmic); altered motion (slow, accelerated, the still, reverse); means for editing shots together including the fade and superimposition; special lenses and special focus (e.g. soft focus).

And this account does not yet comprehend the feature which Eisenstein points to when he says that in a film 'each sequential element is perceived not *next* to the other, but on *top* of the other'.[8] Separate shots edited together on the basis of juxtaposition (contrast, repetition, similarity, and so on) can yield meanings over and above any simple notion that one follows the other. Arnheim's argument picks the work of the Soviet directors in theorising the possibilities of such *montage* to confirm his affirmation of the potential artistic creativeness of film.

Though undoubtedly contributing to our understanding of the

expressive resources of film, none of this eradicates what Arnheim acknowledges when he says the film director is influenced 'by the strong resemblance of his (sic) photographic material to reality'.[9] Other theorists, and notably André Bazin, make that resemblance the central virtue of the medium.

The position outlined in Bazin's essays is hardly mistakable:

> The realism of the cinema follows directly from its photographic nature. Not only does some marvel or some fantastic thing on the screen not undermine the reality of the image, on the contrary it is its most valid justification. Illusion in the cinema is not based as it is in the theatre on convention tacitly accepted by the general public; rather, contrariwise, it is based on the inalienable realism of that which is shown.[10]

> This production by automatic means has radically affected our psychology of the image. The objective nature of photography confers on it a quality of credibility absent from all other picture-making. In spite of any objections our critical spirit may offer, we are forced to accept as real the existence of the object reproduced, actually re-presented, set before us, that is to say, in time and space. Photography enjoys a certain advantage in virtue of this transference of reality from the thing to its reproduction.[11]

> I will distinguish, in the cinema between 1920 and 1940, between two broad and opposing trends: those directors who put their faith in the image and those who put their faith in reality. By 'image' I here mean, very broadly speaking, everything that the representation on the screen adds to the object there represented.[12]

It would, however, be an error to conclude that Bazin thinks cinema copies or reproduces reality as though through a transparent pane of glass. Rather, it is the indexical feature of the photographic image which he stresses – not so much that cinema resembles reality iconically but that, as he writes, it 're-presents' it so that 'the photographic image is the object itself'.[13]

It would also be a mistake not to recognise the evaluative scheme leading Bazin to wish to equate the image with its profilmic reality.[14] He is working with a set of binary oppositions which may be summarised as:

> illusion/nature
> imposition/discovery
> single interpretation/ambiguity
> personal/impersonal
> theatre/cinema
> montage/deep focus and the long take

For Bazin such oppositions map onto – and are provoked by – the contrast between silent cinema, especially in the Soviet tradition, and the films of Jean Renoir and of Italian Neo-Realism. Realism, as Bazin conceives it, is valued because it allows the spectator to be active rather than passive.

Even so, it should be clear that formalist theory (Arnheim) and realist theory (Bazin) differ only because they share a common assumption. Formalist theory values cinema to the extent that it is, in Arnheim's phrase, more than 'the feeble mechanical reproduction of real life': realist theory values cinema to the extent that it adheres to 'a mechanical reproduction in the making of which man plays no part' (the phrase is Bazin's).[15] Both assume that cinema, based as it is in photography, must be judged as in part a mechanical reproduction, whether feeble or convincing.[16] For both approaches the iconic and indexical relation between the film image and the objects it represents entails that a major effect of cinema stands apart from human intervention and resists signification, expression, value. Classic film theory is superseded when this assumption gets overthrown.

Semiotics

A road beyond the naturalist fallacy began to become clear when film theory moved away from models of the visual (cognition, perception and psychology) to theories of language. The most influential account of language, the one that achieved the deepest saturation of contemporary film theory, came from Saussure's *Course in General Linguistics*, first published in 1916.[17]

Before Saussure the study of language had been mainly **diachronic**, directed, that is, at its changing forms across history; Saussure distinguishes his area of concern as **synchronic**, how a language works at a given moment as a rule-governed system. To do this he introduces two further distinctions, between **langue** and **parole**, between **signifier** and **signified**. What anyone utters, their writing or speech, is termed **parole** but the system of a particular language allowing someone to generate a meaningful sentence, according to rules for word-formation and sentence structure, constitutes **langue**.

On this basis Saussure broke with the commonsense notion of 'words' and revived the distinction, known to classical rhetoric, between signifier and signified. While the signifier is made up from the sounds used by a particular language, arranged in a temporal order, the signified consists of the concepts or meanings assigned to any organisation of signifiers. If we hear two people speaking in a language we do not know, we can pick up some of its signifiers but do not have access to the signified meanings that go with them. When signifier and signified are joined together they form a sign.

Signifiers consist only of entirely arbitrary sounds related only to each other in an internally self-consistent system that differs from language to language. It is only through social convention that a string of such sounds (for example a /c/, an /a/ and a /t/) are agreed to mean a certain small furry mammal while an equally arbitrary string (/b/a/t/) can mean a small flying rodent (and something you hit something with). It is very essential to keep in mind that in all this Saussure steps aside from the question of the relation between the verbal sign (a word) and any aspect of reality it may refer to (an actual cat or bat). And it is helpful to recall that words work perfectly well – we know what they mean – even when they could never refer to real objects: dragons for instance.

Saussure predicted that one day there would be *a science that studies the life of signs within society*[18] and named it **semiology** (the term **semiotics** is also used to mean virtually the same thing). He was right, and the implications of the signifier/signified distinction have come to touch many areas of contemporary thought, including film theory.

In 1957 in his path-breaking work, *Mythologies*, the French critic Roland Barthes undertook an analysis of the rapidly developing forms of contemporary popular culture, especially advertising (with its dependence on colour photography), television, cinema. Though these are predominantly visual media Barthes turned for an understanding of them to the work of linguists such as Saussure and Louis Hjelmslev.

At the barber's Barthes reads a copy of *Paris-Match*. On the cover a young black African in French uniform is shown saluting something out of the photograph, presumably the French flag. Barthes suggests that the photograph conceals a hidden meaning which can be revealed if the image is analysed in terms of signifier and signified. Thus the shapes and colours of the flat photographic surface form one set of signifiers which denote a 'literal' meaning (a young man in uniform is saluting). But this sign (signifier plus signified) itself acts as a *new* signifier at another level of meaning with a signified, which Barthes spells out as: '*The French Empire? It's just a fact: look at this good Negro who salutes like one of our own boys*'.[19] Barthes wants to expose the way a familiar visual realism ('This photograph shows what happened on one occasion') covertly installs an ideological meaning (French imperialism).

Developing this account in the early 1960s Barthes introduced the linguistic distinction between denotation and connotation to differentiate between 'literal' representation and its hidden 'symbolic' and ideological meaning. He proposed that while the connotation of a photograph is coded (conforms to a system of rules) its denotation of real objects constitutes a 'message without a code', giving the usual reason that photography reproduces the real directly: 'only the photograph is able to transmit the (literal) information without forming it by means of discontinuous signs and rules of transformation'.[20]

So the problem of realism in photography and the cinema remains unresolved. However, in the mid-60s Christian Metz pursued a rigorous attempt to think through how far cinema could be analysed as itself a language. Though Metz's flexible and developing project was ultimately unsuccessful,[21] it had the consequence of finally pushing film theory beyond the naturalist fallacy.

In film, as in language, the relation between the celluloid strip projected onto a screen, the shaped and patterned visual image, and what that image may represent – a house, a tree, a person – is the relation between signifier and signified. But unlike language that relation is iconic (the image resembles what it represents) and indexical (the image as effect of a photochemical process is caused by what it represents). There is, then, no equivalent in cinema for the arbitrary relation between signifier and signified by which a string of purely abstract phonemes through social convention becomes able to mean a house, a tree or a person.

Yet it does not follow from this that the cinematic image denotes a pure literal meaning untouched by culture and codes, the 'real' as we perceive it. In the first place, human perception of the world is *itself* constructed, not simply given. As the contemporary psychology of perception demonstrates, we learn to perceive reality in the particular ways we do, experiencing what we know rather than what we just see.[22]

And in any case, what we watch on the screen, no matter how firmly it relies on the iconic and indexical methods, is never the real itself but always a reproduction or *re-presentation* of the real. As Metz indicates, by the mere fact that it occurs in a film 'the image of a house does not signify "house", but rather "Here is a house" '.[23] Such representation is the achievement of culture, not nature.[24] To introduce a visual system capable of rendering a recognisable effect of monocular linear perspective took several centuries because the enterprise originated with, is rooted in, and remains inseparable from, ideological conventions and specific cultural practices. Of this Stephen Heath's account of the Quattrocento innovation and 'Narrative Space' (Essay 5) provides brilliant and compelling evidence.

The cinematic image – neither pure nor raw but already processed, constructed – must be thought of as a signifier that stands for something which is absent. The more vividly present the cinematic image appears to make its object, the more it insists that the object is actually lacking, was once there but is there no more – 'made present', as Metz says, 'in the mode of absence'.[25] The more real cinema seems, the more it reminds us of its unreality. So, even before we turn to all those well-known forms of manipulation and construction (the effect of

movement, editing, camera angles and so on) at the seemingly primary
level of photographic realism we encounter the fact that what cinema
represents is always already textualised.

In retrospect it can be seen that when classic film theory treated
cinema as, in part, a mechanical reproduction of reality it conformed to
and reproduced one of the most ancient and insidious binary
oppositions structuring the inheritance of Western culture, that between
speech and writing. As Jacques Derrida has proposed,[26] for over two
millennia writing was regarded as a secondary, mechanical and
artificial derivation from speech, which in contrast was privileged as
primary, living, natural. In speech, thought seems spontaneously
present, able to gain an unmediated apprehension of the world; writing
by contrast appears constructed, inexpressively material. The classic
film theory debate over the 'mechanical' means by which film
reproduces reality imposed the old speech/writing opposition by
supposing that, somehow, there could be human utterance *without*
material and physical intervention at its very basis.

As Norman Bryson points out, painting, so often held up against film
as more humanly expressive, in fact might well be judged the opposite
since it is 'the most material of all the signifying practices'[27], grounded
as it is in the physical materiality of the iconic sign produced through
labour, the body, the chance of the arm and hand. Or one could argue,
with Metz, that theatre is more material than cinema since it depends
more directly on the body and performance, as becomes obvious 'when
a stage actor sneezes' and a ' "real" reality disrupts the reality of the
fiction'.[28] The point is that no one can draw a firm line between the
'human' and 'material' aspects of any form of sign. That cinema's signs
are in part iconic and indexical does not diminish their status as signs.
A shot of a house is a sign ('Here is a house'), not a house. Film is not a
place where reality speaks but is rather a form of writing. And it is
writing all over.

Politics and ideology

Following the classic period, the most important work in film theory
arose from what Stephen Heath refers to as 'the encounter of Marxism
and psychoanalysis on the terrain of semiotics'.[29] All three strands –
semiotics, theories of ideology and of subjectivity – are woven together
in the essays which follow, so that it is hard to recount them here in a
sequential order. Each move is accompanied by a reinterpretation of
older material – after 1968 Marxists interested in cinema re-read Bertolt
Brecht's theatre writings from the 1930s, Althusser's Marxism leads
back to Jacques Lacan and then to Freud. Yet each area of concern,

though in different ways, denies that film should be thought of as a reflection of reality, affirming rather that film is a form of language, an ideological operation, a position offered to the subject.

Just as classic film theory was written with an eye on contemporary film making, so the new theories took off in response to the movies of their time. The 'New Wave' of directors in France who made their first films at the end of the 1950s (Godard, Truffaut, Chabrol and others) revitalised film technique and forced a reassessment (in effect, the discovery) of such classic Hollywood directors as John Ford, Howard Hawks and Alfred Hitchcock. In 1959–60 Resnais's *Hiroshima Mon Amour* came out, as did Truffaut's *Les Quatre Cents Coups* and Godard's *A Bout de Souffle*, while Hollywood marked a radical transformation of genre with Hitchcock's *Psycho*. As the decade progressed cinema became ever more overtly politicised, as was signalled in Godard's move from the individualist anarchism of *Pierrot le Fou* (1965) to the committedly Marxist *Vent d'est* (1970). In 1969 Jean-Louis Comolli and Jean Narboni (Essay 3) can ask, as if for the first time, 'What is a film?', and give the resoundingly confident answer that '*every film is political*'. And so film theory cannot fail to be political as well.

Yet in searching for an avowedly political theory of film, Comolli and Narboni hold onto the insights produced by the semiotics of the preceding ten years; in fact in sympathy with these they affirm that cinema should not be judged as some neutral reproduction of reality for it is 'one of the languages through which the world communicates itself to itself' (Essay 3, p. 46). Too much of classic theory had been contaminated with views and attitudes more pertinent to still photography, or worse, literary and theatrical models. In accord with this the emergent film theory was concerned with the ways in which film was film and not something else.

That principle is strengthened by the work of the French Marxist writer, Louis Althusser, who argues that all forms of social practice, including ideological practice (and so cinema) are relatively autonomous, related to others but each working in its own specific mode.[30] Comolli and Narboni also look back to Brecht who, excited by a similar will to discover a political theory of the theatre, had contrasted the passive position provided for spectators in their consumption of the conventional well-made play with the possibility of radically confrontational drama. Such drama, not just in its narrated themes but through its actual operation as theatre, would make the audience take up an active and critical stance towards their experience of a play and its production.[31] Comolli and Narboni, therefore, turn attention to the effect of different kinds of cinema on the viewer. Through permutation of 'signifier/signified' with 'conservative/radical' they come up with essentially four crude and initial categorisations of film: complicit with dominant ideology both in form and content; radical in both; radical in the operation of the signifier but complicit in ideology; radical in signified meaning but the usual Hollywood in its formal operation.

As the effects of '1968' were followed through at the level of theory, a more subtle discrimination between conventional and radical cinema began to develop. Under the slogan 'L'Imagination au pouvoir' the movement of 1968 tried to make a new society not simply from a sense of obligation but for pleasure, not for justice alone but to realise human potential, to make dreams reality.

Consistent with this belief, attempts to explain the failure of the hopes of 1968 turned to the question of ideology with a renewed interest in psychoanalysis and the notion of the unconscious, especially as theorised by Freud and his French successor, Jacques Lacan. In an essay first published in 1970, 'Ideology and Ideological State Apparatuses', Althusser aimed to understand how contemporary capitalist society reproduced itself so successfully.[32] It depends, he argues, on the reproduction of *people* willing to submit in apparent freedom to the prevailing social hierarchy. This is ensured not just by the threat of force, institutionalised in the police and the army as 'Repressive State Apparatuses', but also by 'Ideological State Apparatuses' (education, the legal system, the family, the media, etc.). What these institutions work on is the subject, taking babies (the merely physical human being) and transforming them into thinking and speaking subjects, able to go off on their own five or six years later and answer individually when the teacher calls their names in school. And this is achieved through a process of **interpellation** – potential subjects are 'hailed' by the institutions and discourses they find themselves within to take up and live into an imaginary identity. That identity is a **misrecognition** but is inescapable since it has the effect of constructing subjects who act and think as having individual identity and choice.

If, as can easily be evidenced, the discourses and practices of post-Renaissance or bourgeois culture circulate around the centrality of the supposedly free-standing and free-thinking individual, then Modernism exemplified a crisis for that sense of individuality. A Modernist cinema, then, would be politically progressive if, in its very textuality, it offered a radical challenge to the seeming autonomy of the viewer, interpellating its subjects in a very different way from what Godard calls 'Nixon-Paramount'.

Politics and subjectivity

While film theory in the Althusserian tradition was certainly attentive to the basic economic forces tending to pull film production into certain modes (Hollywood, the dream factory, trying to ensure production on industrial principles), it also aimed to analyse critically the textual forms taken by conventional realist cinema. As Metz wrote, 'the cinematic institution is not just the cinema industry (which works to fill cinemas, not to empty them), it is also the mental machinery – another industry – which spectators "accustomed to the cinema" have internalised historically and which has adapted them to the consumption of film'.[33]

Especially in Britain, the Althusserian account of how subjects are constituted to think they are free was rapidly generalised into an explicitly political analysis of film. Picking up Brecht's contrast between passive and active spectators and keeping always in mind Godard's own post-1967 movie making, film theory mobilised Althusser's concept of ideological interpellation. It is enlarged as a way to understand, first, how mainstream realist cinema 'hails' its viewer to take up the position it offers, treating the text as natural, obvious, simply *there* to be enjoyed; and to imagine, second, how a film practice might disrupt that position of imaginary security, misrecognised as outside and looking on.

Such film theory was anxious also to co-opt the work in semiotics, to carry through the full implications of a materialism which stressed the materiality of language and the signifier. In this it was aided and encouraged by what linguistics had recently come to offer, especially in regarding the relation between text and reader, addresser and addressee, as these had been led into a marriage with psychoanalysis by Lacan.

While the distinction between signifier and signified serves well for a single term or word, something more is needed to name the process of discourse in which a speaking subject converts a system of language into an act of utterance, and for this Émile Benveniste proposed the opposition between **enunciation** and **enounced**. Enunciation, then, is to enounced as signifier is to signified, or narration to narrated. On this basis Benveniste was prepared to discriminate between discourses marked by signs of enunciation (through such terms as 'I', 'you', 'here', 'now') and others which appear to describe a state of affairs or sequence of events (via 'he', 'she' and 'it'). But to assign discourses to the categories of subjective and objective according to whether explicit marks of personality are present or absent was challenged, first, for linguistics, by Roman Jakobson, and then, more tellingly, by Lacan.

In an essay on shifters (those terms which bear the imprint of a situated addresser), Jakobson contrasts 'the speech act' (*procés de l'énonciation*) with 'the narrated event' (*procés de l'énoncé*): 'four terms are to be distinguished: a narrated event, a speech event, a participant of the narrated event, and a participant of the speech event'.[34] Thus in the utterance, 'She bought a cat yesterday', cat-buying is the narrated event, 'She' is the subject of the enounced (or narrated), enunciation is the act of uttering or listening to the words 'She bought ...' and the speaker or listener is placed as the subject of and for this act of enunciation. Whether a text is marked or unmarked by shifters, there is always a subject for that text, whether it's an objective narrative or first-person discourse. In film one might claim that subjectivity is marked by so-called subjective camera but as the argument over the point-of-view shot illustrates (see Essay 5, pp. 83–8), the viewer is positioned even by the most seemingly documentary objectivity, a conception confirmed by psychoanalysis.

Lacan seizes on Jakobson's categorisation to substantiate his account of subjectivity. For Lacan the human being is provoked into being a subject by a lack or absence (*manque à être*) – a lack we desire to make good by finding plenitude and presence, so imagining ourselves as a full identity. As a speaking human subject I become what I am by internalising the discourses that surround me from birth; but I am split between the apparent fixity of the signified or enounced, and the process of enunciation from which any such fixity derives. Metonymy is the ancient name for the trope which refers to something by an associated term ('the Crown' for 'the Monarchy', for instance), and has come to be used for the way one term seems to be linked to the next in meaningful discourse. In stringing together coherent sentences metonymically I find a stable identity as subject of the enounced but that 'I' is always sliding away from the 'me' subject to the process of enunciation.

In 'The Mirror Stage' (Essay 2) Lacan exemplifies how the 'I' is developed from the reaction, specific to the species, of a baby to its image in a mirror.[35] With jubilation the infant greets, assumes, this external effect as though it were itself as it would like to be. For Lacan my identity is an ideal likeness reflected back from everyone else, developing the moment someone may have said, 'Who's a good little boy, then?' My identity is not something I *recognise* because that would suppose I am *already there* able to do the recognising – rather, it is a misrecognition I internalise and, to that extent, become. Identity on this account is an effect of a dialectic between subject and object, its apparent unity and solidity a consequence of the position I live into in coherent discourse.

It is Lacan's conception of the process of self-identification that Althusser relies on in his essay on ideology. And its implication, as taken up by film theory, is that there is always a subject in and for discourse, split between a more or less fixed position in identification with the subject of the enounced and its actual fluidity as subject of enunciation. 'Film', Metz argues, 'is like the mirror' in the mirror stage[36]: the objects on the screen are absent and the spectator, too, is lacking there but imagines presence by identifying with its seemingly ideal plenitude. With a close attention to the specificities of film practice it becomes possible to establish an opposition between those realist texts which afford their viewers (for the time being) a position of relative coherence by denying the operation of the signifier and those potentially more radical films which manifest the signifier, driving the viewer to acknowledge how temporary and provisional is that great bourgeois enactment, His Majesty the Ego.

Accordingly, Colin MacCabe (Essay 4) exploits semiotics and these theories of subjectivity to account for the realist effect in traditional Hollywood film and the classic nineteenth-century novel. What is said in a language – how a language is *used* – can be distinguished from a higher order or **metalanguage** in which that first **object language** might be discussed (so, if a 'Teach Yourself French' book is written in Mandarin Chinese, French is the object language and Mandarin the metalanguage for it).[37] MacCabe argues that the different discourses of a realist text conform to a hierarchic categorisation between object language and metalanguage.

The term **diegesis** has become current to refer to everything represented 'within' a film. In its diegesis the classic realist film sets up what the characters know and say to each other as object language, a limited knowledge, contrasted with what we learn from the image as metalanguage, the whole truth (apparently) about the characters and their world. Corresponding to the empiricist view that knowledge can be obtained directly through experience, realism invites its reader to 'look through' the metalanguage and so 'see' as if directly what is represented in the object language. MacCabe's analysis of classic realist cinema finds its political context when it argues that the 'classic realist text ensures the position of the subject in a relation of dominant specularity' (Essay 4, p. 58), distancing the viewer so that he or she appears capable of mastering all that the text requires them to know.

'Spaces are born and die like societies' writes Pierre Francastel (cited in Essay 5, p. 70). In 'Narrative Space' Stephen Heath aims to define what is specific to cinema: first, by demonstrating continuity between the representation of space inaugurated by the Quattrocento tradition and modern photography; and, second, by considering how that secure position provided for the viewer (seemingly outside looking in) is threatened by the operation of film as moving pictures, the constant movement – characters across the screen, from one camera angle to the next, from shot to shot, sequence to sequence. His essay argues with close illustration that in the dominant form of cinema (Hollywood realism) 'narrative contains the mobility that could threaten the clarity of vision in a constant renewal of perspective' so that 'space becomes place'. Heath goes against MacCabe in this argument. For while MacCabe suggests that the realist effect in cinema tends to efface the operation of the signifier, Heath argues that we never forget we are watching a film and that the effect is rather to *contain* the signifier, with narration 'held on the narrated, the enunciation on the enounced' (Essay 5, p. 81).

If the mobility of cinema (relative to still photography) necessitates transitions which threaten the viewer's security, those gaps are nevertheless made good, 'achieving a coherence of place and positioning the spectator as the unified and unifying subject of its vision' (p. 77). It did not have to happen that way but in conjunction with the rest of Hollywood practice that is the kind of cinema that came to dominate. Another practice of cinema could operate to deny its subject that coherence, so instating an alternative sense of subjectivity, a different experience (as far as film is concerned) of who we are and how we view.

Whether conceived as MacCabe's exteriorised subject posed in a relation of dominant specularity of Heath's subject, constructed only in terms of the desire for that filmic text, the subject is positioned textually, an implied not actual response. For this reason Fredric Jameson attacks this kind of theorisation on the grounds that it 'brackets the historical situations in which texts are effective' and insists on ideological positions identified by 'purely formal features'.[38] His own essay arising from *Dog Day Afternoon* (Essay 6) therefore interrogates the work of MacCabe and Heath though he shares with them the perception that the filmic text works to make good its own contradictions.

In *A Theory of Literary Production* Pierre Macherey asserts that the aesthetic text can never achieve the completeness and unity it affirms. Always divided against itself, the text exhibits its historical significance in the contradictions, gaps and fissures over which and from which it aims to construct a coherent meaning, especially as narrative.[39] Accepting with Hayden White[40] that for human beings history is only representable as narrative, Jameson asserts that Marxism provides the only possible Great Narrative. If the realities of our historical situation are determined by multinational capitalism, these, in a film, will become visible only in the margins and interstices of what the text tries to say. The attempt to represent the unrepresentable – one which becomes more crucially obstructed by the pervasive commodification of all aesthetic values with postmodernity – can be grasped only through an allegorical reading, such as that which Jameson deploys in persuasive detail for the analysis of *Dog Day Afternoon*.

Politics and gender

But 'the cinematic institution ... is also the mental machinery – another industry – which spectators "accustomed to the cinema" have internalised historically', as Metz says. Film, then, provides pleasure not only at the level of theme by dramatising a narrative but also through the very experience of sitting in the dark to watch moving pictures projected on a screen, a kind of voyeurism. Freud suggests that in one form unconscious drives become deflected into **scopophilia**, a word used to translate the German *Schaulust* or visual pleasure. Beginning in the child's sexual curiosity and innocent voyeurism ('you show me yours and I'll show you mine') scopophilia later becomes linked more definitively with narcissism and a drive for mastery (*Bemächtigungstrieb*). In an adult this could lead to a desire for cinema.[41] On this account, one reason we enjoy film (and perhaps books of film theory) is because you, gentle reader, and I are scopophiliacs who find pleasure in visual representation and in thinking about it.

Freud's extraordinary essay on **fetishism** (Essay 1) – extraordinary, that is, for those unfamiliar with psychoanalysis – inserts the question of gender and sexuality by hardly acknowledging its own assumption that fetishism is particularly masculine. It would explain the disorder in terms of an object set up as substitute for what is imagined to be lacking – a psychic mechanism in which the reality of the fetishised object is known but *disavowed*. For film theory it is crucial that the unfortunate young man of Freud's account takes as a fetish not just the *shine* on the nose but the *glance* at the nose, so fetishising the look itself. Through high-definition photography, recently with colour added, and typically via a fictional narrative, cinema seems able to make real, present and substantial what is known to be absent, missing.

But if fetishism weighs peculiarly on men, is the pleasure of scopophilia merely neutral between men and women? Is the mastery Freud indicates as accompanying that pleasure specially masculinised (as the choice of term suggests) or not? Pursuing these questions, Juliet Mitchell in *Psychoanalysis and Feminism*[42] drew fresh attention to Freud's 1931 account of female sexuality. Since both little girls and little boys are equally active in seeking the figure of the mother during the pre-Oedipal phallic stage, what needs to be explained, Mitchell suggests, is how women's activity and drive may be turned towards a passive aim, unconsciously internalising patriarchy. In view of cinema's dependence on active scopophilia and mastery, it is a pressing question for film theory to ask, with Ann Kaplan, 'Is the gaze male?' (cited in Essay, 11, p. 166).

Laura Mulvey (Essay 7) analyses the reproduction of sexual

imbalance by a visual regime which extends well beyond Hollywood (into magazine photography and advertising, for instance). This regime works through the superimposition of a series of binaries: narcissism/desire; looking/being looked at; active/passive; masculine/feminine. In the dominant cinema men are invited to identify with a male protagonist in looking at and desiring women as objects, while women are to identify with the female figures passively looked at. Women's own desire – and identification with an active figure – become effaced.

'So many times over the years since my "Visual Pleasure and Narrative Cinema" article was published in *Screen*, I have been asked why I only used the *male* third person singular to stand in for the spectator' (Mulvey, Essay 8, p. 125): in answering that question Mulvey brings forward Freud's well-known comment in *Three Essays on the Theory of Sexuality* which denies that sexuality is simply '*biological*' or '*sociological*' (defined neither by the body or by social roles), proposing instead that 'masculine' and 'feminine' are equal attributes of a single subject, equivalent to 'active' and 'passive'.[43] Drawing on this, as well as on Freud's repeated assertion that the human species is constitutionally bisexual in its aims, and noting 'the problems inevitably activated by any attempt to represent the feminine in patriarchal society' (p. 133), Mulvey suggests that the masculinised position offered to the female spectator may reactivate from an early stage a memory of her own 'fantasy of "action" '.

'Visual Pleasure and Narrative Cinema' is outstanding as a single essay which has fostered a small library of subsequent writing. Endorsing Mulvey's analysis of the way cinema offers gendered positions for the spectator's identification, Claire Johnston (Essay 9) explores in detail the contradictions undermining patriarchy in a famous example of *film noir, Double Indemnity*. For Lacan I do not exist outside the sum of identities available from the Other and the Symbolic Order of a given historical society (if, for example, I had been born and lived in Nanking I would have much the same body but a very different identity). But no matter where I'm born I am set the task of winning a coherent identity (which Lacan names as Imaginary) from the discourses and signifiers of the Symbolic Order which precedes and pre-exists me. Lack in the subject is instituted by the Symbolic Order, though under patriarchy such Law is imposed in the Name of the Father, by the disclosure that the Father is a signifier, a name, not a full presence. Johnston puts this theorisation to work in exposing the troubled fashion in which *Double Indemnity* contrives to hold in place conventional definitions of masculine and feminine.

Identification, then, is obviously not a simple binary matter of female spectators identifying with women on the screen, male with men.

Crossing boundaries of gender, identification includes identification with animals (the sheepdog in *Lassie* films), with objects (including landscapes), with narration as opposed to space, as Teresa de Lauretis has argued.[44] And such identifications are comprehended, complexly, within the spectators' identification with themselves as those who enjoy cinema, a particular genre,[45] a particular kind of film. On this basis Elizabeth Cowie (Essay 10) challenges the assumption (implicitly regarded as Mulvey's) that there can be any fixity in the identifications found in such performances. Rather, she argues that 'the sliding of positions is unstoppable', that whatever elaboration a narrative undertakes to close this off, even in the most conventional-seeming film 'subject-positions are variable'.

'Is the gaze male?' That question, first posed inescapably for film theory by Laura Mulvey, has stimulated different efforts to theorise the female spectator for cinema, including Mulvey's own answer in terms of bisexual potentiality, Johnston's more modest demonstration of what exceeds the male gaze, Cowie's argument for multiple positioning. In the 'Introduction' (see Essay 11) to *The Desire to Desire*, a book which ought to be read in its entirety, Mary Ann Doane sums up the 'sometimes confusing array of concepts' which have been mobilised 'to think the relation between female spectator and screen' (p. 167) and concludes that there are 'seemingly insurmountable difficulties in conceptualising the female gaze' (p. 169). It may be that in seeking to define an alternative and authentic female gaze, film theory has been looking for an essence, a given, corresponding in its autonomy and identity to what is supposed as the male gaze. But that would be an unavailing quest since the female spectator 'exists nowhere but as an effect of discourse' (p. 170).[46] Doane suggests that the female gaze may operate aside from the structures of voyeurism and fetishism, structures assuming exteriority and distance in the desire to look, may work through overidentification and a desire to desire. This at least would be more like the effect inscribed by 'the woman's film of the 1940's', her chosen topic for analysis.

If Doane is right that there remains 'an apparent blockage at the level of theory' in understanding the female gaze, the essay by Rob Lapsley and Michael Westlake (Essay 12) runs aslant to the debate initiated with Mulvey and so may open new questions by seeking not so much for a radically alternative position for the viewer but by pushing forward an account of already existing cinema. When Lacan writes that 'in the case of the speaking being the relation between the sexes does not take place',[47] he is not missing the fact that the human species reproduces itself without difficulty. He is concerned to challenge an ideology descending to us from Courtly Love and the Troubadours – the belief that the sexual couple reflect each other in a perfect dyad, so that, as in

'The Good-Morrow' by John Donne, 'My face in thine eye, thine in mine appears'.

It is predictable that Hollywood, in seeking to provide visual plenitude, should complement it with the imagined plenitude of Romantic love. Such love is impossible, Lapsley and Westlake argue, on four grounds. Since identity is constituted by misrecognition, I can never do more than imagine I am reflected in an 'Ideal point' from which 'the Other sees me, in the form I like to be seen'.[48] Since my identification with myself as subject of the enounced depends upon the process of enunciation, my identity is always vanishing in front of me down the sentences as I speak – I am never *there* to love. At a primary level, the plenitude I desire (*La Chose*) is itself made by lack, a constitutive lack no seeming plenitude can ever fully exclude. And fourth, Romantic love is demonstrably a historical construction with no reality outside a particular culture.

Yet mainstream cinema (Godard represents an exception here) has developed various strategies to efface the lack at the heart of love – eradication of the Other, idealisation of a woman as The Woman, fulfilment deferred. A main effect of Hollywood narrativisation is to put off Romantic happiness to some other future, or place it irrevocably in the past, or translate it into a conditional mode ('if only …'). Even the Oedipus complex, Lapsley and Westlake consider, may be only Romantic love at its deepest level of misrecognition. And they hint but do not declare concurrence with Rainer Fassbinder when he wrote, in connection with the films of Douglas Sirk, that for both men and women 'love is the best, most insidious, most effective instrument of social repression'.[49]

Although Lapsley and Westlake refer to Mulvey, they resist the temptation to bring together their analysis of the absence of the sexual relation with her account of the visual regime which instates 'Woman as Image, Man as Bearer of the Look'. Narrative in film enables the lovers' acts of looking at the other to alternate, giving a strong effect of reciprocity. But a painting, such as Titian's *Venus of Urbino* (1538), registers the actual asymmetry of the relation: her potentially adoring gaze can only reflect the spectator (implicitly male) as he would wish, on condition that her own active look and desire are rendered, very literally, impossible (she is in a painting).

Although a position is implied by the selection of these essays and extracts rather than others, and also in the summary remarks on each, I have tried deliberately to refrain from criticism and comment. I shall end this 'Introduction' with three conclusions.

Supersession of the naturalist fallacy is the foundation on which contemporary film theory is constructed. Accepting that film is not nature but culture, not a reproduction of the real but a sign, film theory since 1968 has made available for critical discussion not just the manifestly creative aspects of cinema but everything that happens when you enjoy a movie. Claire Johnston's analysis of *Double Indemnity*, for example, gains purchase on every aspect of the text, including those in which the willed project of the narrative shows how the text differs from itself. While classic theory, working with an opposition between reality and construction, always ignored certain features of a film as being outside discussion, the new theory does not. At the end of his 'Concluding Statement' to the *Style in Language* conference of 1958, Roman Jakobson told the story of a tribe reproached by missionaries for not wearing clothes. But, they said, you wear no clothes on your face, and we are face all over.[50] The aesthetic text, including film, signifies all over, and film theory achieves maturity when it can respond adequately to that challenge.

Although different writers adopt different stances, the new theory conforms to some common assumptions. The cinematic text must be grasped in terms of its full semiotic complexity. It is always ideological, operating to dramatise and so promote certain forms of power (whether these relate to gender, class, race, nation). Film is also a form of phantasy, offering meanings and pleasures which need to be understood through some use of psychoanalysis, however sceptical (having deployed a scrupulously psychoanalytic mode, Lapsley and Westlake finish with a cautionary note on the use of psychoanalysis). And film always includes its viewing subject, offering a position to the spectator – one which requires analysis in terms of subjectivity. On this, though, it is important to remember that the implied viewer is not the empirical viewer, the position afforded by the text and described on the basis of the text is not the same as that of any actual film-goer.

The analysis of film in terms of semiotics, theories of ideology, of subjectivity and of gender, as the essays collected testify, does not always lead to the same answers, in some doctrinaire fashion. But these are the questions that need to be posed to the aesthetic text. Contemporary theory has worked them through with exceptional rigour and seriousness. This means it is well in advance of literary criticism, for example, or art history, or any comparable account of aesthetic texts.

I am most grateful to David Rodowick, Kate McGowan and John O. Thompson for helpful comments on this collection. My thanks are due particularly to the staff at Longman for their support. And I would like to say that the idea for this book was first suggested by the late Ray Selden.

I have marked '*sic*' only for the first instance when an essay uses a masculine term to mean men and women.

Notes

1. See THOMAS KUHN, *The Structure of Scientific Revolutions*, 2nd rev. edn (Chicago: Chicago University Press, 1970); and RICHARD RORTY, *Philosophy and the Mirror of Nature* (Oxford: Blackwell, 1980).

2. ROLAND BARTHES, *Writing Degree Zero* (London: Cape, 1967); but see particularly *S/Z* (London: Cape, 1975).

3. NORMAN BRYSON, *Vision and Painting: The Logic of the Gaze* (London: Macmillan, 1983), p. 65.

4. Louis-Jacques-Mandé Daguerre (1789–1851) developed a process for producing a photographic image on copper plate.

5. CHARLES BAUDELAIRE, 'Curiosités esthétiques', *Oeuvres Complètes*, ed. Jacques Crédet (Paris: Louis Conard, 1923), 19 vols, vol. 19, pp. 268–9.

6. PETER WOLLEN drew attention to the relevance of Peirce's work for film theory in *Signs and Meaning in the Cinema* , 3rd edn (London: Secker and Warburg, 1972).

7. RUDOLF ARNHEIM, *Film as Art* (London: Faber, 1958), p. 37. *Film as Art* is effectively a reprint with corrections of *Film* (London: Faber, 1933); for further comments on Arnheim, see HEATH, Essay 5, pp. 78–9.

8. SERGEI EISENSTEIN, *Film Form: Essays in Film Theory* (London: Dennis Dobson, 1963), p. 49.

9. ARNHEIM, op. cit., p. 38. For the argument that all Eisenstein's complexification of editing does nothing to challenge the naturalist fallacy, see COLIN MACCABE, below, pp. 58–62.

10. ANDRÉ BAZIN, *What is Cinema?* (Berkeley: University of California Press, 1967 and 1971), 2 vols, vol. I, p. 108.

11. BAZIN, op. cit., pp. 13–14.

12. BAZIN, op. cit., p. 24.

13. BAZIN, op. cit., p. 14. Bazin's work, in the form of essays, is exploratory as much as it is definitive, and a more qualified view emerges in 'An Aesthetic of Reality', *What is Cinema?*, vol. 2, pp. 16–40.

14. See LAPSLEY and WESTLAKE, *Film Theory: An Introduction* (Manchester: Manchester University Press, 1988), pp. 159–60; this is far and away the best critical introduction to contemporary film theory.

15. BAZIN, op. cit., vol. 1, p. 12.

16. NOEL CARROLL in *Philosophical Problems of Classical Film Theory* (Princeton: Princeton University Press, 1988) argues that the formalist theorists defend film as art in a way that seems 'to accept the premise that if film were mechanical recording, then film would not be art' (p. 26).

17. See FERDINAND DE SAUSSURE, *Course in General Linguistics*, tr. Wade Baskin (New York: Philosophical Library, 1959).

18. Ibid., p. 16 (italics original).

19. Ibid., p. 124.

20. ROLAND BARTHES, 'Rhetoric of the Image' (1964) in *Image-Music-Text*

(London: Fontana/Collins, 1977), p. 43; see also 'The Photographic Message' (1961) in the same volume.

21. Reasons for this are well explained by LAPSLEY and WESTLAKE in *Film Theory: an Introduction*, pp. 38–46.

22. See, for example, RICHARD GREGORY, *Eye and Brain: the Psychology of Seeing*, 3rd edn (London: Weidenfeld and Nicolson, 1977); MAURICE MERLEAU-PONTY adduces solid evidence that animals simply do not experience reality as discrete individual objects which retain the same identity from one situation into another; see *The Structure of Behaviour* (London: Methuen, 1965), pp. 110–28.

23. METZ, *Film Language*, p. 116. So Metz argues that cinema 'can be considered as a *language*, to the extent that it orders signifying elements within ordered arrangements different from those of spoken idioms – and to the extent that these elements are not traced on the perceptual configurations of reality itself (which does not tell stories). Filmic manipulation transforms what might have been a mere visual transfer of reality into discourse' (p. 105).

24. METZ suggests that the cinematic message is subject to rules both in 'perception itself (systems for structuring space, "figures", and "backgrounds", etc.), to the degree that It already constitutes a system of acquired intelligibility, which varies according to different "cultures" ' as well as in 'recognition and identification of visual or auditive objects appearing on the screen – that is to say, the ability (which is also culturally acquired) to manipulate correctly the denoted material of the film', *Film Language: a Semiotics of the Cinema* (New York: Oxford University Press, 1974), p. 62 fn.

25. METZ, *Psychoanalysis and Cinema: The Imaginary Signifier* (London: Macmillan, 1982), p. 44.

26. See JACQUES DERRIDA, *Of Grammatology* (Baltimore: Johns Hopkins University Press, 1976).

27. BRYSON, op. cit., p. 85.

28. METZ, *Film Language*, p. 11. See UMBERTO ECO's brilliant argument that actions performed in the theatre are signs, that even if someone actually ties their shoelaces on stage it is to be taken as a sign of tying shoelaces, 'Semiotics of Theatrical Performance' in *Literature in the Modern World*, ed. Dennis Walder (Oxford: Oxford University Press, 1990), pp. 115–22.

29. STEPHEN HEATH, '*Jaws*, ideology and film theory', *Times Higher Education Supplement*, 26 March 1976, p. 11. Another important strand, which I have not had enough space to represent in this collection, is largely empiricist and based in a cognitive psychology. *The Classical Hollywood Cinema* by DAVID BORDWELL et al. (London: Routledge and Kegan Paul, 1985) represents a sustained and detailed attempt to explain Hollywood's commitment to realism in terms of economic and ideological factors. BORDWELL's *Narration in the Fiction Film* (London: Methuen, 1985) draws upon a form of cognitive psychology to analyse filmic narrative, as does EDWARD BRANIGAN's *Narrative Comprehension and Film* (London and New York: Routledge, 1992). Such accounts address the semiotic system, the rules and codes instanced in a particular text and enabling us to follow it (what JULIA KRISTEVA names as the *phenotext*) while the work of STEPHEN HEATH, COLIN MacCABE, LAURA

MULVEY and others directs itself at the semiotic process acting on the spectator in the experience of a particular film and so to the process of the unconscious in the reading of a text (what Kristeva distinguishes as the *genotext* (see KRISTEVA, 'The System and the Speaking Subject', reprinted in *A Critical and Cultural Theory Reader*, ed. Antony Easthope and Kate McGowan (Buckingham: Open University Press and Toronto: Toronto University Press, 1992), pp. 77–80; also HEATH, Essay 5, pp. 85–6 and 88–90). Limits to the understanding of film via cognitive psychology are acknowledged when EDWARD BRANIGAN in *Narrative Comprehension* writes that 'At the centre of the psychoanalytic method is a search for what is invisible and implicit and what may never be known ... I believe that cognitive psychology, like other reception theories, needs a drive theory' (p. 124).

30. See LOUIS ALTHUSSER, *For Marx* (London: New Left Books, 1977).

31. See *Brecht on Theatre*, ed. John Willett (London: Methuen, 1964).

32. See ALTHUSSER, *Lenin and Philosophy*, 2nd edn (London: New Left Books, 1977).

33. METZ, *Psychoanalysis and Cinema*, p. 7.

34. ROMAN JAKOBSON, 'Shifters, Verbal Categories, and the Russian Verb' in *Word and Language* (The Hague and Paris: Mouton, 1971).

35. See JACQUES LACAN 'The Mirror Stage' in *Écrits: A Selection* (London: Tavistock, 1977), pp. 1–7; and see also Essay 12, pp. 182–3.

36. METZ, *Psychoanalysis and Cinema*, p. 45.

37. For the distinction between object language and metalanguage, see ALFRED TARSKI, 'The Semantic Conception of Truth' in *Readings in Philosophical Analysis*, ed. H. Feigl and W. Sellar (New York: Appleton-Century-Crofts, 1949).

38. JAMESON, *The Political Unconscious* (Ithaca: Cornell University Press, 1981), p. 283.

39. See PIERRE MACHEREY, *A Theory of Literary Production* (London: Routledge and Kegan Paul, 1978).

40. See WHITE, *Metahistory* (Baltimore: Johns Hopkins University Press, 1983); see also JEAN-FRANÇOIS LYOTARD, *The Postmodern Condition* (Manchester: Manchester University Press, 1983) (French, 1979).

41. For an account of the historical importance of the effect of scopophilia, see ANTONY EASTHOPE, *Poetry and Phantasy* (Cambridge: Cambridge University Press, 1989).

42. See MITCHELL, *Psychoanalysis and Feminism* (London: Allen Lane, 1974).

43. SIGMUND FREUD, *Standard Edition* (London: Hogarth Press and the Institute of Psycho-Analysis, 1953–76), 22 vols, 7: 218–19.

44. DE LAURETIS in *Alice Doesn't: Feminism, Semiotics, Cinema* (London: Macmillan and Bloomington: Indiana University Press, 1984) advances a subtle and far-reaching account of how narration and the space such narrative traverses encourage correspondingly masculine and feminine identifications; see also Essay 11, pp. 167–9.

45. See CONSTANCE PENLEY, 'The Avant-garde and its Imaginary' in *The Future of an Illusion: Film, Feminism and Psychoanalysis* (Minneapolis: University of Minnesota Press, 1989), pp. 3–28, for a brilliant account of how, faced with the radical disruptions of an avant-garde film text, the spectators may find an identification with themselves through *epistemophilia*, as one, that is, who can master the difficulties of films of this kind.

46. TORIL MOI has acutely discredited notions of essence which may lie behind the idea of *écriture féminine* as theorised in some of the work of Hélène Cixous and Luce Irigaray; see *Sexual/Textual Politics* (London: Methuen, 1985).

47. LACAN, 'God and the *Jouissance* of The Woman' in *Feminine Sexuality*, ed. Juliet Mitchell and Jacqueline Rose (London: Macmillan, 1982), p. 138.

48. LACAN, *The Four Fundamental Concepts of Psycho-Analysis* (London: Hogarth Press, 1977), p. 268.

49. FASSBINDER, 'Six Films by Douglas Sirk', *New Left Review*, **91** (May/June 1975): 92.

50. JAKOBSON, 'Concluding Statement: Linguistics and Poetics' in *Style in Language* ed. Thomas Sebeok (Cambridge, Mass.: MIT Press, 1960), p. 370.

Part One

Vision and Phantasy

1 Fetishism*

SIGMUND FREUD

Sigmund Freud was the German founder of psychoanalysis. Born in 1856, he fled from Nazism to London in 1938 and died there the year after. Collected as the *Standard Edition* and translated into English by James Strachey, his works include *The Interpretation of Dreams* (1900), *Jokes and their Relation to the Unconscious* (1905), *Three Essays on the Theory of Sexuality* (1905) and *Beyond the Pleasure Principle* (1920). He wrote about art not only in his book, *Leonardo da Vinci* (1910), but in a number of essays on 'Creative Writers and Day-Dreaming', on Michelangelo, psychopathic characters in drama, *The Merchant of Venice*, Rebecca West in Ibsen's *Rosmersholm*, Dostoevsky (these are now collected in a volume on *Art and Literature* published by Penguin in 1985). See 'Introduction', p. 15.

In the last few years I have had an opportunity of studying analytically a number of men whose object-choice was dominated by a fetish. There is no need to expect that these people came to analysis on account of their fetish. For though no doubt a fetish is recognized by its adherents as an abnormality, it is seldom felt by them as the symptom of an ailment accompanied by suffering. Usually they are quite satisfied with it, or even praise the way in which it eases their erotic life. As a rule, therefore, the fetish made its appearance in analysis as a subsidiary finding.

For obvious reasons the details of these cases must be withheld from publication; I cannot, therefore, show in what way accidental circumstances have contributed to the choice of a fetish. The most extraordinary case seemed to me to be one in which a young man had exalted a certain sort of 'shine on the nose' into a fetishistic precondition. The surprising explanation of this was that the patient had been brought up in an English nursery but had later come to

*Reprinted from *Standard Edition of the Complete Psychological Works*, trans. James Strachey (London: Hogarth Press and the Institute of Psycho-Analysis, 1953–74), 24 vols, vol. 21, pp. 147–57.

Germany, where he forgot his mother-tongue almost completely. The fetish, which originated from his earliest childhood, had to be understood in English, not German. The 'shine on the nose' [in German *'Glanz auf der Nase'*] – was in reality a *'glance* at the nose'. The nose was thus the fetish, which, incidentally, he endowed at will with the luminous shine which was not perceptible to others.

In *every instance*, the meaning and the purpose of the fetish turned out, in analysis, to be the same. It revealed itself so naturally and seemed to me so compelling that I am prepared to expect the same solution in all cases of fetishism. When now I announce that the fetish is a substitute for the penis, I shall certainly create disappointment; so I hasten to add that it is not a substitute for any chance penis, but for a particular and quite special penis that had been extremely important in early childhood but had later been lost. That is to say, it should normally have been given up, but the fetish is precisely designed to preserve it from extinction. To put it more plainly: the fetish is a substitute for the woman's (the mother's) penis that the little boy once believed in and – for reasons familiar to us – does not want to give up.[1]

What happened, therefore, was that the boy refused to take cognizance of the fact of his having perceived that a woman does not possess a penis. No, that could not be true: for if a woman had been castrated, then his own possession of a penis was in danger; and against that there rose in rebellion the portion of his *narcissism* which Nature has, as a precaution, attached to that *particular organ*. In later life a grown man may perhaps experience a similar panic when the cry goes up that Throne and Altar are in danger, and similar illogical consequences will ensue. If I am not mistaken, Laforgue would say in this case that the boy 'scotomizes' his perception of the woman's lack of a penis.[2] A new technical term is justified when it describes a new fact or emphasizes it. This is not so here. The oldest word in our psychoanalytic terminology, 'repression', already relates to this pathological process. If we wanted to differentiate more sharply between the vicissitude of the *idea* as distinct from that of the *affect*,[3] and reserve the word *'Verdrängung'* ['repression'] for the affect, then the correct German word for the vicissitude of the idea would be *'Verleugnung'* ['disavowal'].[4] 'Scotomization' seems to me particularly unsuitable, for it suggests that the perception is entirely wiped out, so that the result is the same as when a visual impression falls on the blind spot in the retina. In the situation we are considering, on the contrary, we see that the perception has persisted, and that a very energetic action has been undertaken to maintain the disavowal. It is not true that, after the child has made his observation of the woman, he has preserved unaltered his belief that women have a phallus. He has retained that belief, but he has also given it up. In the conflict between the weight of the unwelcome perception and the force of his counter-wish, a compromise has been reached, as is only possible under the dominance of the unconscious laws of thought – the primary processes. Yes, in his mind the woman *has* got a penis, in spite of everything; but this penis is no longer the same as it was before. Something else has taken its place, has been appointed its substitute, as it were, and now inherits the interest which was formerly directed to its predecessor. But this interest suffers an extraordinary increase as well, because the horror of castration has set up a memorial to itself in the creation of this substitute. Furthermore, an aversion, which is never absent in any fetishist, to the real female genitals remains a *stigma indelebile* of the repression that has taken place. We can now see what the fetish achieves and what it is that maintains it. It remains a token of triumph over the threat of castration and a protection against it. It also saves the fetishist from becoming a homosexual, by endowing women with the characteristic which makes them tolerable as sexual objects. In later life, the fetishist feels that he enjoys yet another advantage from his substitute for a genital. The meaning of the fetish is not known to other people, so the fetish is not withheld from him: it is easily accessible and he can readily obtain the sexual satisfaction attached to it. What other men have to woo and make exertions for can be had by the fetishist with no trouble at all.

Probably no male human being is spared the fright of castration at the sight of a female genital. Why some people become homosexual as a consequence of that impression, while others fend it off by creating a fetish, and the great majority surmount it, we are frankly not able to explain. It is possible that, among all the factors at work, we do not yet know those which are decisive for the rare pathological results. We must be content if we can explain what has happened, and may for the present leave on one side the task of explaining why something has *not* happened.

One would expect that the organs or objects chosen as substitutes for the absent female phallus would be such as appear as symbols of the penis in other connections as well. This may happen often enough, but is certainly not a deciding factor. It seems rather that when the fetish is instituted some process occurs which reminds one of the stopping of memory in traumatic amnesia. As in this latter case, the subject's interest comes to a halt half-way, as it were; it is as though the last impression before the uncanny and traumatic one is retained as a fetish. Thus the foot or shoe owes its preference as a fetish – or a part of it – to the circumstances that the inquisitive boy peered at the woman's genitals from below, from her legs up; fur and velvet – as has long been suspected – are a fixation of the sight of the pubic hair, which should have been followed by the longed-for sight of the female member; pieces of underclothing, which are so often chosen as a fetish, crystallize the moment of undressing, the last moment in which the woman could still be regarded as phallic. But I do not maintain that it is invariably possible to discover with certainty how the fetish was determined.

An investigation of fetishism is strongly recommended to anyone who still doubts the existence of the castration complex or who can still believe that fright at the sight of the female genital has some other ground – for instance, that it is derived from a supposed recollection of the trauma of birth.[5]

For me, the explanation of fetishism had another point of theoretical interest as well. Recently, along quite speculative lines, I arrived at the proposition that the essential difference between neurosis and psychosis was that in the former the ego, in the service of reality, suppresses a piece of the id, whereas in a psychosis it lets itself be induced by the id to detach itself from a piece of reality. I returned to this theme once again later on.[6] But soon after this I had reason to regret that I had ventured so far. In the analysis of two young men I learned that each – one when he was two years old and the other when he was ten – had failed to take cognizance of the death of his beloved father – had 'scotomized' it – and yet neither of them had developed a psychosis. Thus a piece of reality which was undoubtedly important had been disavowed by the ego, just as the unwelcome fact of women's castration is disavowed in fetishists. I also began to suspect that similar occurrences in childhood are by no means rare, and I believed that I had been guilty of an error in my characterization of neurosis and psychosis. It is true that there was one way out of the difficulty. My formula needed only to hold good where there was a higher degree of differentiation in the psychical apparatus; things might be permissible to a child which would entail severe injury to an adult.

But further research led to another solution of the contradiction. It turned out that the two young men had no more 'scotomized' their father's death than a fetishist does the castration of women. It was only one current in their mental life that had not recognized their father's death; there was another current which took full account of that fact. The attitude which fitted in with the wish and the attitude which fitted in with reality existed side by side. In one of my two cases this split had formed the basis of a moderately severe obsessional neurosis. The patient oscillated in every situation in life between two assumptions: the one, that his father was still alive and was hindering his activities; the other, opposite one, that he was entitled to regard himself as his father's successor. I may thus keep to the expectation that in a psychosis the one current – that which fitted in with reality – would have in fact been absent.

Returning to my description of fetishism, I may say that there are many and weighty additional proofs of the divided attitude of fetishists to the question of the castration of women. In very subtle instances both the disavowal and the affirmation of the castration have found their way into the construction of the fetish itself. This was so in the case of a man whose fetish was an athletic support-belt which could also be worn as bathing drawers. This piece of clothing covered up the genitals entirely and concealed the distinction between them. Analysis showed that it signified that women were castrated and that they were not castrated; and it also allowed of the hypothesis that men were castrated, for all these possibilities could equally well be concealed under the belt – the earliest rudiment of which in his childhood had been the fig-leaf on a statue. A fetish of this sort, doubly derived from contrary ideas, is of course especially durable. In other instances the divided attitude shows itself in what the fetishist does with his fetish, whether in reality or in his imagination. To point out that he reveres his fetish is not the whole story; in many cases he treats it in a way which is obviously equivalent to a representation of castration. This happens particularly if he has developed a strong identification with his father and plays the part of the latter; for it is to him that as a child he ascribed the woman's castration. Affection and hostility in the treatment of the fetish – which run parallel with the disavowal and the acknowledgement of castration – are mixed in unequal proportions in different cases, so that the one or the other is more clearly recognizable. We seem here to approach an understanding, even if a distant one, of the behaviour of the '*coupeur de nattes*'.[7] In him the need to carry out the castration which he disavows has come to the front. His action contains in itself the two mutually incompatible assertions: 'the woman has still got a penis' and 'my father has castrated the woman'. Another variant, which is also a parallel to fetishism in social psychology, might be seen in the Chinese custom of mutilating the female foot and then revering it like a fetish after it has been mutilated. It seems as though the Chinese male wants to thank the woman for having submitted to being castrated.

In conclusion we may say that the normal prototype of fetishes is a man's penis, just as the normal prototype of inferior organs is a woman's real small penis, the clitoris.[8]

Notes

1. This interpretation was made as early as 1910, in my study on Leonardo da Vinci, without any reasons being given for it. [See Chapter III of *Leonardo da Vinci* study, *Standard Edition*, v. 11, pp. 57–137.]

2. I correct myself, however, by adding that I have the best reasons for supposing that Laforgue would not say anything of the sort. It is clear from his own remarks [Laforgue, 'Verdrängung und Skotomisation',

Internationale Zeitschrift Psychoanalytische v. 12, 54, p. 352] that 'scotomization' is a term which derives from descriptions of dementia praecox, which does not arise from a carrying-over of psychoanalytic concepts to the psychoses and which has no application to developmental processes or to the formation of neuroses. In his exposition in the text of his paper, the author has been at pains to make this incompatibility clear.

3. [This is considered in a passage near the middle of the paper on 'Repression'(*Standard Edition*, v. 14, pp. 141–58).]

4. [Some discussion of Freud's use of this term and of the English rendering of it appears in an Editor's footnote to the paper on 'The Infantile Genital Organization' [*Standard Edition*, v. 19, p. 143]. It may be remarked that in Chapter VIII of the *Outline of Psycho-Analysis* [*Standard Edition*, v. 23, pp. 139–207] Freud makes a different distinction between the uses of the two words: 'repression' applies to defence against internal instinctual demands and 'disavowal' to defence against the claims of external reality.]

5. [Cf. OTTO RANK, *Das Trauma der Geburt* (Vienna: Internationale Psychoanalytische Bibliothek, 1924, pp. 22–4; *The Trauma of Birth* (London: Kegan Paul, 1929)).]

6. 'Neurosis and Psychosis' (*Standard Edition*, v. 19, pp. 147–53) and 'The Loss of Reality in Neurosis and Psychosis' (*Standard Edition*, v. 19. pp. 181–7).

7. [A pervert who enjoys cutting off the hair of females. Part of the present explanation was given by Freud in his study of Leonardo (1910), see Chapter III of *Leonardo da Vinci, Standard Edition*, v. 11, pp. 57–137.]

8. [This is an allusion to Adler's insistence on 'organ-inferiority' as the basis of all neuroses. Cf. a footnote to the paper on 'Some Psychical Consequences of the Anatomical Distinction between the Sexes' (*Standard Edition*, v. 19, p. 251), and a longer discussion in Lecture 31 of the *New Introductory Lectures* (*Standard Edition*, v. 22, pp. 1–182).]

2   The Mirror Stage*

JACQUES LACAN

Born in 1901, Jacques Lacan trained as a Freudian analyst. From 1953 in Paris he held weekly seminars which were later attended by Althusser, Barthes, Derrida and Kristeva (among others). Some of these seminars were published as *The Four Fundamental Concepts of Psycho-Analysis* in 1973 (English, 1977). His collection, *Écrits*, was published in 1966 (English, 1977), and a further group of essays, under the title *Feminine Sexuality*, appeared in English translation in 1982. Since his death in 1981, his complete works, prepared by Jacques-Alain Miller, are slowly being published. See 'Introduction', pp. 12–13.

The conception of the mirror stage that I introduced at our last congress, thirteen years ago, has since become more or less established in the practice of the French group. However, I think it worthwhile to bring it again to your attention, especially today, for the light it sheds on the formation of the *I* as we experience it in psychoanalysis. It is an experience that leads us to oppose any philosophy directly issuing from the *Cogito*.

Some of you may recall that this conception originated in a feature of human behaviour illuminated by a fact of comparative psychology. The child, at an age when he is for a time, however short, outdone by the chimpanzee in instrumental intelligence, can nevertheless already recognize as such his own image in a mirror. This recognition is indicated in the illuminative mimicry of the *Aha-Erlebnis*, which Köhler sees as the expression of situational apperception, an essential stage of the act of intelligence.

This act, far from exhausting itself, as in the case of the monkey, once the image has been mastered and found empty, immediately rebounds in the case of the child in a series of gestures in which he experiences in play the relation between the movements assumed in the image and the

---

*Reprinted from *Écrits: A Selection*, trans. Alan Sheridan (London: Tavistock, 1977), pp. 1–7.

reflected environment, and between this virtual complex and the reality it reduplicates – the child's own body, and the persons and things, around him.

This event can take place, as we have known since Baldwin, from the age of six months, and its repetition has often made me reflect upon the startling spectacle of the infant in front of the mirror. Unable as yet to walk, or even to stand up, and held tightly as he is by some support, human or artificial (what, in France, we call a '*trotte-bébé*'), he nevertheless overcomes, in a flutter of jubilant activity, the obstructions of his support and, fixing his attitude in a slightly leaning-forward position, in order to hold it in his gaze, brings back an instantaneous aspect of the image.

For me, this activity retains the meaning I have given it up to the age of eighteen months. This meaning discloses a libidinal dynamism, which has hitherto remained problematic, as well as an ontological structure of the human world that accords with my reflections on paranoiac knowledge.

We have only to understand the mirror stage *as an identification*, in the full sense that analysis gives to the term: namely, the transformation that takes place in the subject when he assumes an image – whose predestination to this phase-effect is sufficiently indicated by the use, in analytic theory, of the ancient term *imago*.

This jubilant assumption of his specular image by the child at the *infans* stage, still sunk in his motor incapacity and nursling dependence, would seem to exhibit in an exemplary situation the symbolic matrix in which the I is precipitated in a primordial form, before it is objectified in the dialectic of identification with the other, and before language restores to it, in the universal, its function as subject.

This form would have to be called the Ideal-I,[1] if we wished to incorporate it into our usual register, in the sense that it will also be the source of secondary identifications, under which term I would place the functions of libidinal normalization. But the important point is that this form situates the agency of the ego, before its social determination, in a fictional direction, which will always remain irreducible for the individual alone, or rather, which will only rejoin the coming-into-being (*le devenir*) of the subject asymptotically, whatever the success of the dialectical syntheses by which he must resolve as I his discordance with his own reality.

The fact is that the total form of the body by which the subject anticipates in a mirage the maturation of his power is given to him only as *Gestalt*, that is to say, in an exteriority in which this form is certainly more constituent than constituted, but in which it appears to him above all in a contrasting size (*un relief de stature*) that fixes it and in a symmetry that inverts it, in contrast with the turbulent movements that the subject feels are animating him. Thus, this *Gestalt* – whose pregnancy should be regarded as bound up with the species, though its motor style remains scarcely recognizable – by these two aspects of its appearance, symbolizes the mental permanence of the *I* at the same time as it prefigures its alienating destination; it is still pregnant with the correspondences that unite the *I* with the statue in which man projects himself, with the phantoms that dominate him, or with the automaton in which, in an ambiguous relation, the world of his own making tends to find completion.

Indeed, for the *imagos* – whose veiled faces it is our privilege to see in outline in our daily experience and in the penumbra of symbolic efficacity[2] – the mirror-image would seem to be the threshold of the visible world, if we go by the mirror disposition that the *imago of one's own body* presents in hallucinations or dreams, whether it concerns its individual features, or even its infirmities, or its object-projections; or if we observe the role of the mirror apparatus in the appearances of the *double*, in which psychical realities, however heterogeneous, are manifested.

That a *Gestalt* should be capable of formative effects in the organism is attested by a piece of biological experimentation that is itself so alien to the idea of psychical causality that it cannot bring itself to formulate its results in these terms. It nevertheless recognizes that it is a necessary condition for the maturation of the gonad of the female pigeon that it should see another member of its species, of either sex; so sufficient in itself is this condition that the desired effect may be obtained merely by placing the individual within reach of the field of reflection of a mirror. Similarly, in the case of the migratory locust, the transition within a generation from the solitary to the gregarious form can be obtained by exposing the individual, at a certain stage, to the exclusively visual action of a similar image, provided it is animated by movements of a style sufficiently close to that characteristic of the species. Such facts are inscribed in an order of homeomorphic identification that would itself fall within the larger question of the meaning of beauty as both formative and erogenic.

But the facts of mimicry are no less instructive when conceived as cases of heteromorphic identification, in as much as they raise the problem of the signification of space for the living organism – psychological concepts hardly seem less appropriate for shedding light on these matters than ridiculous attempts to reduce them to the supposedly supreme law of adaptation. We have only to recall how Roger Caillois (who was then very young, and still fresh from his breach with the sociological school in which he was trained) illuminated the subject by using the term '*legendary psychasthenia*' to classify morphological mimicry as an obsession with space in its derealizing effect.

I have myself shown in the social dialectic that structures human knowledge as paranoiac[3] why human knowledge has greater autonomy than animal knowledge in relation to the field of force of desire, but also why human knowledge is determined in that 'little reality' (*ce peu de réalité*), which the Surrealists, in their restless way, saw as its limitation. These reflections lead me to recognize in the spatial captation manifested in the mirror-stage, even before the social dialectic, the effect in man of an organic insufficiency in his natural reality – in so far as any meaning can be given to the word 'nature'.

I am led, therefore, to regard the function of the mirror-stage as a particular case of the function of the *imago*, which is to establish a relation between the organism and its reality – or, as they say, between the *Innenwelt* and the *Umwelt*.

In man, however, this relation to nature is altered by a certain dehiscence at the heart of the organism, a primordial Discord betrayed by the signs of uneasiness and motor unco-ordination of the neo-natal months. The objective notion of the anatomical incompleteness of the pyramidal system and likewise the presence of certain humoral residues of the maternal organism confirm the view I have formulated as the fact of a real *specific prematurity of birth* in man.

It is worth noting, incidentally, that this is a fact recognized as such by embryologists, by the term *foetalization*, which determines the prevalence of the so-called superior apparatus of the neurax, and especially of the cortex, which psycho-surgical operations lead us to regard as the intraorganic mirror.

This development is experienced as a temporal dialectic that decisively projects the formation of the individual into history. The *mirror stage* is a drama whose internal thrust is precipitated from insufficiency to anticipation – and which manufactures for the subject, caught up in the lure of spatial identification, the succession of phantasies that extends from a fragmented body-image to a form of its totality that I shall call orthopaedic – and, lastly, to the assumption of the armour of an alienating identity, which will mark with its rigid structure the subject's entire mental development. Thus, to break out of the circle of the *Innenwelt* into the *Umwelt* generates the inexhaustible quadrature of the ego's verifications.

This fragmented body – which term I have also introduced into our system of theoretical references – usually manifests itself in dreams when the movement of the analysis encounters a certain level of aggressive disintegration in the individual. It then appears in the form of disjointed limbs, or of those organs represented in exoscopy, growing wings and taking up arms for intestinal persecutions – the very same that the visionary Hieronymus Bosch has fixed, for all time, in painting, in their ascent from the fifteenth century to the imaginary zenith of modern man. But this form is even tangibly revealed at the organic level, in the lines of 'fragilization' that define the anatomy of phantasy, as exhibited in the schizoid and spasmodic symptoms of hysteria.

Correlatively, the formation of the *I* is symbolized in dreams by a fortress, or a stadium – its inner arena and enclosure, surrounded by marshes and rubbish-tips, dividing it into two opposed fields of contest where the subject flounders in quest of the lofty, remote inner castle whose form (sometimes juxtaposed in the same scenario) symbolizes the id in a quite startling way. Similarly, on the mental plane, we find realized the structures of fortified works, the metaphor of which arises spontaneously, as if issuing from the symptoms themselves, to designate the mechanisms of obsessional neurosis – inversion, isolation, reduplication, cancellation and displacement.

But if we were to build on these subjective givens alone – however little we free them from the condition of experience that makes us see them as partaking of the nature of a linguistic technique – our theoretical attempts would remain exposed to the charge of projecting themselves into the unthinkable of an absolute subject. This is why I have sought in the present hypothesis, grounded in a conjunction of objective data, the guiding grid for a *method of symbolic reduction*.

It establishes in the *defences of the ego* a genetic order, in accordance with the wish formulated by Miss Anna Freud, in the first part of her great work, and situates (as against a frequently expressed prejudice) hysterical repression and its returns at a more archaic stage than obsessional inversion and its isolating processes, and the latter in turn as preliminary to paranoiac alienation, which dates from the deflection of the specular *I* into the social *I*.

This moment in which the mirror-stage comes to an end inaugurates, by the identification with the *imago* of the counterpart and the drama of primordial jealousy (so well brought out by the school of Charlotte Bühler in the phenomenon of infantile *transitivism*), the dialectic that will henceforth link the *I* to socially elaborated situations.

It is this moment that decisively tips the whole of human knowledge into mediatization through the desire of the other, constitutes its objects in an abstract equivalence by the co-operation of others, and turns the *I* into that apparatus for which every instinctual thrust constitutes a danger, even though it should correspond to a natural maturation – the very normalization of this maturation being henceforth dependent, in man, on a cultural mediation as exemplified, in the case of the sexual object, by the Oedipus complex.

In the light of this conception, the term primary narcissism, by which analytic doctrine designates the libidinal investment characteristic of that moment, reveals in those who invented it the most profound awareness of semantic latencies. But it also throws light on the dynamic opposition between this libido and the sexual libido, which the first analysts tried to define when they invoked destructive and, indeed, death instincts, in order to explain the evident connection between the narcissistic libido and the alienating function of the I, the aggressivity it releases in any relation to the other, even in a relation involving the most Samaritan of aid.

In fact, they were encountering that existential negativity whose reality is so vigorously proclaimed by the contemporary philosophy of being and nothingness.

But unfortunately that philosophy grasps negativity only within the limits of a self-sufficiency of consciousness, which, as one of its premises, links to the *méconnaissances* that constitute the ego, the illusion of autonomy to which it entrusts itself. This flight of fancy, for all that it draws, to an unusual extent, on borrowings from psychoanalytic experience, culminates in the pretention of providing an existential psychoanalysis.

At the culmination of the historical effort of a society to refuse to recognize that it has any function other than the utilitarian one, and in the anxiety of the individual confronting the 'concentrational'[4] form of the social bond that seems to arise to crown this effort, existentialism must be judged by the explanations it gives of the subjective impasses that have indeed resulted from it; a freedom that is never more authentic than when it is within the walls of a prison; a demand for commitment, expressing the impotence of a pure consciousness to master any situation; a voyeuristic–sadistic idealization of the sexual relation; a personality that realizes itself only in suicide; a consciousness of the other that can be satisfied only by Hegelian murder.

These propositions are opposed by all our experience, in so far as it teaches us not to regard the ego as centred on the *perception-consciousness system*, or as organized by the 'reality principle' – a principle that is the expression of a scientific prejudice most hostile to the dialectic of knowledge. Our experience shows that we should start instead from the *function of méconnaissance* that characterizes the ego in all its structures, so markedly articulated by Miss Anna Freud. For, if the *Verneinung* represents the patent form of that function, its effects will, for the most part, remain latent, so long as they are not illuminated by some light reflected on to the level of fatality, which is where the id manifests itself.

We can thus understand the inertia characteristic of the formations of the I, and find there the most extensive definition of neurosis – just as the captation of the subject by the situation gives us the most general formula for madness, not only the madness that lies behind the walls of asylums, but also the madness that deafens the world with its sound and fury.

The sufferings of neurosis and psychosis are for us a schooling in the passions of the soul, just as the beam of the psychoanalytic scales, when we calculate the tilt of its threat to entire communities, provides us with an indication of the deadening of the passions in society.

At this junction of nature and culture, so persistently examined by modern anthropology, psychoanalysis alone recognizes this knot of imaginary servitude that love must always undo again, or sever.

For such a task, we place no trust in altruistic feeling, we who lay bare the aggressivity that underlies the activity of the philanthropist, the idealist, the pedagogue, and even the reformer.

In the recourse of subject to subject that we preserve, psychoanalysis may accompany the patient to the ecstatic limit of the '*Thou art that*', in which is revealed to him the cipher of his mortal destiny, but it is not in our mere power as practitioners to bring him to that point where the real journey begins.

Notes

1. Throughout this article I leave in its peculiarity the translation I have adopted for Freud's *Ideal-Ich* (i.e. 'je–idéal'), without further comment, other than to say I have not maintained it since.

2. CLAUDE LÉVI -STRAUSS , *Structural Anthropology* (New York: Basic Books, 1963) chapter X.

3. [LACAN] 'Aggressivity in Psychoanalysis' (another paper collected in *Écrits* [*Écrits: A Selection*, trans. Sheridan (London: Tavistock, 1977)]).

4. '*Concentrationnaire*', an adjective coined after the Second World War (this article was written in 1949) to describe the life of the concentration camp. In the hands of certain writers it became, by extension, applicable to many aspects of 'modern' life (Translator).

Part Two

Ideology and Subjectivity

3 Cinema/Ideology/Criticism (1)*

JEAN-LOUIS COMOLLI and JEAN NARBONI

Jean-Louis Comolli and Jean Narboni were senior members of the collective which edited *Cahiers du Cinéma* in the crucial period after 1968 during which, alongside the journal *Cinéthique*, it was committed to developing an explicit and radical theory of cinema. They also participated in the long, collective analysis, 'John Ford's *Young Mr Lincoln*' published in *Cahiers du Cinéma*, **223**, in 1970. In 1975 Comolli directed *La Cecilia*, a film about Italian anarchists in Brazil. See 'Introduction', pp. 9–10.

Scientific criticism has an obligation to define its field and methods. This implies awareness of its own historical and social situation, a rigorous analysis of the proposed field of study, the conditions which make the work necessary and those which make it possible, and the special function it intends to fulfil.

It is essential that we at *Cahiers du Cinéma* should now undertake just such a global analysis of our position and aims. Not that we are starting entirely from zero. Fragments of such an analysis have been coming out of material we have published recently (articles, editorials, debates, answers to readers' letters) but in an imprecise form and as if by accident. They are an indication that our readers, just as much as we ourselves, feel the need for a clear theoretical base to which to relate our critical practice and its field, taking the two to be indivisible. 'Programmes' and 'revolutionary' plans and declarations tend to become an end in themselves. This is a trap we intend to avoid. Our objective is not to reflect upon what we 'want' (would like) to do, but upon what we *are* doing and what we *can* do, and this is impossible without an analysis of the present situation.

*Translated by Susan Bennett, reprinted from *Cahiers du Cinéma*, **216** (October 1969): 11–15.

I. Where?

(a) First, our situation. *Cahiers* is a group of people working together; one of the results of our work appearing as a magazine.[1] A magazine, that is to say, a particular product, involving a particular amount of work (on the part of those who write it, those who produce it and, indeed, those who read it). We do not close our eyes to the fact that a product of this nature is situated fairly and squarely inside the economic system of capitalist publishing (modes of production, spheres of circulation, etc.). In any case it is difficult to see how it could be otherwise today, unless one is led astray by Utopian ideas of working 'parallel' to the system. The first step in the latter approach is always the paradoxical one of setting up a false front, a 'neo-system' alongside the system from which one is attempting to escape, in the fond belief that it will be able to negate the system. In fact all it can do is reject it (idealist purism) and consequently it is very soon jeopardized by the enemy upon which it modelled itself.[2] This 'parallelism' works from one direction only: It touches only one side of the wound, whereas we believe that both sides have to be worked upon. And the danger of the parallels meeting all too speedily in infinity seems to us sufficient to argue that we had better stay in the finite and allow them to remain apart.

This assumed, the question is: what is our attitude to our situation? In France the majority of films, like the majority of books and magazines, are produced and distributed by the capitalist economic system and within the dominant ideology. Indeed, strictly speaking all are, whatever expedient they adopt to try and get around it. This being so, the question we have to ask is: which films, books and magazines allow the ideology a free, unhampered passage, transmit it with crystal clarity, serve as its chosen language? And which attempt to make it turn back and reflect itself, intercept it and make it visible by revealing its mechanisms, by blocking them?

(b) For the situation in which we are *acting* is the field of cinema (*Cahiers* is a film magazine),[3] and the precise object of our study is the history of a film: how it is produced, manufactured, distributed,[4] understood.

What is the film today? This is the relevant question; not, as it possibly once was: what is the cinema? We shall not be able to ask that again until a body of knowledge, of theory, has been evolved (a process to which we certainly intend to contribute) to inform what is at present an empty term, with a concept. For a film magazine the question is also: what work is to be done in the field constituted by films? And for *Cahiers* in particular: what is our specific function in this field? What is to distinguish us from other 'film magazines'?

II. The films

What is a film? On the one hand it is a particular product, manufactured within a given system of economic relations, and involving labour (which appears to the capitalist as money) to produce – a condition to which even 'independent' film-makers and the 'new cinema' are subject – assembling a certain number of workers for this purpose (even the director, whether he is Moullet or Oury, is in the last analysis only a film worker). It becomes transformed into a commodity, possessing exchange value, which is realized by the sale of tickets and contracts, and governed by the laws of the market. On the other hand, as a result of being a material product of the system, it is also an ideological product of the system, which in France means capitalism.[5]

No film-maker can, by his own individual efforts, change the economic relations governing the manufacture and distribution of his films. (It cannot be pointed out too often that even film-makers who set out to be 'revolutionary' on the level of message and form cannot effect any swift or radical change in the economic system – deform it, yes, deflect it, but not negate it or seriously upset its structure. Godard's recent statement to the effect that he wants to stop working in the 'system' takes no account of the fact that any other system is bound to be a reflection of the one he wishes to avoid. The money no longer comes from the Champs-Elysées but from London, Rome or New York. The film may not be marketed by the distribution monopolies but it is shot on film stock from another monopoly – Kodak.) Because every film is part of the economic system it is also a part of the ideological system, for 'cinema' and 'art' are branches of ideology. None can escape: somewhere, like pieces in a jigsaw, all have their own allotted place. The system is blind to its own nature, but in spite of that, indeed because of that, when all the pieces are fitted together they give a very clear picture. But this does not mean that every film-maker plays a similar role. Reactions differ.

It is the job of criticism to see where they differ, and slowly, patiently, not expecting any magical transformations to take place at the wave of a slogan, to help change the ideology which conditions them.

A few points, which we shall return to in greater detail later: *every film is political*, inasmuch as it is determined by the ideology which produces it (or within which it is produced, which stems from the same thing). The cinema is all the more thoroughly and completely determined because unlike other arts or ideological systems its very manufacture mobilizes powerful economic forces in a way that the production of literature (which becomes the commodity 'books', does not – though once we reach the level of distribution, publicity and sale, the two are in rather the same position).

Clearly, the cinema 'reproduces' reality: this is what a camera and film stock are for – so says the ideology. But the tools and techniques of film-making are a part of 'reality' themselves, and furthermore 'reality' is nothing but an expression of the prevailing ideology. Seen in this light, the classic theory of cinema that the camera is an impartial instrument which grasps, or rather is impregnated by, the world in its 'concrete reality' is an eminently reactionary one. What the camera in fact registers is the vague, unformulated, untheorized, unthought-out world of the dominant ideology. Cinema is one of the languages through which the world communicates itself to itself. They constitute its ideology for they reproduce the world as it is experienced when filtered through the ideology. (As Althusser defines it, more precisely: 'Ideologies are perceived-accepted-suffered cultural objects, which work fundamentally on men by a process they do not understand. What men express in their ideologies is not their true relation to their conditions of existence, but how they react to their conditions of existence which presupposes a real relationship and an imaginary relationship.') So, when we set out to make a film, from the very first shot, we are encumbered by the necessity of reproducing things not as they really are but as they appear when refracted through the ideology. This includes every stage in the process of production: subjects, 'styles', forms, meanings, narrative traditions *all* underline the general ideological discourse. The film is ideology presenting itself to itself, talking to itself, learning about itself. Once we realize that it is the nature of the system to turn the cinema into an instrument of ideology, we can see that the film-maker's first task is to show up the cinema's so-called 'depiction of reality'. If he can do so there is a chance that we will be able to disrupt or possibly even sever the connection between the cinema and its ideological function.

The vital distinction between films today is whether they do this or whether they do not.

(a) The first and largest category comprises those films which are imbued through and through with the dominant ideology in pure and unadulterated form, and give no indication that their makers were even aware of the fact. We are not just talking about so-called 'commercial' films. The *majority* of films in all categories are the unconscious instruments of the ideology which produces them. Whether the film is 'commercial' or 'ambitious','modern' or 'traditional', whether it is the type that gets shown in art houses, or in smart cinemas, whether it belongs to the 'old' cinema or the 'young' cinema, it is most likely to be a re-hash of the same old ideology. For all films are commodities and therefore objects of trade, even those whose discourse is explicitly political – which is why a rigorous definition of what constitutes 'political' cinema is called for at this moment when it is being widely promoted.[6] This merging of ideology and film is reflected in the first instance by the fact that audience demand and economic response have also been reduced to one and the same thing. In direct continuity with political practice, ideological practice reformulates the social need and backs it up with a discourse. This is not a hypothesis, but a scientifically-established fact. The ideology is talking to itself; it has all the answers ready before it asks the questions. Certainly there is such a thing as public demand, but 'what the public wants' means 'what the dominant ideology wants'. The notion of a public and its tastes was created by the ideology to justify and perpetuate itself. And this public can only express itself via the thought-patterns of the ideology. The whole thing is a closed circuit, endlessly repeating the same illusion.

The situation is the same at the level of artistic form. These films totally accept the established system of depicting reality: 'bourgeois realism' and the whole conservative box of tricks: blind faith in 'life', 'humanism', 'common sense', etc. A blissful ignorance that there might be something wrong with this whole concept of 'depiction' appears to have reigned at every stage in their production, so much so, that to us it appears a more accurate gauge of pictures in the 'commercial' category than box-office returns. Nothing in these films jars against the ideology, or the audience's mystification by it. They are very reassuring for audiences for there is no difference between the ideology they meet every day and the ideology on the screen. It would be a useful complementary task for film critics to look into the way the ideological system and its products merge at all levels: to study the phenomenon whereby a film being shown to an audience becomes a monologue, in which the ideology talks to itself, by examining the success of films by, for instance, Melville, Oury and Lelouch.

(b) A second category is that of films which attack their ideological assimilation on two fronts. Firstly, by direct political action, on the level of the 'signified', i.e. they deal with a directly political subject. 'Deal with' is here intended in an active sense: they do not just discuss an issue, reiterate it, paraphrase it, but use it to attack the ideology (this presupposes a theoretical activity which is the direct opposite of the ideological one). This act only becomes politically effective if it is linked with a breaking down of the traditional way of depicting reality. On the level of form, *Unreconciled, The Edge* and *Earth in Revolt* all challenge the concept of 'depiction' and mark a break with the tradition embodying it.

We would stress that only action on both fronts, 'signified' and 'signifiers' [7] has any hope of operating against the prevailing ideology. Economic/political and formal action have to be indissolubly wedded.

(c) There is another category in which the same double action operates, but 'against the grain'. The content is not explicitly political, but in some way becomes so through the criticism practised on it through its form.[8] To this category belong *Méditerranée, The Bellboy, Persona…* . For *Cahiers* these films ((b) and (c)) constitute the essential in the cinema, and should be the chief subject of the magazine.

(d) Fourth case: those films, increasingly numerous today, which have an explicitly political content (Z is not the best example as its presentation of politics is unremittingly ideological from first to last; a better example would be *Le Temps de Vivre*) but which do not effectively criticize the ideological system in which they are embedded because they unquestioningly adopt its language and its imagery.

This makes it important for critics to examine the effectiveness of the political criticism intended by these films. Do they express, reinforce, strengthen the very thing they set out to denounce? Are they caught in the system they wish to break down… ? (see (a)).

(e) Five: films which seem at first sight to belong firmly within the ideology and to be completely under its sway, but which turn out to be so only in an ambiguous manner. For though they start from a non-progressive standpoint, ranging from the frankly reactionary through the conciliatory to the mildly critical, they have been worked upon, and work, in such a real way that there is a noticeable gap, a dislocation, between the starting point and the finished product. We disregard here the inconsistent – and unimportant – sector of films in which the director makes a *conscious* use of the prevailing ideology, but leaves it absolutely straight. The films we are talking about throw up obstacles in the way of the ideology, causing it to swerve and get off course. The cinematic framework lets us see it, but also shows it up and denounces it. Looking at the framework one can see two moments in it: one holding it back within certain limits, one transgressing them. An internal criticism is taking place which cracks the film apart at the seams. If one reads the film obliquely, looking for symptoms; if one looks beyond its apparent formal coherence, one can see that it is riddled with cracks: it is splitting under an internal tension which is simply not there in an ideologically innocuous film. The ideology thus becomes subordinate to the text. It no longer has an independent existence: it is *presented* by the film. This is the case in many Hollywood films for example, which while being completely integrated in the system and the ideology end up by partially dismantling the system from within. We must find out what makes it possible for a film-maker to corrode the ideology by restating it in the terms of his film: if he sees his film simply as a blow in favour of liberalism, it will be recuperated instantly by the ideology; if, on the other hand, he conceives and realizes it on the deeper level of imagery, there is a chance that it will turn out to be more disruptive. Not, of course, that he will be able to break the ideology itself, but simply its reflection in his film. (The films of Ford, Dreyer, Rossellini, for example.)

Our position with regard to this category of films is: that we have absolutely no intention of joining the current witch-hunt against them. They are the mythology of their own myths. They criticize themselves, even if no such intention is written into the script, and it is irrelevant and impertinent to do so for them. All we want to do is to show the process in action.

(f) Films of the live cinema (*cinéma direct*) variety, group one (the larger of the two groups). These are films arising out of political (or, it would probably be more exact to say: social) events or reflections, but which make no clear differentiation between themselves and the non-political cinema because they do not challenge the cinema's traditional, ideologically-conditioned method of 'depiction'. For instance a miner's strike will be filmed in the same style as *Les Grandes Familles*. The makers of these films suffer under the primary and fundamental illusion that if they once break off the ideological filter of narrative traditions (dramaturgy, construction, domination of the component parts by a central idea, emphasis on formal beauty) reality will then yield itself up in its true form. The fact is that by doing so they only break off one filter, and not the most important one at that. For reality holds within itself no hidden kernel of self-understanding, of theory, of truth, like a stone inside a fruit. We have to manufacture those. (Marxism is very clear on this point, in its distinction between 'real' and 'perceived' objects.) Cf. *Chiefs* (Leacock and a good number of the May films).

This is why supporters of *cinéma direct* resort to the same idealist terminology to express its role and justify its successes as others use about products of the greatest artifice: 'accuracy', 'a sense of lived experience', 'flashes of intense truth', 'moments caught live', 'abolition of all sense that we are watching a film' and finally: fascination. It is that magical notion of 'seeing is understanding': ideology goes on display to prevent itself from being shown up for what it really is, contemplates itself but does not criticize itself.

(g) The other kind of 'live cinema'. Here the director is not satisfied with the idea of the camera 'seeing through appearances', but attacks the basic problem of depiction by giving an active role to the concrete stuff of his film. It then becomes productive of meaning and is not just a passive receptacle for meaning produced outside it (in the ideology): *La Règne du Jour, La Rentrée des Usines Wonder*.

III. Critical function

Such, then, is the field of our critical activity: these films, within the ideology, and their different relations to it. From this precisely defined field spring four functions: (1) in the case of the films in category (a):

49

show what they are blind to; how they are totally determined, moulded, by the ideology; (2) in the case of those in categories (b), (c) and (g), read them on two levels, showing how the films operate critically on the level of signified and signifiers; (3) in the case of those types (d) and (f), show how the signified (political subject matter) is always weakened, rendered harmless, by the absence of technical/theoretical work on the signifiers; (4) in the case of those in group (e) point out the gap produced between film and ideology by the way the films work, and show how they work.

There can be no room in our critical practice either for speculation (commentary, interpretation, de-coding even) or for spacious raving (of the film-columnist variety). It must be a rigidly factual analysis of what governs the production of a film (economic circumstances, ideology, demand and response) and the meanings and forms appearing in it, which are equally tangible.

The tradition of frivolous and evanescent writing on the cinema is as tenacious as it is prolific, and film analysis today is still massively pre-determined by idealistic presuppositions. It wanders farther abroad today, but its method is still basically empirical. It has been through a necessary stage of going back to the material elements of a film, its signifying structures, its formal organization. The first steps here were undeniably taken by André Bazin, despite the contradictions that can be picked out in his articles. Then followed the approach based on structural linguistics (in which there are two basic traps, which we fell into – phenomenological positivism and mechanistic materialism). As surely as criticism had to go through this stage, it has to go beyond. To us, the only possible line of advance seems to be to use the theoretical writing of the Russian film-makers of the twenties (Eisenstein above all) to elaborate and apply a critical theory of the cinema, a specific method of apprehending rigorously defined objects, in direct reference to the method of dialectical materialism.

It is hardly necessary to point out that we know that the 'policy' of a magazine cannot – indeed, should not – be corrected by magic overnight. We have to do it patiently, month by month, being careful in our own field to avoid the general error of putting faith in spontaneous change, or attempting to rush in a 'revolution' without the preparation to support it. To start proclaiming at this stage that the truth has been revealed to us would be like talking about 'miracles' or 'conversion'. All we should do is to state what work is already in progress and publish articles which relate to it, either explicitly or implicitly.

We should indicate briefly how the various elements in the magazine fit into this perspective. The essential part of the work obviously takes place in the theoretical articles and the criticisms. There is coming to be less and less of a difference between the two, because it is not our concern to add up the merits and defects of current films in the interests of topicality, nor, as one humorous article put it 'to crack up the product'. The interviews, on the other hand, and also the 'diary' columns and the list of films, with the dossiers and supplementary material for possible discussion later, are often stronger on information than theory. It is up to the reader to decide whether these pieces take up any critical stance, and if so, what.

Notes

1. Others include distribution, screening and discussion of films in the provinces and the suburbs, sessions of theoretical work (see 'Montage', No 210).

2. Or tolerated, and jeopardized by this very toleration. Is there any need to stress that it is the tried tactic of covertly repressive systems not to harass the protesting fringe? They go out of their way to take no notice of them, with the double effect of making one half of the opposition careful not to try their patience too far and the other half complacent in the knowledge that their activities are unobserved.

3. We do not intend to suggest by this that we want to erect a corporatist fence round our own field, and neglect the infinitely larger field where so much is obviously at stake politically. Simply, we are concentrating on that precise point of the spectrum of social activity in this article, in response to precise operational needs.

4. A more and more pressing problem. It would be inviting confusion to allow it to be tackled in bits and pieces and obviously we have to make a unified attempt to pose it theoretically later on. For the moment we leave it aside.

5. Capitalist ideology. This term expresses our meaning perfectly, but as we are going to use it without further definition in this article, we should point out that we are not under any illusion that it has some kind of 'abstract essence'. We know that it is historically and socially determined, and that it has multiple forms at any given place and time, and varies from historical period to historical period. Like the whole category of 'militant' cinema, which is totally vague and undefined at present. We must (a) rigorously define the function attributed to it, its aims, its side effects (information, arousal, critical reflection, provocation 'which always has *some* effect' ...); (b) define the exact political line governing the making and screening of these films – 'revolutionary' is too much of a blanket term to serve any useful purpose here; and (c) state whether the supporters of militant cinema are in fact proposing a line of action in which the cinema would become the poor relation, in the illusion that the less the cinematic aspect is worked on, the greater the strength and clarity of the 'militant' effect will be. This would be a way of avoiding the contradictions of **parallel cinema** and getting embroiled in the problem of deciding whether 'underground' films should be included in the category, on the pretext that their relationship to drugs and sex, their preoccupation with form, might possibly establish new relationships between film and audience.

6. As also the category of militant cinema, today completely vague and indeterminate. We must (a) specify rigorously the function attributed to it, its intended aims, the hoped-for effect (information, warning, critical reflection, provocation 'from which something will always result'), and *on whom*; (b) define what exact political line these films are made and shown within, and not be content with the vague qualification of 'revolutionary', a hold-all; (c) announce whether, in these terms, an activity is being offered which treats cinema as a poor relation, under the illusion that the less cinema works, the more the 'militant' effect will grow in strength and clarity. All this is necessary to avoid the contradictions of, for example, the 'parallel cinema', indefinitely engulfed in the problem of whether 'underground' films should be included in the category, using the excuse that their relation to drugs or sex, their formalist preoccupations, are capable of inaugurating new modes of the relation film-spectator.

7. We are not shutting our eyes to the fact that it is an oversimplification (employed here because operationally easier) to make such sharp distinction between the two terms. This is particularly so in the case of the cinema, where the signified is more often than not a product of the permutations of the signifiers, and the sign has dominance over the meaning.

8. This is not a magical doorway out of the system of 'depiction' (which is particularly dominant in the cinema) but rather a rigorous, detailed, large-scale work on this system – what conditions make it possible, what mechanisms render it innocuous. The method is to draw attention to the system, so that it can be seen for what it is, to make it serve one's own ends, condemn itself out of its own mouth. Tactics employed may include 'turning cinematic syntax upside-down' but it cannot be just that. Any old film nowadays can upset the normal chronological order in the interests of looking vaguely 'modern'. But *The Exterminating Angel* and *The Diary of Anna Magdalena Bach* (though we would not wish to set them up as a model) are rigorously chronological without ceasing to be subversive in the way we have been describing, whereas in many a film the mixed-up time sequence simply covers up a basically naturalistic conception. In the same way, perceptual confusion (avowed intent to act on the unconscious mind, changes in the texture of the film, etc.) are not sufficient in themselves to get beyond the traditional way of depicting 'reality'. To realize this, one has only to remember the unsuccessful attempts there have been of the 'lettriste' or new kinds of onomatopoeia. In the one and the other case only the most 'zaoum' type to give back its infinity to language by using nonsense words superficial level of language is touched. They create a new code, which operates on the level of the impossible, and has to be rejected on any other, and is therefore not in a position to transgress the normal.

4 *From* Realism and the Cinema: Notes on Some Brechtian Theses*

COLIN MACCABE

Colin MacCabe now divides his career between the British Film Institute and the University of Pittsburgh. He was on the Editorial Board
of *Screen* in the 1970s, and his publications include *James Joyce and the
Revolution of the Word* (1978) and *Theoretical Essays* (1985). See
'Introduction', pp. 12–13.

The classic realist text

> Criticism, at least Marxist criticism, must proceed methodically and
> concretely in each case, in short scientifically. Loose talk is of no
> help here, whatever its vocabulary. In no circumstances can the
> necessary guide-lines for a practical definition of realism be derived
> from literary works alone. (Be like Tolstoy – but without his
> weaknesses! Be like Balzac – only up-to-date!) Realism is an issue
> not only for literature: it is a major political, philosophical and
> practical issue and must be handled and explained as such – as a
> matter of general human interest.[1]

One of the difficulties of any discussion about realism is the lack of any
really effective vocabulary with which to discuss the topic. Most
discussions turn on the problems of the production of discourse which
will fully adequate the real. This notion of adequacy is accepted both by
the realists and indeed by the anti-realists whose main argument is that
no discourse can ever be adequate to the multifarious nature of the real.
This notion of the real is, however, I wish to suggest, a notion which is
tied to a particular type of literary production – the nineteenth-century
realist novel. The dominance of this novel form is such that people still
tend to confuse the general question of realism with the particular

* Reprinted from *Screen*, **15**: 2 (Summer 1974): 7–27.

forms of the nineteenth-century realist novel. In order to make the discussion clearer I want therefore to attempt to define the structure which typifies the nineteenth-century realist novel and to show how that structure can also be used to describe a great number of films. The detour through literature is necessary because, in many ways, the structure is much more obvious there and also because of the historical dominance of the classic realist novel over much film production. What to a large extent will be lacking in this article is the specific nature of the film form but this does not seem to me to invalidate the setting up of certain essential categories from which further discussion must progress. The structure I will attempt to disengage I shall call the classic realist text and I shall apply it to novels and films.

A classic realist text may be defined as one in which there is a hierarchy amongst the discourses which compose the text and this hierarchy is defined in terms of an empirical notion of truth. Perhaps the easiest way to understand this is through a reflection on the use of inverted commas within the classic realist novel. While those sections in the text which are contained in inverted commas may cause a certain difficulty for the reader – a certain confusion *vis-à-vis* what really is the case – this difficulty is abolished by the unspoken (or more accurately the unwritten) prose that surrounds them. In the classical realist novel the narrative prose functions as a metalanguage that can state all the truths in the object language – those words held in inverted commas – and can also explain the relation of this object language to the real. The metalanguage can thereby explain the relation of this object language to the world and the strange methods by which the object languages attempt to express truths which are straightforwardly conveyed in the metalanguage. What I have called an unwritten prose (or a metalanguage) is exactly that language, which while placing other languages between inverted commas and regarding them as certain material expressions which express certain meanings, regards those same meanings as finding transparent expression within the metalanguage itself. Transparent in the sense that the metalanguage is not regarded as material; it is dematerialised to achieve perfect representation – to let the identity of things shine through the window of words. For in so far as the metalanguage is treated itself as material – it, too, can be reinterpreted; new meanings can be found for it in a further metalanguage. The problem is the problem that has troubled western thought since the pre-Socratics recognised the separation between what was said and the act of saying. This separation must be thought both as time and space – as the space, which in the distance from page to eye or mouth to ear allows the possibility of misunderstanding – as the time taken to traverse the page or listen to an utterance which ensures the deferred interpretation of words which are always only defined by what follows. The problem is that in the moment that we say a sentence the meaning (what is said) seems fixed and evident but what is said does not exist solely for the moment and is open to further interpretations. Even in this formulation of the problem I have presupposed an original moment when there is strict contemporaneity between the saying and what is said, but the difficulty is more radical for there is no such original moment. The separation is always already there as we cannot locate the presence of what is said – distributed as it is through space – nor the present of what is said – distributed as it is through time.

This separation bears witness to the real as articulated. The thing represented does not appear in a moment of pure identity as it tears itself out of the world and presents itself, but rather is caught in an articulation in which each object is defined in a set of differences and oppositions.

It is this separation that the unwritten text attempts to *anneal*, to make whole, through denying its own status as writing – as marks of material difference distributed through time and space. Whereas other discourses within the text are considered as material which are open to re-interpretation, the narrative discourse simply allows reality to appear and denies its own status as articulation. This relationship between discourses can be clearly seen in the work of such a writer as George Eliot. In the scene in *Middlemarch* where Mr Brooke goes to visit the Dagleys' farm we read two different languages. One is the educated, well-meaning, but not very intelligent discourse of Mr Brooke and the other is the uneducated, violent and very nearly unintelligible discourse of the drunken Dagley. But the whole dialogue is surrounded by a metalanguage, which being unspoken is also unwritten, and which places these discourses in inverted commas and can thus discuss these discourses' relation to truth – a truth which is illuminatingly revealed in the metalanguage. The metalanguage reduces the object languages into a simple division between form and content and extracts the meaningful content from the useless form. One can see this process at work in the following passage which ends the scene:

> He [Mr Brooke] had never been insulted on his own land before, and had been inclined to regard himself as a general favourite (we are all apt to do so, when we think of our own amiability more than what other people are likely to want of us). When he had quarrelled with Caleb Garth twelve years before he had thought that the tenants would be pleased at the landlord's taking everything into his own hands.
>
> Some who follow the narrative of this experience may wonder at the midnight darkness of Mr Dagley; but nothing was easier in

those times than for a hereditary farmer of his grade to be ignorant, in spite somehow of having a rector in the twin parish who was a gentleman to the backbone, a curate nearer at hand who preached more learnedly than the rector, a landlord who had gone into everything, especially fine art and social improvement and all the lights of Middlemarch only three miles off.[2]

This passage provides the necessary interpretations for the discourses that we have read earlier in the chapter. Both the discourses of Dagley and Mr Brooke are revealed as springing from two types of ignorance which the metalanguage can expose and reveal. So we have Mr Brooke's attitude to what his tenants thought of him contrasted with the reality which is available through the narrative prose. No discourse is allowed to speak for itself but rather it must be placed in a context which will reduce it to a simple explicable content. And in the claim that the narrative prose has direct access to a final reality we can find the claim of the classic realist novel to present us with the truths of human nature. The ability to reveal the truth about Mr Brooke is the ability that guarantees the generalisations of human nature.

Thus then a first definition of the classic realist text – but does this definition carry over into films where it is certainly less evident where to locate the dominant discourse? It seems to me that it does and in the following fashion. The narrative prose achieves its position of dominance because it is in the position of knowledge and this function of knowledge is taken up in the cinema by the narrative of events. Through the knowledge we gain from the narrative we can split the discourses of the various characters from their situation and compare what is said in these discourses with what has been revealed to us through narration. The camera shows us what happens – it tells the truth against which we can measure the discourses. A good example of this classical realist structure is to be found in Pakula's film *Klute*. This film is of particular interest because it was widely praised for its realism on its release. Perhaps even more significantly it tended to be praised for its realistic presentation of the leading woman, Bree (played by Jane Fonda).

In *Klute* the relationship of dominance between discourses is peculiarly accentuated by the fact that the film is interspersed with fragments of Bree talking to her psychiatrist. This subjective discourse can be exactly measured against the reality provided by the unfolding of the story. Thus all her talk of independence is portrayed as finally an illusion as we discover, to no great surprise but to our immense relief, what she really wants is to settle down in the mid-West with John Klute (the detective played by Donald Sutherland) and have a family. The final sequence of the film is particularly telling in this respect. While Klute and Bree pack their bags to leave, the soundtrack records Bree at her last meeting with her psychiatrist. Her own estimation of the situation is that it most probably won't work but the reality of the image ensures us that this is the way it will really be. Indeed Bree's monologue is even more interesting – for in relation to the reality of the image it marks a definite advance on her previous statements. She has gained insight through the plot development and like many good heroines of classic realist texts her discourse is more nearly adequate to the truth at the end of the film than at the beginning. But if a progression towards knowledge is what marks Bree, it is possession of knowledge which marks the narrative, the reader of the film and John Klute himself. For Klute is privileged by the narrative as the one character whose discourse is also a discourse of knowledge. Not only is Klute a detective and thus can solve the problem of his friend's disappearance – he is also a man, and a man who because he has not come into contact with the city has not had his virility undermined. And it is as a full-blooded man that he can know not only the truth of the mystery of the murders but also the truth of the woman Bree. Far from being a film which goes any way to portraying a woman liberated from male definition (a common critical response), *Klute* exactly guarantees that the real essence of woman can only be discovered and defined by a man.

The analysis sketched here is obviously very schematic but what, hopefully, it does show is that the structure of the classic realist text can be found in film as well. That narrative of events – the knowledge which the film provides of how things really are – is the metalanguage in which we can talk of the various characters in the film. What would still remain to be done in the elaboration of the structure of the classic realist text in cinema is a more detailed account of the actual mechanisms by which the narrative is privileged (and the way in which one or more of the characters within the narrative can be equally privileged) and also a history of the development of this dominant narrative. On the synchronic level it would be necessary to attempt an analysis of the relationship between the various types of shot and their combination into sequences – are there for example certain types of shot which are coded as subjective and therefore subordinate to others which are guaranteed as objective? In addition how does music work as the guarantee or otherwise of truth? On the diachronic level it would be necessary to study how this form was produced – what relationship obtains between the classic realist text and technical advances such as the development of the talkie? What ideological factors were at work in the production and dominance of the classic realist text?

To return, however, to the narrative discourse. It is necessary to attempt to understand the type of relations that this dominant discourse produces. The narrative discourse cannot be mistaken in its identifications because the narrative discourse is not present as discourse – as articulation. The unquestioned nature of the narrative discourse entails that the only problem that reality poses is to go and look and see what *Things* there are. The relationship between the reading subject and the real is placed as one of pure specularity. The real is not articulated – it is. These features imply two essential features of the classic realist text:

1 The classic realist text cannot deal with the real as contradictory.
2 In a reciprocal movement the classic realist text ensures the position of the subject in a relation of dominant specularity.

The classic realist text as progressive art

> In general, do not be content with providing an insight into the literature of the country in question, but follow the details of literary life itself. Consider literary phenomena as events and as social events. (Principles for the review *Das Wort*.)[3]

It may be objected that the account that I have given of the classic literary text is deficient in the following extremely important fashion. It ignores what is the usual criterion for realism, that is to say subject matter. The category of the classic realist text lumps together in book and film *The Grapes of Wrath* and *The Sound of Music*, *L'Assommoir* and *Toad of Toad Hall*. In order to find a criterion with which to make distinctions within the area of the classic realist text it is necessary to reflect on contradiction. I have stated that the classic realist text cannot deal with the real in its contradiction because of the unquestioned status of the representation at the level of the dominant discourse. In order to understand how contradiction can be dealt with it is necessary to investigate the workings of an operation that is often opposed to representation, namely montage.

In his essay on 'Word and image' in *The Film Sense*, Eisenstein defines montage. Amongst numerous examples of montage he quotes the following from Ambrose Bierce's *Fantastic Fables*:

> A Woman in widow's weeds was weeping upon a grave.
> 'Console yourself, madam' said a Sympathetic Stranger.
> 'Heaven's mercies are infinite. There is another man somewhere, beside your husband, with whom you can still be happy.'
> 'There was,' she sobbed – 'there was, but this is his grave.'[4]

Eisenstein explains the effect of this fable in terms of an interaction between the visual representations in the story. The woman is a representation and so is the mourning dress – they are, in Eisenstein's terms, objectively representable – but the juxtaposition of these representations gives rise to a new image that is not representable – namely that the woman is a widow. It is the expectation created by the juxtaposition which is undercut by the final line uttered by the woman. For the moment we shall only notice the following point:

1 that Eisenstein, concerned very largely with a simple definition of representation, fails to recognise that widow is just as objective a representation as woman or mourning dress and

2 that montage involves both an interaction between representations and a shock.

Eisenstein continues his explanation by expanding his distinction between representation (the raw material of the montage) and image (that which is produced by the montage itself).

> Take a white circular disc of average size and smooth surface, its circumference divided into sixty equal parts. At every fifth division is set a figure in the order of succession of 1 to 12. At the centre of the disc are fixed two metal rods, moving freely on their fixed ends, pointed at their free ends, one being equal to the radius of the disc, the other rather shorter. Let the longer pointed rod have its free end resting at the figure 12 and the shorter in succession pointing towards the figures 1, 2, 3 and so on up to 12. This will comprise a series of geometrical representations of successive relations of the two metal rods to one another expressed in the dimensions 30, 60, 90 degrees, and so on up to 360 degrees.
>
> If, however, this disc is provided with a mechanism that imparts steady movement to the metal rods, the geometrical figure formed on the surface acquires a special meaning: it is now not simply a *representation*, it is an *image* of time.[5]

The confusion that led Eisenstein to count woman and mourning dress as representable but widow as non-representable can be seen at work again in this passage. Eisenstein thinks of the world as being composed of basic objects available to sight which are then linked together in various ways by the perceiving subject with the aid of his past experiences. That this is his position is made abundantly clear in the passage which follows the passage I have just quoted. He takes the example of Vronsky looking at his watch, after Anna Karenina has told him that she is pregnant, and being so shocked that he sees the position of the hands but not the time. Thus the position of the hands is the primitive object in the world and the time is what the human subject creates through his linking of this object with other items of his experience. Montage is thus, for Eisenstein, in this passage (which must not be confused with Eisenstein's cinematic practice), the manipulation of definite representations to produce images in the mind of the spectator. But now it can be seen that this definition of montage does not contradict representation at all. If we understand by representation the rendering of identities in the world then Eisenstein's account of montage is not opposed to representation but is simply a secondary process which comes after representation. Eisenstein would have montage linking onto representation but not in any sense challenging it. The representation starts from an identity in the world which it re-presents, the montage starts from representations, identities, and combines them to form an image.

Eisenstein's acceptance of representation can be seen in those passages where representation is contrasted with montage. For Eisenstein the opposite to montage is 'affadavit-exposition' which he defines as '*in film terms; representations shot from a single set-up*'.[6] Thus montage is the showing of the same representation from different points of view. And it is from this point that we can begin to challenge Eisenstein's conception of montage. A point of view suggests two things. Firstly a view – something that is seen – and secondly a location from which the view may be had, the sight may be seen. Thus the suggestion is that there are different locations from which we can see. But in all cases the sight remains the same – the activity of representation is not the determining factor in the sight seen but simply the place from where it is seen. The inevitable result of this is that there is something the same which we all see but which appears differently because of our position. But if there is identity; if there is something over and above the views which can be received at different points then this identity must be discernable from some other 'point of view'. And this neutral point of view is exactly the 'representations shot from a single set-up'.

What is at work in Eisenstein's argument is the idea that there is some fixed reality which is available to us from an objective point of view (the single set-up). Montage is simply putting these fixed elements together in such a way that the subject brings forth other elements in his experience – but without any change in the identities, the elements that are being rendered. It is essential to realise that this account leaves both subject and object unchallenged and that montage becomes a kind of super-representation which is more effective at demonstrating the real qualities of the object through the links it can form within the subject. Thus Eisenstein would analyse the Bierce story as the representation of a given set of elements which are first organised in one way then in another. There are, however, no such set of fixed elements in the Bierce story. It is not that there is a set of elements which the reader composes 'in his mind' but rather that these elements are already determined by the method of representation. What Eisenstein ignores is that the method of representation (the language: verbal or cinematic) determines in its structural activity (the oppositions which can be articulated) both the places where the object 'appears' and the 'point' from which the object is seen. It is this point which is exactly the place allotted to the reading subject.

A careful analysis of the Bierce story may enable us to discover how montage operates and why that operation is difficult to grasp. We can read three different discourses at work in the Bierce story (a discourse being defined as a set of significant oppositions). The narrative discourse, the discourse of the Sympathetic Stranger and the discourse of the Woman. The question is whether as Eisenstein holds, the narrative discourse represents simply a woman and a mourning dress. But 'woman' is not some simple identity as Eisenstein would have us believe. Whereas the Sympathetic Stranger identifies woman in terms of religion and state – thus our relationships are determined in heaven and are institutionalised by the state on earth – the Woman determines her own identity as 'woman' in terms of desire and transgression – relationships are formed through the transgressing of the state's institutions and this transgression is linked with a certain sexuality; for relationships between a man and a woman outside the bond of holy matrimony are explicitly sexual. We can now understand that the montage works through a contest between the identities offered by the different discourses in the Bierce story, the woman's statement jars with what has gone before so that we re-read it – the identifications that we made (that were made for us) are undermined by new ones. What is thrown into doubt is exactly the identity (the nature) of woman and this doubt is achieved through the 'shock' of the woman's statement as the identity already proffered is subverted. It is also clear from this analysis that there is no neutral place from which we can see the view and where all the points are located. There is no possible language of 'affadavit-exposition' that would show the scene 'as it really is'. For how we see the scene will be determined by the way in which we identify 'woman' – and this determination is a feature of the available discourses; the discourses in which 'woman' can figure.

We are still, however, left with the problem of how we can mistake this effect of montage, as I have suggested Eisenstein has done, and the answer to this question can be found in the apparent similarity of the discourses in the Bierce story. For the three discourses are so similar that we can be persuaded to read them as one. All that is missing from the first and second is provided by the third. The third discourse can be read as 'closing' the text. For with the information thus given to us we can read the previous discourses in a 'final' – that is to say *once and for all* – manner. We can fill in the gaps in the first two discourses – see the real identities which are mistaken. But this is to ignore the fact that what is at question in the story are different discourses. Different discourses can be defined in discourses in which different oppositions are possible. Although at one level – the level of the legal relationship to the body and the grave – both discourses coincide (she *is* or *is not* the wife), at another level there are a set of oppositions of an emotional nature (she *does* or *does not* mourn some man) which the stranger cannot articulate outside the oppositions determined by the legal relationship. Bierce's story, through the coincidences between the discourses on one level, suggests to Eisenstein a set of identities in the world. But the identities rest in the discourses. Thus opposed to Eisenstein's concept of montage resting on the juxtapositions of identities already rendered, we could talk of montage as the effect generated by a conflict of discourse in which the oppositions available in the juxtaposed discourses are contradictory and in conflict.

All this by way of explaining that the classic realist text (a heavily 'closed' discourse) cannot deal with the real in its contradictions and that in the same movement it fixes the subject in a point of view from which everything becomes obvious. There is, however, a level of contradiction into which the classic realist text can enter. This is the contradiction between the dominant discourse of the text and the dominant ideological discourses of the time. Thus a classic realist text in which a strike is represented as a just struggle in which oppressed workers attempt to gain some of their rightful wealth would be in contradiction with certain contemporary ideological discourses and as such might be classified as progressive. It is here that subject matter enters into the argument and where we can find the justification for Marx and Engels's praise of Balzac and Lenin's texts on the revolutionary force of Tolstoy's texts which ushered the Russian peasant on to the stage of history. Within contemporary films one could think of the films of Costa-Gavras or such television documentaries as *Cathy Come Home*. What is, however, still impossible for the classic realist text is to offer any perspectives for struggle due to its inability to investigate contradiction. It is thus not surprising that these films tend either to be linked to a social democratic conception of progress – if we reveal injustices then they will go away – or certain *ouvrieriste* tendencies which tend to see the working class, outside any dialectical movement, as the simple possessors of truth. It is at this point that Brecht's demand that literary and artistic productions be regarded as social events gains its force. The contradictions between the dominant discourse in a classic realist text and the dominant ideological discourses at work in a society are what provide the criteria for discriminating within the classic realist text. And these criteria will often resolve themselves into questions of subject-matter. That this tends to leave open any question about the eternal values of art is not something that should worry us. As Brecht remarks:

> To be frank, I do not set such an excessively high value on the concept of endurance. How can we foresee whether future generations will wish to preserve the memory of these figures [*figures created by Balzac or Tolstoy*]? (Balzac and Tolstoy will scarcely be in a position to oblige them to do so, however ingenious the methods with which they set their plots in motion.) I suspect it will depend on whether it will be a socially relevant statement if someone says: 'That' (and 'that' will refer to a contemporary) 'is a Père Goriot character'. Perhaps such characters will not survive? Perhaps they precisely arose in a cramping web of relations of a type which will no longer exist.[7]

Moments of subversion and strategies of subversion

> The practical methods of the revolution are not revolutionary, they are dictated by the class struggle. It is for this reason that great writers find themselves ill at ease in the class struggle, they behave as though the struggle was already finished, and they deal with the new situation, conceived as collectivist, which is the aim of the revolution. The revolution of the great writers is permanent.[8]

In the last issue of *Screen* we published Franco Fortini's text on 'The writer's mandate' (1974) which took the position that art is that area which deals with the irreconcilable contradictions of life over and beyond the particular contradictions of the class struggle and of their successful resolution in the revolution. It was suggested in the editorial that, in order to avoid a fall into romantic and ultra-left positions, these irreconcilable differences had to be theorised within the scientific concepts offered to us by psychoanalysis. Freud's theory is a theory of the construction of the subject: the entry of the small infant into language and society and the methods by which it learns what positions, as subject, it can take up. This entry into the symbolic (the whole cultural space which is structured, like language through a set of differences and oppositions) is most easily traced in the analytic situation through that entry which is finally determining for the infant – the problem of sexual difference. Freud's insight is that the unproblematic taking up of the position of the subject entails the repression of the whole mechanism of the subject's construction. The subject is seen as the founding source of meanings – unproblematically standing outside an articulation in which it is, in fact, defined. This view of the subject as founding source is philosophically encapsulated in Descartes' *cogito*: I think, therefore I am – the 'I' in simple evidence to itself provides a moment of pure presence which can found the enterprise of analysing the world. Jacques Lacan, the French psychoanalyst, has read Freud as reformulating the Cartesian *cogito* and destroying the subject as source and foundation – Lacan rewrites the *cogito*, in the light of Freud's discoveries as, I think where I am not and I am where I do not think. We can understand this formulation as the indicating of the fundamental misunderstanding (*méconnaissance*) which is involved in the successful use of language (or any other area of the symbolic which is similarly structured) in which the subject is continually ignored as being caught up in a process of articulation to be taken as a fixed place founding the discourse. The unconscious is that effect of language which escapes the conscious subject in the distance between the act of signification in which the subject passes from signifier to signifier and what is signified in which the subject finds himself in place as, for example, the pronoun 'I'. The importance of phenomena like verbal slips is that they testify to the existence of the unconscious through the distance between what was said and what the conscious subject intended to say. They thus testify to the distance between the subject of the act of signification and the conscious subject (the ego). In this distance there is opened a gap which is the area of desire. What is essential to all of those psychic productions which Freud uses in the analytic interpretation is that they bear witness to the lack of control of the conscious subject over his discourses. The mechanisms of the unconscious can indeed be seen as the mechanisms of language. Condensation is the work of metaphor which brings together two signifieds under one signifier and displacement is the constant process along the signifying chain. The ego is constantly caught in this fundamental misunderstanding (*méconnaissance*) about language in which from an illusory present it attempts to read only one signified as present in the metaphor and attempts to bring the signifying chain to an end in a perpetually deferred present ... What Brecht suggests in his comments on the spectator in the cinema is that the very position offered to the spectator is one that guarantees the necessary re-production of labour power. It is the cinema's ability to place the spectator in the position of a unified subject that ensures the contradiction between his working activity which is productive and the leisure activity in which he is constantly placed as consumer. Althusser makes the very important point in his essay that ideology is not a question of ideas circulating in people's heads but is inscribed in certain material practices. The reactionary practice of the cinema is that which involves this petrification of the spectator in a position of pseudo-dominance offered by the metalanguage. This metalanguage, resolving as it does all contradictions, places the spectator outside the realm of contradiction and of action – outside of production.

Two films which suggest a way of combating this dominance of the metalanguage, without falling into an agnostic position vis-à-vis all discourses (which would be the extreme of a subversive cinema – intent merely on disrupting any position of the subject) are *Kuhle Wampe* (the film in which Brecht participated) and Godard-Gorin's *Tout Va Bien*. In both films the narrative is in no way privileged as against the characters. Rather the narrative serves simply as the method by which various situations can be articulated together. The emphasis is on the particular scenes and the knowledge that can be gained from them rather than the providing of a knowledge which requires no further activity – which just is there on the screen. Indeed the presentation of the individual's discourses is never stripped away from the character's actions but is involved in them. Whether it is a question of the petit-bourgeois and the workers discussing the waste of coffee in the S-Bahn or the various monologues in *Tout Va Bien* – it is not a question of the discourses being presented as pure truth content which can be measured against the truth provided by the film. Rather the discourses are caught up in certain modes of life which are linked to the place of the agent in the productive process. The unemployed workers know that waste is an inevitable part of the capitalist process because they experience it every day in their search for work. Equally the workers in the meat factory know that the class struggle is not finished for they experience the exploitation of their labour in such concrete details as the time that is allowed them to go to the toilet. The film does not provide this knowledge ready-made in a dominant discourse but in the contradictions offered, the reader has to produce a meaning for the film (it is quite obvious in films of this sort that the meaning produced will depend on the class-positions of the reader). It is this emphasis on the reader as producer (more obvious in *Tout Va Bien* which is in many ways more Brechtian than *Kuhle Wampe*) which suggests that these films do not just offer a different representation for the subject but a different set of relations to both the fictional material and 'reality'.

Very briefly this change could be characterised as the introduction of time (history) into the very area of representation so that it is included within it. It is no accident that both films end with this same emphasis on time and its concomitant change. 'But who will change the world' (*Kuhle Wampe*) – 'We must learn to live historically' (*Tout Va Bien*) – this emphasis on time and change embodied both within the film and in the position offered to the reader suggests that a revolutionary socialist ideology might be different in form as well as content. It also throws into doubt Barthes's thesis that revolutionary art is finally caught in the same space of representation that has persisted for 2,000 years in the West. This monolithic conception of representation ignores the fact that post-Einsteinian physics offers a conception of representation in which both subject and object are no longer caught in fixed positions but caught up in time.

It might be thought that this possibility of change, of transformation – in short, of production – built into the subject-object relation (which could no longer be characterised in this simple fashion) simply reduplicates the Hegelian error of final reconciliation between the orders of being and consciousness. But this is not so in so far as this possibility of change built into the relation does not imply the inevitable unfolding of a specific series of changes but simply the possibility of change – an area of possible transformations contained within the relation.

It seems that some such account must be offered if one wishes to allow the possibility of a revolutionary art. Otherwise it seems inevitable that art can simply be progressive or subversive and Brecht's whole practice would be a marriage of the two, in which subversive effects were mechanically used simply to aid the acceptance of the progressive content of his work.

A definite category: reactionary art

> It is our metaphysicians of the press, our partisans of 'art' who would like more emphasis on 'fate' in human processes. For a long time now fate, which was once a sublime notion, has been nothing more than a mediocre received idea: by reconciling himself to his condition, man arrives at that so longed for 'transfiguration' and 'interiorisation'. It is equally a pure notion of the class struggle: one class 'determines' the fate of the other.[9]

One fashionable way of receiving and recuperating Brecht, which has been at work since the beginning of the Cold War, is to see him as a satirist ridiculing his contemporary society and the excesses of capitalism and fascism. This approach negates the productive element in Brecht's work and turns the techniques for the production of alienation effects into pure narcissistic signals of an 'intellectual' work of 'art'. A very typical example of this vulgarisation and de-politicisation of Brecht can be seen in Lindsay Anderson's *O Lucky Man!* An explicitly Brechtian film – the loosely connected scenes are counter-pointed by the Alan Price songs – the film pretends to offer a tableau of England in 1973 much as *Tout Va Bien* attempts to offer a tableau of France in 1972. But whereas in the French film the tableaux are used to reflect the contradictions within the society – the different articulations of reality – in the English film the tableaux are all used to express a stereotyped reality of England which the spectator is invited to enjoy from his superior position. The scenes may seem to be dominant over the reality revealed by the narrative but as the film progresses along its endless development it becomes obvious that the narrative simply confirms the evident truths which are offered to us on the screen. And these truths turn out to be that endless message of the reactionary petit-bourgeois intellectual – that we can do nothing against the relentless and evil progress of society (run as it is by a bunch of omnipotent capitalists with the morality of gangsters) except note our superiority to it. A longer analysis of the film might well be in order were it not for the fact that Walter Benjamin had already written the definitive critique of this particularly impoverished artistic strategy. It is perhaps a testament to the paucity of petit-bourgeois imagination in the era of monopoly capitalism that what Benjamin wrote forty years ago about the satirical poet Erich Kästner (1974) can be applied word for word to *O Lucky Man!*

Notes

1. BERTOLT BRECHT, *Gesammelte Werke* 20 vols (Frankfurt: Suhrkamp Verlag, 1967), vol. 19, p. 307.

2. GEORGE ELIOT, *Middlemarch* (Harmondsworth: Penguin, 1968), pp. 432–33.

3. BRECHT, op. cit., vol. 19, p. 307.

4. SERGEI EISENSTEIN, *The Film Sense* (London: Faber, 1968), pp. 14–15.

5. Ibid., p. 20.

6. Ibid., p. 37.

7. BRECHT, op. cit., vol. 19, pp. 308–9.

8. BRECHT, op. cit., vol. 18, p. 16.

9. BRECHT, op. cit., vol. 17, pp. 169–70.

5 *From* Narrative Space*

Stephen Heath

Stephen Heath teaches in the English Faculty of the University of Cambridge. He was for several years on the Editorial Board of *Screen*. His publications include *The Nouveau Roman: A Study in the Practice of Writing, Vertige du déplacement* (1974, a book on the work of Roland Barthes), *Questions of Cinema* 1981) and *The Sexual Fix* (1982). See 'Introduction', pp. 13–14.

It is precise that 'events *take place*'. (Michael Snow)

Photography and cinema share the camera. Photography is a mode of projecting and fixing solids on a plane surface, of producing images; cinema uses the images produced by photography to reproduce movement, the motion *of* the flow of the images playing on various optical phenomena (φ-effect, retinal persistence) to create the illusion of a single movement *in* the images, an image of movement. Phenomenologically, the result is characterized as 'neither absolutely two-dimensional nor absolutely three-dimensional, but something between'.[1] The 'something between' is the habitual response to the famous 'impression of reality' in cinema and it is this impression, this reality that are of concern here in their implications for a consideration of space in film.

Stress has been laid in recent work on the situation of cinema in terms of a development of codes of figuration inherited from the Quattrocento, notably codes of perspective. The focus of attention thus defined is, exactly, the camera: 'a camera productive of a perspective code directly constructed on the model of the scientific perspective of the Quattrocento' (Marcelin Pleynet)[2] the stress, in other words, is on the camera as machine for the reproduction of objects (of solids) in the form of images realized according to the laws of the rectilinear propagation of light rays, which laws constitute the perspective

---

*Reprinted from *Screen*, **17**: 3 (Autumn 1976): 68–112.

effect. In this connection, there are already a number of remarks
and clarifications to be made, remarks that will bear on
Quattrocento perspective, the photograph and cinema, and in that
order.

The perspective system introduced in the early years of the fifteenth
century in Italy (developing above all from Florence) is that of *central
projection*: 'It is the art of depicting three-dimensional objects upon a
plane surface in such a manner that the picture *may* affect the eye of an
observer in the same way as the natural objects themselves.... . A
perfectly deceptive illusion can be obtained only on *two conditions*: (a)
the spectator shall use only one eye, (b) this eye has to be placed in the
central point of perspective (or, at least, quite near to this point)'.[3] The
component elements of that account should be noted: the possible exact
match for the eye of picture and object, the deceptive illusion; the centre
of the illusion, the eye in place. What is fundamental is the idea of the
spectator at a window, an *'aperta finestra'* that gives a view on the world
– framed, centred, harmonious (the *'istoria'*). Alberti, in his treatise *Della
Pittura* written circa 1435, talks of the picture plane as of a pane of glass
on which the world in view can be traced: 'Painters should only seek to
present the form of things seen on this plane as if it were of transparent
glass. Thus the visual pyramid could pass through it, placed at a
definite distance with definite lights and a definite position of centre in
space and a definite place in respect to the observer.'[4] The cost of such
fixed centrality is the marginal distortion which ensues when the
observer's eye is not correctly in position in the centre of the perspective
projection but pulls to the edge (like Benson's gaze in *Suspicion*, which
then receives the shock of another – confusing – painting).
Anamorphosis is the recognition and exploitation of the possibilities of
this distortion; playing between 'appearance' and 'reality', it situates the
centre of the projection of the painting (or of a single element, as in
Holbein's 'The Ambassadors' in the National Gallery) obliquely to the
side, the sense of the painting – its representation – only falling into
place (exactly) once the position has been found. Galileo abhorred these
perversions of the 'normal' view into a turmoil of lines and colours
('una confusa e inordinata mescolanza di linee e di colori'[5]) but,
developed in the course of the sixteenth century and particularly
appreciated in the following two centuries, they can be seen as a
constant triumph of central perspective, a kind of playful liberation
from its constraints that remains nevertheless entirely dependent on its
system, a ceaseless confirmation of the importance of centre and
position. What must be more crucially emphasized is that the ideal of a
steady position, of a unique embracing centre, to which Galileo refers
and to which anamorphosis pays its peculiar homage, is precisely that:
a powerful *ideal*. To say this is not simply to acknowledge that the

practice of painting from the Quattrocento on is far from a strict adherence to the perspective system but demonstrates a whole variety of 'accommodations' (in certain paintings, for example, buildings will be drawn with one centre according to central perspective while a separate centre will then be chosen for each set of human figures); it is also to suggest that there is a real utopianism at work, the construction of a code – in every sense a *vision* – projected onto a reality to be gained in all its hoped-for clarity much more than onto some naturally given reality; a suggestion that merely repeats the conclusions of Francastel in his study of the birth of Quattrocento space: 'It was a question for a society in process of total transformation of a space in accordance with its actions and its dreams.... It is men who create the space in which they move and express themselves. Spaces are born and die like societies; they live, they have a history. In the fifteenth century, the human societies of Western Europe organized, in the material and intellectual senses of the term, a space completely different from that of the preceding generations; with their technical superiority, they progressively imposed that space over the planet.'[6] For five centuries men and women *exist at ease* in that space; the Quattrocento system provides a practical representation of the world which in time appears so natural as to offer its real representation, the immediate translation of reality in itself.

The conception of the Quattrocento system is that of a scenographic space, space set out as spectacle for the eye of a spectator. Eye and knowledge come together, subject, object and the distance of the steady observation that allows the one to master the other; the scene with its strength of geometry and optics. Of that projected utopia, the camera is the culminating realization (the **camera obscura**, described by Giambattista della Porta in 1589 in a treatise on optics, commands attention in the wake of the spread of the Quattrocento system); the images it furnishes become, precisely, the currency of that vision, that space:

> Strong as the mathematical convention of perspective had become in picture making before the pervasion of photography, that event definitely clamped it on our vision and our beliefs about 'real' shapes, etc. The public has come to believe that geometrical perspective, so long as it does not involve unfamiliar points of view, is 'true', just as a long time ago it believed that the old geometry of Euclid was 'the truth'.
>
> Every day we see photographs which are central perspective images. If another system were applied to the art of painting one could believe that one was living in a bilingual country.[7]

In so far as it is grounded in the photograph, cinema will contribute to the circulation of this currency, will bring with it monocular perspective, the positioning of the spectator-subject in an identification with the camera as the point of a sure and centrally embracing view (Metz draws further conclusions from this identification in his essay 'The Imaginary Signifier').[8]

'Our field of vision is full of solid objects but our eye (like the camera) sees this field from only one station point at a given moment...'[9] The comparison of eye and camera in the interests of showing their similarity has come to seem irresistible: our eye like the camera, with its stationary point, its lens, its surface on which the image is captured, and so on. In fact, of course, any modern scientific description of the eye will go on to indicate the limits of the comparison. Our eye is never seized by some static spectacle, is never some motionless recorder; not only is our vision anyway binocular, but one eye alone sees in time: constant *scanning* movements to bring the different parts of whatever is observed to the fovea, movements necessary in order that the receptive cells produce fresh neuro-electric impulses, immediate activity of memory inasmuch as there is no brute vision to be isolated from the visual experience of the individual inevitably engaged in a specific socio-historical situation. In a real sense, the ideological force of the photograph has been to 'ignore' this in its presentation as a coherent image of vision, an image that then carries over into a suggestion of the world as a kind of sum total of possible photographs, a spectacle to be recorded in its essence in an instantaneous objectification for the eye (it would be worth considering the ideological determinations and resonances of the development and commercialization of polaroid photography); a world, that is, conceived outside of process and practice, empirical scene of the confirmed and central master-spectator, serenely 'present' in tranquil rectilinearity (a curvilinear perspective, for which arguments of 'optical realism' can be adduced if need be, comfortably rejected as out of true, as 'wrong').

Cinema is involved with photograph and camera, its principal matter of expression that of moving photographic images ('principal' as we know it in its history), its prime achievement that of the creation of the 'impression of reality' – 'neither absolutely two-dimensional nor absolutely three-dimensional, but something between'. The latter description reads in many ways like an account of the effect of depth of field which gives very much the possibility of a cued construction of space in accordance with the Quattrocento system. Yet cinema can also use in one and the same film quite other projections (lenses with long focal length, for example), projections which approximate more or less, but differently, to the perspective model; simply, angles and distances change, the centre shifts its points. It may well be that classically cinema acquires 'the mobility of the eye' while preserving the contained and delimited visual field on which 'correct' perspectives depend, but the mobility is nevertheless difficult: movement of figures 'in' film, camera movement, movement from shot to shot; the first gives at once a means of creating perspective (the movements of the figures in a shot can 'bring out' the space, show relative positions, suggest depth) and a problem of 'composition' (film is said to destroy the 'ordinary laws' of pictorial organization because of its moving figures which capture attention against all else); the second equally produces problems of composition and, though often motivated in the manuals by some extension of the eye-camera comparison (the camera executes the same movements as the head; horizontal panning is turning the head, etc.), is strictly regulated in the interests of the maintenance of scenographic space (the version of space, indeed, which determines the justifying comparison); the third, again apt to receive the comparative motivation ('In so far as the film is photographic and reproduces movement, it can give us a life-like semblance of what we see, in so far as it employs editing, it can exactly reproduce the *manner* in which we normally see it'[10]), effectively indicates the filmic nature of film space, film as constantly the construction of a space (thus Branigan will conclude that 'that space exists only at twenty-four frames per second'[11]). The ideal of space remains that of photographic vision which brings with it the concern to sustain the camera as eye; in the sense of the detached, untroubled eye discussed earlier, an eye free from the body, outside process, purely looking (no matter, finally, if the falsity of the eye-camera comparison be admitted since it can be retrieved with a confirming twist: the eye in cinema is the *perfect* eye, the steady and ubiquitous control of the scene passed from director to spectator by virtue of the cinematic apparatus:

> The director's aim is to give an *ideal* picture of the scene, in each case placing his camera in such a position that it records most effectively the particular piece of action or detail which is dramatically significant. He becomes, as it were, a ubiquitous observer, giving the audience at each moment of the action the best possible viewpoint.[12]

The ideal, however, is a construction, the mobility acquired is still not easy, the shifting centre needs to be settled along the film in its making scenes, its taking place; space will be difficult.

To put it another way: mobility is exactly what is *possible* in film, complicit – the possibility of holding film within a certain vision, thereby 'perfected' – and radical – the possibility of film disturbing that vision, with which none the less it is immediately involved, historically, industrially, ideologically. Cinema is not simply and specifically ideological 'in itself'; but it is developed in the context of concrete and specific ideological determinations which inform as well the 'technical' as the 'commercial' or 'artistic' sides of that development. For Marey, cinema did nothing 'to rid the eye of any of its illusions' since set up precisely to play on the illusions of a conventional vision, to 'reproduce life' as Lumière put it; for Vertov, cinema could be made to challenge that vision by constructions of dissociations in time and space that would produce the contradictions of the alignment of camera-eye and human-eye in order to displace the subject-eye of the social-historical individual into an operative – transforming – relation to reality. Film is dominantly articulated in the interests of the 'theatrical cinema' Vertov sought to shatter, the world of the scene and the stasis of its relations of vision, but Brecht, and Benjamin with him, will see in the very fact of the succession of film images a certain contradiction to be exploited against the theatre, for a different vision, a different space. In its developments and possibilities, its constraints and disruptions, it is the whole question of space in film that must now be examined further.

The examination of space in film may be divided for the moment into two: the examination of space 'in frame', of the space determined by the frame, held within its limits; the examination of space 'out of frame', the space beyond the limits of the frame, there in its absence and given back, as it were, in the editing of shot with shot or in camera movement with its reframings. The division can be maintained long enough to allow an order for the remarks that follow, remarks which will finally suggest more clearly its inadequacy.

Screen, frame: Notions of screen and frame are fundamental in the elaboration of the perspective system. Leonardo da Vinci writes: 'Perspective is nothing else than seeing a place (or objects) behind a pane of glass, quite transparent, on the surface of which the objects behind that glass are drawn. These can be traced in pyramids to the point in the eye, and these pyramids are intersected on the glass pane.'[13] The pane is at once a frame, the frame of a window, and a screen, the

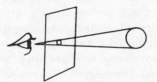

area of projection on which what is seen can be traced and fixed; from the Quattrocento on, the 'pane' delimits and holds a view, the painter's canvas as a screen situated between eye and object, point of interception of the light rays (see figure). It is worth noting, indeed, in Renaissance (and post-Renaissance) painting the powerful attraction of the window as theme, the fascination with the rectangle of tamed light, the luminously defined space of vision. In Ghirlandaio's 'Vecchio e bambino' (Louvre, Paris), Titian's 'Isabel di Portogallo' (Prado, Madrid) or Dürer's 'Selbstbildnis' (Prado), for example, a window opens to the right, behind the figure portrayed, on to the perspective of a distant horizon; the figure placed almost as by a cinema screen, the sudden illumination of another view, a frame of light to which we are invited to attend. More important, however, is to grasp the very idea of the frame as fully historical in the developments it is given. Before the fifteenth century, frames hardly exist, other than as the specific architectural setting that is to be decorated (wall, altarpiece, or whatever); it is during that century that frames begin to have an independent reality, this concomitant with the growth of the notion itself of 'a painting' (the first instance of the use of the word 'frame' in an artistic sense recorded by the *Oxford English Dictionary* is *c*. 1600). The new frame is symmetrical (the centred rectangle, clearly 'composable') and inevitable (the Quattrocento system cannot be realized without it, it becomes a reflex of 'natural' composition). Significantly, it brings with it the easel (first recorded instance *c*. 1634 – 'a frame or easel called by artists'), 'significantly' because the easel is precisely dependent on the idea of 'a painting' as single, central view. The painter stands as spectator in front of his easel (in this history it is men who are the professionals of painting, the authoritative gaze), capturing on the canvas screen the scene behind onto which it gives and which it sets as such; no longer englobed in the area of the painting (dome or arch or ceiling), the painter is definitely upright, an eye on the world, an eye that stations itself, with the easel carried from place to place, much like a tripod. Easel painting, that is, established along with perspective system and camera obscura (the latter itself rapidly becomes a portable apparatus for the mobile painter), is a step in the direction of the camera, a camera that will provide screen and frame and the image reflected, fixed, painted with light: a camera that will culminate this whole vision.

'Frame' describes the material unit of film ('the single transparent photograph in a series of such photographs printed on a length of cinematographic film', 'twenty-four frames a second') and, equally, the film image in its setting, the delimitation of the image on screen (in Arnheim's *Film as Art*, for example, 'frame' and 'delimitation' are assumed as synonymous). Framing, determining and laying out the frame, is quickly seen as a fundamental cinematic act, the moment of the very 'rightness' of the image: 'framing, that is to say, bringing the image to the place it must occupy', a definition taken from a manual for teachers written in the 1920s.[14] Quickly too, and in consequence, it becomes the object of an aesthetic attention concerned to pose decisively the problems of the composition of the frame, of what Eisenstein calls 'mise en cadre'.

'There it is, our 1.33 to 1 rectangle, it will tolerate precious little tampering with at all' (Hollis Frampton).[15] The compositional rectangle is there, carried through into cinema, space is structured within its frame, areas are assigned position in relation to its edges. In a sense, moreover, the constraint of the rectangle is even greater in cinema than in painting: in the latter, its proportions are relatively free; in the former, they are limited to a standard aspect ratio (Frampton's 1.33 to 1 rectangle, the aptly named 'academy frame') or, as now, to a very small number of ratios,[16] with techniques such as masking the sides of the frame to change the size of the rectangle in general disfavour. Hence the rectangle must be mastered – 'Maîtriser le rectangle', the title of one of the key sections in a modern manual for young people. Hence the rules for mastery, rules which come straight from the Quattrocento system, its balanced vision and the composition of the clarity thus decided; so, from the same modern manual:

> To consider the rectangle as a surface crossed by lines of force ... and with strong points (the points of intersection of those lines) is to guarantee it a solid base structure and to refuse the notion of it as a sort of visual hold-all;
> If, therefore, we have to place an actor in this rectangle, one of the best places will be that which follows one of the lines of force in question. And the face, 'strong point' of the human person, will be placed at one of the strong points of the rectangle;
> A second character will naturally be placed at one of the strong points ...;
> Let us quickly note when we come to 'landscapes' how inharmonious is a division of the surface which does not correspond to the famous 'third' and how placing the horizon midway in the frame is only apparently logical.[17]

In cinema, however, these rules also have their 'excess', there is always a further court of appeal – life itself, the very aim of cinema: 'But cinema is life, is movement. The cinéaste must not fall into the traps of a plastic aesthetic. Failure to remember the rules of framing will often bring agreeable surprises, for it is not without truth that the world is already, in itself, harmonious.'[18]

If life enters cinema as movement, that movement brings with it nevertheless its problems of composition in frame, as was mentioned earlier in the discussion of perspective. In fact, composition will organize the frame in function of the human figures in their actions; what enters cinema is a logic of movement and it is this logic that centres the frame. Frame space, in other words, is constructed as narrative space. It is narrative significance that at any moment sets the space of the frame to be followed and 'read', and that determines the development of the filmic cues in their contributions to the definition of space in frame (focus pull, for example, or back-lighting). Narrative contains the mobility that could threaten the clarity of vision in a constant renewal of perspective; space becomes place – narrative as the taking place of film – in a movement which is no more than the fulfilment of the Renaissance impetus, an impetus that a De Kooning can describe as follows:

> It was up to the artist to measure out the exact space for a person to die in or to be dead already. The exactness of the space was determined or, rather inspired by whatever reason the person was dying or being killed for. The space thus measured out on the original plane of the canvas surface became a 'place' somewhere on the floor.[19]

What is crucial is the conversion of seen into scene, the holding of signifier on signified: the frame, composed, centred, narrated, is the point of that conversion.

Cinema as 'life in its truth as scene', the frame as the instance of such a vision. Metz talks here of the regime 'of the primal scene and the keyhole': 'the rectangular screen permits every type of fetishism, all the effects of "just-before", since it places at exactly the height it wants the sharp vibrant bar which stops the seen... .'[20] The fascination of the scene is there, and from the beginnings of cinema with its tableaux, its dramatic masks (including the keyhole-shaped matte; as in *A Search for Evidence*, AM & B 1903), its occasional thematic directnesses (in *Gay Shoe Clerk*, Edison Co. 1903, which involves a flirtatious shoe clerk, an attractive young lady and her chaperone armed with an umbrella, a cut-in close-up shows the young lady's ankle with the clerk's hand gripping her foot into the shoe[21]); the fetishism is there, with the edge, the limit, the setting, the careful place, and from Alberti on – witness that whole series of machines and devices for the production of a certain distance of image, a sure illusion of scrutiny. Simply, the 'just-before' in film is spatially moving, the itinerary of a fixity perpetually gained, and the frame stands – acts – in relation to that.

As for the screen, it receives and gives the frame, its flatness halts the image and lays the base of that triangle for which the spectator's eye provides the apex. Doubtless there is a sheer pleasure for the position of the eye in the very fact of the projection of the frames onto and from the screen, in their 'hitting the screen'[22]; a space is established with no 'behind' (it is important that the Lumière brothers should set the screen as they do in the Grand Café and not with the audience on either side of a translucent screen, that cinema architecture should take its forms in consequence, that there should be no feeling of machinery to the side of or beyond the screen, that the screen should be one of the most stable elements in cinema's history), a pure expanse that can be invested with depth. The screen, that is, is at once ground, the surface that supports the projected images, and background, its surface caught up in the cone of light to give the frame of the image. Ground and background are one in the alignment of frame and screen, the 'on screen in frame' that is the basis of the spatial articulations a film will make, the start of its composition.[23]

Psychoanalysis, it may be briefly added, has come to stress the dream as itself projected on a screen: the *dream screen*, blank surface present in dreams though mostly 'unseen', covered over by the manifest content of the projected dream; a screen that represents the breast (infinitely extensive centre of the baby's visual space) and then also sleep (the desire for sleep) as an original ground of pleasure 'before' difference, 'before' identity, 'before' symbolization.[24] In cinema, the images pass (twenty-four per second), the screen remains; covered but there, specified – the images of this or that film – but the same – the satisfying projection of a basic oneness. The force of this relation, however, must be understood: it is the passing of the images that produces the constancy of the screen; without those images the screen is 'empty', with them it is an impression, a surface-ground that the film and the spectator find as the frames hit the screen, that they find intact, safely *in* the background (revealing and disturbing moment when a character in a film throws something, as is said, 'at the screen').[25]

Movement, transitions: From the very first, as though of right, human figures enter film, spilling out of the train, leaving the factory or the photographic congress, *moving* – this is the movies, these are moving pictures. The figures move in the frame, they come and go, and there is then need to change the frame, reframing with a camera movement or moving to another shot. The transitions thus effected pose acutely the problem of the filmic construction of space, of achieving a coherence of place and positioning the spectator as the unified and unifying subject of its vision. It is this process of construction, indeed, which is often regarded as the power of cinema and as defining the overall reality of film as that of a kind of generalized 'trick effect': 'if several successive images represent a space under different angles, the spectator, victim of the "trick effect", spontaneously perceives the space as unitary... .'[26]

Early films are typically organized as a series of fixed scenes, with a strict unity of time and place. The example was cited above of *Tom, Tom,*

The Piper's Son which tells the well-known story in 'eight snappy scenes', simply joined the one after the other as so many *tableaux*. The actions of the characters in frame, as though on a stage, make out the sense of the image, centre the eye in paths of reading, but within the limits of the distance of the fixed frontal view which creates difficulties of effectively maintaining such a centred perception given the continual wealth of movements and details potentially offered by the photographic image (Ken Jacobs in his film of the same title minutely explores the surface of *Tom, Tom, The Piper's Son*, refilming from the screen and finding in so doing not just 'other' actions but also 'central' actions not easily grasped or possibly even missed in the original – as, for instance, the handkerchief stealing in the opening shot). Those difficulties, in the context of its commercial exploitation, are fundamental for cinema's development. The centre is the movement, not movements but the logic of a consequent and temporally coherent action. The vision of the image is its narrative clarity and that clarity hangs on the negation of space for place, the constant realization of centre in function of narrative purpose, narrative movement: 'Negatively, the space is presented so as not to distract attention from the dominant actions: positively, the space is "used up" by the presentation of narratively important settings, character traits ("psychology"), or other causal agents.'[27] Specific spatial cues – importantly, amongst others, those depending on camera movement and editing – will be established and used accordingly, centring the flow of the images, taking place.

Which is to say, of course, that the *tableau* space of the early films is intolerable in its particular fixity, must be broken up in the interests of the unity of action and place and subject view as that unity is conceived from the narrative models of the novelistic that cinema is dominantly exploited to relay and extend. Burch puts it well: 'It was necessary to be able to film objects or people close up – to isolate a face, a hand, an accessory (as the discourse of the novel does) – but avoiding any disorientation of the spectator in respect of his or her own "reasoned" analysis of the spatial continuum... .'[28] The need is to cut up and then join together in a kind of spatial *Aufhebung* that decides a superior unity, the binding of the spectator in the space of the film, the space it realizes. In the late 1930s and early 1940s, the average shot length of a full-length Hollywood film has been estimated at about 9–10 seconds,[29] but that fragmentation is the condition of a fundamental continuity.

> There are no jerks in time or space in real life. Time and space are continuous. Not so in film. The period of time that is being photographed may be interrupted at any point. One scene may be immediately followed by another that takes place at a totally

different time. And the continuity of space may be broken in the same manner.[30]

Why is it, Arnheim goes on to ask, that the 'juggling with space' possible in film (and including the breaking of a single 'real life' space into 'several successive images ... under different angles') does not cause discomfort? The answer refers back to the 'something-between' status of film previously mentioned:

> Film gives simultaneously the effect of an actual happening and of a picture. A result of the 'pictureness' of film is, then, that a sequence of scenes that are diverse in time and space is not felt as arbitrary.... If film photographs gave a very strong spatial impression, montage probably would be impossible. It is the partial unreality of the film picture that makes it possible.[31]

The emphasis on the 'pictureness' of the image is crucial here (there would be problems of cutting for spatial unity with holography): the space constructed in film is exactly *a filmic construction*. Thus Mitry, for example, will write that shots are like 'cells', 'distinct spaces the succession of which, however, reconstitutes a homogeneous space, but a space *unlike* that from which these elements were subtracted'.[32]

The conception at work in such descriptions can be seen (even if in this or that writer that conception may be inflected 'aesthetically', turned in the direction of film as 'art'). The filmic construction of space is recognized in its difference but that difference is the term of an ultimate similarity (indeed, a final 'illusion'); the space is 'unlike' but at the same time 'reconstitutes', using elements lifted from real space. In fact, we are back in the realm of 'composition', where composition is now the laying out of a succession of images in order to give the picture, to produce the implication of a coherent ('real') space; in short, to create continuity.

The compositional rules for spatial clarity and continuity are sufficiently well known not to need extended discussion at this stage; it will be enough merely to stress one or two of their determinations. Firstly, the establishment of fixed patterns of clarity for the variation of scale of shot in a scene: there are 'normal ways' of organizing dialogue scenes, action scenes, and so on[33]; these systems allowing for a certain free play – 'exceptions' – within their overall structure in the interests of 'dramatic effect' ('In the normal way, it is almost certainly better to cut the scenes as we have indicated, but ... there may be exceptions when the rules need to be modified to convey certain dramatic effects.').[34] What may be remembered above all in this context is the extreme importance attached to providing an overall view, literally the

'master-shot' that will allow the scene to be dominated in the course of
its reconstitution narratively as dramatic unity ('Even where a sequence
starts on a detail, it is important that the whole setting should be shown
at some stage'[35]). Take the beginning of *Jaws*: a beach party with the
camera tracking slowly right along the line of the faces of the
participants until it stops on a young man looking off; eyeline cut to a
young woman who is thus revealed as the object of his gaze; cut to a
high-angle shot onto the party that shows its general space, its situation,
before the start of the action with the run down to the ocean and the
first shark attack – the shot serves, that is, as a kind of master fold in the
sequence, setting it correctly in place. Secondly, the establishment of the
180-degree and 30-degree rules. The former matches screen space and
narrative space (the space represented in the articulation of the images),
ground and background; with its help, 'one will always find the same
characters in the same parts of the screen'.[36] The 180-degree line that the
camera is forbidden to cross answers exactly to the 180-degree line of
the screen behind which the spectator cannot and must not go, in front
of which he or she is placed within the triangle of representation, the
space of the image projected, that is repeated in the very terms of the
fiction of the imaged space. As for the latter, a 'quick, simple rule that
issues directly from the necessities of cinematic fragmentation' and that
avoids the 'disagreeable sensation' of a 'jump in space',[37] it is finally
nothing other than a specific perspective rule for a smooth line of
direction in film, for the achievement of a smooth line in from shot to
shot. Thirdly and lastly, following on from those more particular
remarks, the establishment generally as a powerful evidence, as a
natural basis, of the idea of continuity as smoothness in transitions: the
rules of the filmic construction of space on screen (master-shot,
180-degree and 30-degree rules, matching on action, eyeline matching,
field/reverse field, etc.) background the image flow into a unified
subject-space, immediately and fully continuous, reconstitutive:
'Making a smooth cut means joining two shots in such a way that the
transition does not create a noticeable jerk and the spectator's illusion of
seeing a continuous piece of action is not interrupted.'[38]

Continuity in these terms is also decisive with regard to transitions
and changes of frame effected by camera movement. 'Imperceptible'
reframing movements, more definite pans and tracking shots are
developed in the interests of the narrative composition of space in
relation to the actions of the characters[39]; here, too, rules are elaborated
accordingly, the camera having, for instance, to impregnate space with
the anticipation of action: 'if the actor is accompanied by a movement of
the camera, more "room" must be left in front of him or her than
behind, so as to figure sensorially the space to be crossed'.[40] In this
respect, it is worth bearing in mind the extent to which the

sequence-shot-with-deep-focus long take valued by Bazin in his account of 'the evolution of cinematic language' can stay within such a conception of space. The narrative of a Welles or a Wyler in Bazin's account is carried through in a manner that retains the particular effects to be derived from 'the unity of the image in time and space', a manner that refines and draws out the essential 'realism' of cinema; a realism in which space is all important: 'the cinematographic image can be emptied of all reality save one – the reality of space'.[41] The space of *Citizen Kane* or *The Best Years of Our Lives* is still entirely dramatic, however; heightened indeed in its drama: as was suggested earlier, deep focus allows composition for a high degree of perspective ('depth of field' exactly), and this can be increased over the long take with its potential definition of a complex action in a single shot, its filling out of movements and positions in a temporally visible demonstration of space as narrative place.[42] It should anyway be noted that the average shot length overall of *Citizen Kane* is 12 seconds, 'about average for its period',[43] and it remains true that classically continuity is built on fragmentation rather than the long take – on a segmentation for recomposition that can bind the spectator in the strong articulations of the unity it seeks to create. Elsewhere, Bazin was to refer to the version of the spatial realism he ontologically cherished provided by Italian Neo-Realism; a version that might show the possibilities of the long take away from an absorbed dramatic space; and so, by contrast, the force of the classical continuity in that dependence on segmentation-articulation and its effective inclusion of the longer take within its terms of spatial construction.

Those terms, as they have been described here, are the terms of a constant welding together: screen and frame, ground and background, surface and depth, the whole setting of movements and transitions, the implication of space and spectator in the taking place of film as narrative. The classical *economy* of film is its organization thus as organic unity and the *form* of that economy is narrative, the *narrativization* of film. Narrative, as it were, determines the film which is contained in its process in that determination, this 'bind' being itself a process – precisely the narrativization. The narration is to be held on the narrated, the enunciation on the enounced; filmic procedures are to be held as narrative instances (very much as 'cues'), exhaustively, without gap or contradiction. What is sometimes vaguely referred to as 'transparency' has its meaning in this narrativization: the proposal of a discourse that disavows its operations and positions in the name of a signified that it proposes as its pre-existent justification. 'Transparency', moreover, is entirely misleading in so far as it implies that narrativization has necessarily to do with some simple 'invisibility' (anyway impossible – no one has yet seen a signified without a signifier). The narration may well be given as visible in its filmic procedures; what is crucial is that it be given as visible *for the narrated* and that the spectator be caught up in the play of *that* process, that the *address* of the film be clear (does anyone who has watched, say, *The Big Sleep* seriously believe that a central part of Hollywood films, differently defined from genre to genre, was not the address of a process with a movement of play and that that was not a central part of their pleasure?).

Within this narrativization of film, the role of the character-look has been fundamental for the welding of a spatial unity of narrative implication. In so many senses, every film is a veritable drama of vision and this drama has thematically and symptomatically 'returned' in film since the very beginning: from the fascination of the magnifying glass in *Grandma's Reading Glass* to Lina's short-sightedness in *Suspicion* to the windscreen and rear-view mirror of *Taxi Driver*, from the keyhole of *A Search for Evidence* to the images that flicker reflected over Brody's glasses in *Jaws* as he turns the pages of the book on sharks, finding the images of the film to come and which he will close as he closes the book; not to mention the extended dramatizations such as *Rear Window* or *Peeping Tom*. How to make sense in film if not through vision, film with its founding ideology of vision as truth? The drama of vision in the film returns the drama of vision of the film: the spectator will be bound to the film as spectacle as the world of the film is itself revealed as spectacle on the basis of a narrative organization of look and point of view that moves space into place through the image-flow; the character, figure of the look, is a kind of perspective within the perspective system, regulating the world, orientating space, providing directions – and for the spectator.

Film works at a loss, the loss of the divisions, the discontinuities, the absences that structure it – as, for example, the 'outside' of the frame, off-screen space, the *hors-champ*. Such absence is the final tragedy of a Bazin, who wants to believe in cinema as a global consciousness of reality, an illimitation of picture frame and theatre scene –

> The screen is not a frame like that of a picture, but a mask which allows us to see a part of the event only. When a person leaves the field of the camera, we recognize that he or she is out of the field of vision, though continuing to exist identically in another part of the scene which is hidden from us. The screen has no wings … [44]

– but who can only inspect the damage of 'camera angles or prejudices',[45] acknowledge none the less the frame, the scene, the mask, the hidden, the absent. The sequence-shot-with-deep-focus long take functions as a utopia in this context – the ideal of a kind of 'full angle', without prejudices, but hence too without cinema; the ideal recognized in *Bicycle Thieves*, 'plus de cinéma'.[46]

Burch writes that 'off-screen space has only an intermittent or, rather, *fluctuating* existence during any film, and structuring this fluctuation can become a powerful tool in a film-maker's hands'.[47] The term 'fluctuation' is excellent, yet it must be seen that the work of classical continuity is not to hide or ignore off-screen space but, on the contrary, to contain it, to regularize its fluctuation in a constant movement of reappropriation. It is this movement that defines the rules of continuity and the fiction of space they serve to construct, the whole functioning according to a kind of metonymic lock in which off-screen space becomes on-screen space and is replaced in turn by the space it holds off, each joining over the next. The join is conventional and ruthlessly selective (it generally leaves out of account, for example, the space that might be supposed to be masked at the top and bottom of the frame, concentrating much more on the space at the sides of the frame or on that 'in front', 'behind the camera', as in variations of field/reverse field), and demands that the off-screen space recaptured must be 'called for', must be 'logically consequential', must arrive as 'answer', 'fulfilment of promise' or whatever (and not as difference or contradiction) – must be narrativized. Classical continuity, in other words, is an order of the pregnancy of space in frame; one of the narrative acts of a film is the creation of space[48] but what gives the moving space its coherence in time, decides the metonymy as a 'taking place', is here 'the narrative itself', and above all as it crystallizes round character as look and point of view. The fundamental role of these is exactly their pivotal use as a mode of organization and organicization, the joining of a film's constructions, the stitching together of the overlaying metonymies.

'If in the left of the frame an actor in close-up is looking off right, he has an empty space in front of him; if the following shot shows an empty space to the left and an object situated to the right, then the actor's look appears to cross an orientated, rectilinear, thus logical space: it seems to bear with precision on the object. One has an eye-line match.'[49] The look, that is, joins form of expression – the composition of the images and their disposition in relation to one another – and form of content – the definition of the action of the film in the movement of looks, exchanges, objects seen, and so on. Point of view develops on the basis of this joining operation of the look, the camera taking the position of a character in order to show the spectator what he or she sees.[50] Playing on the assumption of point of view, a film has an evident means of placing its space, of giving it immediate and holding significance; Burch talks of the establishment of an organization founded on the 'traditional dichotomy between the "subjective camera" (which "places the spectator in the position of a character") and the "objective camera" (which makes the spectator the ideal, immaterial "voyeur" of a pro-filmic pseudo-reality)'.[51]

This account, however, requires clarification. The point-of-view shot is 'subjective' in that it assumes the position of a subject-character but to refer to that assumption in terms of 'subjective camera' or 'subjective image' can lead to misunderstanding with regard to the functioning of point of view. Subjective images can be many things; Mitry, for example, classifies them into five major categories:

> the purely mental image (more or less impracticable in the cinema); the truly subjective or analytical image (i.e. what is looked at without the person looking), which is practicable in small doses; the semi-subjective or associated image (i.e. the person looking + what is looked at, which is in fact looked at from the view-point of the person looking), the most generalizable formula; the complete sequence given over to the imaginary, which does not raise special problems; and finally the memory image, which is in principle simply a variety of the mental image but, when presented in the form of a flash-back with commentary, allows for a specific filmic treatment which is far more successful than in the case of other mental images.[52]

The point-of-view shot includes 'the semi-subjective or associated image' (its general mode) and 'the truly subjective or analytical image' (its pure mode, as it were) in that classification but not necessarily any of the other categories (a memory sequence, for instance, need not contain any point-of-view shots); what is 'subjective' in the point-of-view shot is its spatial positioning (its place), not the image or the camera.

To stress this is to stress a crucial factor in the exploitation of the film image and its relation to point-of-view organization. Within the terms of that organization, a true subjective image would effectively need to mark its subjectivity *in the image itself*. Examples are common: the blurred image of Gutman in *The Maltese Falcon* is the subjective image of the drugged Spade; the blurring of focus marks the subjectivity of the image, exclusively Spade's, and the spectator is set not simply *with* Spade but *as* Spade. They are also limited, since they depend exactly on some recognizable – marking – distortion of the 'normal' image, a narratively motivated aberration of vision of some kind or another (the character is drugged, intoxicated, short-sighted, terrified ... down to he or she running, with hand-held effects of the image 'jogging', or even walking, with regular speed of camera movement forward matched on

a shot that effectively establishes the character as in the process of
walking; the latter represents the lowest limit on the scale since the
camera movement is there a weak subjective marking of the image
which itself remains more or less 'normal' – except, of course, and hence
this limit position of the banal action of walking, that the normal image
is precisely static, that movement in a central perspective system can
quickly become a problem of vision). The implication of this, of course,
is then the strength of the unmarked image as a constant third person –
the vision of picture and scene, the Quattrocento view, Burch's 'voyeur'
position – *which is generally continued within point-of-view shots
themselves*; the point-of-view shot is marked as subjective in its
emplacement but the resulting image is still finally (or rather firstly)
objective, the objective sight of what is seen from the subject position
assumed. Indicatively enough, the general mode of the point-of-view
shot is the shot which shows both what is looked at and the person
looking. Instances of the pure shot, showing what is looked at without
the person looking, however, are equally conclusive. Take the shot in
Suspicion of the telegram that Lina receives from Johnnie to tell her of
his intention to attend the Hunt Ball: the telegram is clearly shown from
Lina's reading position and the end of the shot – the end of the reading
– is marked by her putting down her glasses onto the telegram lying on
a table, the glasses thus coming down into frame; the position of the
shot is marked as subjective with Lina but the image nevertheless
continues to be objective, 'the real case' for the narrative.[53]

Point of view, that is, depends on an overlaying of first and third
person modes. There is no radical dichotomy between subjective
point-of-view shots and objective non-point-of-view shots; the latter
mode is the continual basis over which the former can run in its
particular organization of space, its disposition of the images. The
structure of the photographic image – with its vision, its scene, its
distance, its normality – is to the film somewhat as language is to the
novel: the grounds of its representations, which representations can
include the creation of an acknowledged movement of point of view.
This is the sense of the spectator identification with the camera that is so
often remarked upon (Benjamin: 'the audience's identification with the
actor is really an identification with the camera'; Metz: 'the spectator
can do no other than identify with the camera').[54] The spectator must *see*
and this structuring vision is the condition of the possibility of the
disposition of the images via the relay of character look and viewpoint
which pulls together vision and narrative. Emphasis was laid earlier on
the structures of the structuring vision that founds cinema; what is
emphasized now is the dependence of our very notion of point of view
on those structures; dependence at once in so far as the whole
Quattrocento system is built on the establishment of point of view, the

central position of the eye, and in so far as the mode of representation thus defined brings with it fixity and movement in a systematic complicity of interaction – brings with it, that is, the 'objective' and the 'subjective', the 'third person' and the 'first person', the view and its partial points, and finds this drama of vision as the resolving action of its narratives.

Identification with the camera, seeing, the 'ideal picture' of the scene: 'the usual scene in a classical film is narrated as if from the point of view of an observer capable of moving about the room'.[55] Such movement may be given in editing or by camera movement within a shot, and the importance accruing to some master view that will define the space of the mobility has been noted. Movement, in fact, will be treated as a supplement to produce precisely the 'ideal *picture*' (going to the movies is going to the pictures): on the basis of the vision of the photographic image, that is, it will provide the 'total' point of view of an observer capable of moving about the room without changing anything of the terms of that vision, the scene laid out for the central observer (and spectator); every shot or reframing adds a difference, but that difference is always the same image, with the organization – the continuity, the rules, the matches, the pyramid structures – constantly doing the sum of the *scene*.

That said, it remains no less true, as has again been noted and as will become important later on, that movement represents a potentially radical disturbance of the smooth stability of the scenographic vision (hence the need for a systematic organization to contain it). Such a disturbance, however, is not as simple as is sometimes suggested and it is necessary briefly to consider at this stage two instances of disturbance as they are conventionally described; both bear on the mobility of the camera.

The first is that of what Branigan characterizes as the impossible place: 'To the extent that the camera is located in an "impossible" place, the narration questions its own origin, that is, suggests a shift in narration.'[56] 'Impossible', of course, is here decided in respect of the 'possible' positions of the observer moving about, the disturbance involved seen as a disjunction of the unity of narration and narrated, enunciation and enounced. Thus defined, impossible places are certainly utilized in classical narrative cinema, with examples ranging from the relatively weak to the relatively strong. At one end of the range, the weak examples would be any high or low angles that are not motivated as the point of view of a character; or, indeed, any high or low angles that, while so motivated, are nevertheless sufficiently divergent from the assumed normal upright observing position as to be experienced as in some sense 'impossible' in their peculiarity (the most celebrated – and complex – example is the dead-man-in-the-coffin point

of view in *Vampyr*).[57] At the other end, the strong examples – those
intended by Branigan – can be illustrated by a description of two shots
from *Killer's Kiss*: (1) as Davey, the boxer-hero, is seen stooping to feed
his goldfish, there is a cut to a shot through the bowl, from the other
side, of his face peering in as the feed drops down; since the bowl is on
a table against a wall, the place taken by the camera is not possible; (2)
Rappello, the dance-hall owner, furious at being left by the heroine, is
drinking in a back-room, its walls covered with posters and prints; a
close-up of a print showing two men leering from a window is followed
by a shot of Rappello who throws his drink at the camera ('at the
screen'!); a crack appears as the drink runs down a plate of glass;
impossibly, the shot was from 'in' the print. The second – and related –
instance of disturbance is that of the development of camera movement
as a kind of autonomous figure; what Burch calls 'the camera
designated as an "omnipotent and omniscient" (i.e. manipulative and
pre-cognitive) presence'.[58] This presence too is utilized in classical
narrative cinema and weak and strong examples can once more be
indicated. In *Taxi Driver*, Travis Bickle is seen phoning Betsy after the
porno-film fiasco; as he stands talking into the pay-phone, fixed on a
wall inside a building, the camera tracks right and stops to frame a long
empty corridor leading out to the street; when Travis finishes his call,
he walks into frame and exits via the corridor. The tracking movement
designates the camera with a certain autonomy – there is an effect of a
casual decision to go somewhere else, off to the side of the narrative –
but the example is ultimately weak: the corridor is eventually brought
into the action with Travis's exit and, more importantly, it has its
rhyming and thematic resonances – the corridors in the rooming-house
used by Iris, the marked existential atmosphere of isolation, nothingness,
etc. Stronger examples are provided in the work of an Ophuls or a
Welles – the spectacular tracking shot at the start of *Touch of Evil* or the
intense mobility in many of the shots at the end of that same film.

These two instances of disturbance have been characterized here in
their existence in established cinema simply to make one or two points
directly in the context of the present account. Thus, the examples given
of autonomy of camera movement are all clearly operating in terms of
'style' (Welles, Ophuls, the tics of a new American commercial cinema
that has learnt a consciousness of style). The crucial factor is not the
valuation of camera movement, be it autonomous, but the point at
which a certain work on the camera in movement produces the
normality of the third person objective basis as itself a construction,
gives it as role or fiction and breaks the balance of the point-of-view
system. Similarly, the examples of the impossible place from *Killer's
Kiss*, which also have their reality as stylistic marking in the film, are
without critically disruptive extension in themselves, are simply *tricks*

(in the sense of spatial prestidigitations): the impossible place is entirely possible if held within a system that defines it *as such*, that it confirms in its signified exceptionality. The felt element of trick, moreover, raises the general point of the realization of film as process. It is too readily assumed that the operation – the determination, the effect, the pleasure – of classical cinema lies in the attempt at an invisibility of process, the intended transparency of a kind of absolute 'realism' from which all signs of production have been *effaced*. The actual case is much more complex and subtle, and much more telling. Classical cinema does not efface the signs of production, it *contains* them, according to the narrativization described above. It is that process that is the action of the film for the spectator – what counts is as much the representation as the represented, is as much the production as the product. Nor is there anything surprising in this: film is not a static and isolated object but a series of relations with the spectator it imagines, plays and sets as subject in its movement. The process of film is then perfectly available to certain terms of excess – those of that movement in its subject openings, its energetic controls. 'Style' is one area of such controlled excess, as again, more powerfully, are genres in their specific version of process. The musical is an obvious and extreme example with its systematic 'freedom' of space – crane choreography – and its shifting balances of narrative and spectacle; but an example that should not be allowed to mask the fundamental importance of the experience of process in other genres and in the basic order of classical cinema on which the various genres are grounded. Which is to say, finally, that radical disturbance is not to be linked to the mere autonomization of a formal element such as camera movement; on the contrary, it can only be effectively grasped as a work that operates at the expense of the classical suppositions of 'form' and 'content' in cinema, posing not autonomies but contradictions in the process of film and its narrative-subject binding.

The construction of space as a term of that binding in classical cinema is its implication for the spectator in the taking place of film as narrative; implication-process of constant refinding – space regulated, orientated, continued, reconstituted. The use of look and point-of-view structures – exemplarily, the field/reverse field figure (not necessarily dependent, of course, on point-of-view shots)[59] – is fundamental to this process that has been described in terms of suture, a stitching or tying as in the surgical joining of the lips of a wound.[60] In its movement, its framings, its cuts, its intermittences, the film ceaselessly poses an absence, a lack, which is ceaselessly recaptured for – one needs to be able to say 'forin' – the film, that process binding the spectator as subject in the realization of the film's space.

In psychoanalysis, 'suture' refers to the relation of the individual as subject to the chain of its discourse where it figures missing in the guise of a stand-in; the subject is an effect of the signifier in which it is represented, stood in for, taken place (the signifier is the narration of the subject).[61] Ideological representation turns on – supports itself from – this 'initial' production of the subject in the symbolic order (hence the crucial role of psychoanalysis, as potential science of the construction of the subject, with historical materialism), directs it as a set of images and fixed positions, metonymy stopped into fictions of coherence. What must be emphasized, however, is that stopping – the functioning of suture in image, frame, narrative, etc. – is exactly a process: it counters a productivity, an excess, that it states and restates in the very moment of containing in the interests of coherence – thus the film frame, for example, exceeded from within by the outside it delimits and poses and has ceaselessly to recapture (with post-Quattrocento painting itself, images are multiplied and the conditions are laid for a certain mechanical reproduction that the photograph will fulfil, the multiplication now massive, with image machines a normal appendage of the subject). The process never ends, is always *going on*; the construction-reconstruction has always to be renewed; machines, cinema included, are there for that – and their ideological operation is not only in the images but in the suture.

The film poses an image, not immediate or neutral,[62] but posed, framed and centred. Perspective-system images bind the spectator in place, the suturing central position that is the sense of the image, that sets its scene (in place, the spectator *completes* the image as its subject). Film too, but it also moves in all sort of ways and directions, flows with energies, is potentially a veritable festival of affects. Placed, that movement is all the value of film in its development and exploitation: reproduction of life and the engagement of the spectator in the process of that reproduction as articulation of coherence. What moves in film, finally, is the spectator, immobile in front of the screen. Film is the regulation of that movement, the individual as subject held in a shifting and placing of desire, energy, contradiction, in a perpetual retotalization of the imaginary (the set scene of image and subject). This is the investment of film in narrativization; and crucially for a coherent space, the unity of place for vision.

Once again, however, the investment is in the process. Space comes in place through procedures such as look and point-of-view structures, and the spectator with it as subject in its realization. A reverse shot folds over the shot it joins and is joined in turn by the reverse it positions; a shot of a person looking is succeeded by a shot of the object looked at which is succeeded in turn by a shot of the person looking to confirm the object as seen; and so on, in a number of multiple imbrications. *Fields* are made, *moving* fields, and the process includes not just the completions but the definitions of absence for completion. The suturing operation is in the process, the give and take of absence and presence, the play of negativity and negation, flow and bind. Narrativization, with its continuity, closes, and is that movement of closure that shifts the spectator as subject in its terms: the spectator is the *point* of the film's spatial relations – the turn, say, of shot to reverse shot – their subject-passage (point-of-view organization, moreover, doubles over that passage in its third/first person layerings). Narrativization is scene and movement, movement and scene, the reconstruction of the subject in the pleasure of that balance (with genres as specific instances of equilibrium) – *for* homogeneity, containment. What is foreclosed in the process is not its production – often signified as such, from genre instances down to this or that 'impossible' shot – but the terms of the unity of that production (narration on narrated, enunciation on enounced), the other scene of its vision of the subject, the outside – heterogeneity, contradiction, history – of its coherent address.

Notes

1. R. ARNHEIM, *Film as Art* (London: Faber, 1969), p. 20.

2. Cf. M. PLEYNET, Interview (With Gérard Leblanc), *Cinéthique*, no. 3 (1969).

3. G. TEN DOESSCHATE, *Perspective: Fundamentals, Controversials, History* (Nieuwkoop: B. de Graaf, 1964), pp. 6–7.

4. LEON BATTISTA ALBERTI, *On Painting* (New Haven and London: Yale U.P., 1966), p. 51.

5. GALILEO, *Opere*, ed. A. Favaro, vol. IX (Florence: Edizione nazionale, p. 129. [A recent book by ERNEST B. GILMAN , *The Curious Perspective: Literary and Pictorial Wit in the Seventeenth Century* (New Haven and London: Yale U.P., 1978), stresses – as in effect does Galileo – a parodic, almost subversive implication of the use of anamorphosis: 'Although the curious perspective system would have been impossible without the achievement of a systematic linear perspective in the earlier Renaissance, its effect was to parody, question, and even undermine the central cognitive assumption behind perspective representation' (p. 233). It remains, however, that the 'wit' of anamorphosis is constantly a reference to a rational and stable system that it assumes in the very moment it parodies or questions and is thus always available as a final image of order; as witness the idea of anamorphosis in a passage from Leibniz on universal harmony quoted by Gilman (p. 97); 'It is as in the inventions of perspective, where certain lovely drawings appear only as confusion, until one finds their true point of view or sees them by means of a certain glass or mirror... . Thus the apparent deformities of our little world come together as beauties in the greater world, and there is nothing opposed to the unity of a universally perfect principle.' What is clear and important is that the Renaissance perspective system opens the

way to an assurance and a trap for the look, the vision of the subject, to an *illusion* of *reality*, in the play of which two terms a whole problematic of representation is established – a problematic in which cinema is engaged, *moves*.]

6. P. FRANCASTEL, *Études de sociologie de l'art* (Paris: Denoël, 1970), pp. 136–7.

7. W. M. IVINS, *Art and Geometry* (New York: Dover, 1964), p. 108; TEN DOESSCHATE, op. cit., p. 157.

8. C. METZ, 'Le signifiant imaginaire', *Communications*, 23 (1975): 35–7; translation, 'The Imaginary Signifier', *Screen*, **16**: 2 (Summer 1975): 52–4.

9. ARNHEIM, op. cit., p. 18.

10. E. LINDGREN, *The Art of the Film* (London: Allen & Unwin, 1948), p. 54.

11. E. BRANIGAN, 'The Space of *Equinox Flower*', *Screen*, **17**: 2 (Summer 1976): 104.

12. K. REISZ and G. MILLAR , *The Technique of Film Editing* (New York and London: Hastings House, 1968), p. 215.

13. J. P. RICHTER (ed.), *The Literary Works of Leonardo da Vinci*, vol. 1 (London: Oxford U.P., 1939), p. 150. The figure is Leonardo's own, ibid. [Leonardo was much exercised by difficulties in the match between the Albertian perspective system and visual appearances, exploring elsewhere the possibility of an alternative system based on a spherical optics; cf. J. WHITE, *The Birth and Rebirth of Pictorial Space* (Boston: Boston Book and Art Shop, 1967), pp. 207–15.]

14. E. REBOUL, *Le Cinéma scolaire et éducateur* (Paris: Presses Universitaires de France, 1926).

15. HOLLIS FRAMPTON, Interview with Simon Field and Peter Sainsbury, *Afterimage*, 4 (Autumn 1972): 65.

16. Frampton writes elsewhere: 'The film frame is a rectangle, rather anonymous in its proportions, that has been fiddled with recently in the interests of publicising, so far as I can see, nothing much more interesting than the notions of an unbroken and boundless horizon. The wide screen glorifies, it would seem, frontiers long gone: the landscapes of the American corn-flats and the Soviet steppes; it is accommodating to the human body only when that body is lying in state. Eisenstein once proposed that the frame be condensed into a "dynamic" square, which is as close to a circle as a rectangle can get, but his arguments failed to prosper.' 'The Withering Away of the State of Art', *Artforum* (December 1974): 53.

17. *Apprendre le cinéma*, special issue of *Image et son*, no. 194 bis (May 1966): 119, 121.

18. Ibid., p. 123.

19. Quoted by ROSALIND KRAUSS in 'A View of Modernism', *Artforum* (September 1972): 50. Krauss comments: 'Perspective is the visual correlate of causality that one thing follows the next in space according to rule ... perspective space carried with it the meaning of narrative: a succession of events leading up to and away from this moment; and within that temporal succession – given as a spatial analogue – was secreted the "meaning" of both that space and those events.'

20. C. METZ, 'Histoire/discours' in J. Kristeva, J. -C. Milner and N. Ruwet (eds), *Langue, discours, société* (Paris: Seuil, 1975), p. 304; translation, 'History/Discourse', *Edinburgh '76 Magazine* (1976): 23.

21. A still from the shot can be found in Niver, op. cit., p. 36.

22. 'There must be a lot of essential pleasure just in the films when they hit the screen – I heard this expression yesterday, "to hit the screen", that's fantastic in English. Hit the screen – this is really what the frames do. The projected frames hit the screen.' PETER KUBELKA, Interview with Jonas Mekas, *Structural Film Anthology*, p. 102.

23. It can be noted that much independent film work has been concerned to experience dislocations of screen and frame; Sharits, for example, writes: 'When a film "loses its loop" it allows us to see a blurred strip of jerking frames; this is quite natural and quite compelling subject material. When this non-framed condition is intentionally induced, a procedure I am currently exploring, it could be thought of as a "anti-framing".' PAUL SHARITS, 'Words per page', *Afterimage*, 4 (Autumn 1972): 40. For an attempt by a film-maker to provide a theoretical formulation of such dislocation using the notion of a 'second screen' (in fact, the frame on screen in a narrative coherence of ground/background) that independent cinema will destroy ('in independent cinema, there is no second screen'), see CLAUDINE EIZYKMAN, *La jouissance-cinéma* (Paris: Bourgois, 1976), esp. pp. 147–51.

24. B. D. LEWIN, 'Sleep, the Mouth, and the Dream Screen', *Psychoanalytic Quarterly*, **XV** (1946): 419–34.

25. Discussion of screen and dream screen is suggested at the close of a recent article by GUY ROSOLATO, 'Souvenir-écran', *Communications*, 23 (1975): 86–7. See also my 'Screen Images, Film Memory', *Edinburgh '76 Magazine* (1976): 33–42.

26. C. METZ, *Essais sur la signification au cinéma*, vol. II (Paris: Klincksieck, 1972), p. 189.

27. K. THOMPSON and D. BORDWELL, 'Space and Narrative in the Films of Ozu', *Screen*, **17**: 2 (Summer 1976): 42. For an initial discussion of procedures of image centring ('specification procedures'), see my 'Film and System: Terms of Analysis' part II, *Screen*, **16**: 2 (Summer 1975): 99–100.

28. NOËL BURCH, 'De *Mabuse* à *M*: le travail de Fritz Lang', in *Cinéma Théorie Lectures*, special issue of the *Revue d'Esthétique* (Paris: Klincksieck, 1973), p. 229.

29. See BARRY SALT, 'Statistical Style Analysis of Motion Pictures', *Film Quarterly* (Fall 1974): 13–22.

30. ARNHEIM, op. cit., p. 27.

31. Ibid., p. 32.

32. J. MITRY, *Esthétique et psychologie du cinéma*, vol. II (Paris: Editions Universitaires, 1965), p. 10.

33. BRANIGAN gives the schema of the inverted pyramid structure characteristic of classical Hollywood film, art. cit., p. 75. ('1. Establishing Shot (a major variant: we see a detail of the scene, then pull back or cut to the establishing shot). 2. Long Shot (master shot). 3. Medium Two-Shot. 4. Reverse Angles

(over-the-shoulder shots). 5. Alternating Medium Close-ups. 6. Cut-away (or Insert). 7. Alternating Medium Close-ups. 8. Re-establishing Shot (usually a reverse angle or two-shot).')

34. Reisz and Millar, op. cit., pp. 224–5.

35. Ibid., pp. 225–6.

36. *Apprendre le cinéma*, p. 142.

37. Ibid., p. 151.

38. Reisz and Millar, op. cit., p. 216. To emphasize the reality of this smoothness as construction rather than 'reflection', it can be noted that the Navajo Indians studied by Worth and Adair, though capable of producing the 'correct' continuity (for example, by matching on action), were very far from the 'rules' in their films, articulating another system of space as an area of action (in which 'jumps' from the standpoint of the vision of the rules became essential continuities); cf. Sol Worth and John Adair, *Through Navajo Eyes* (Bloomington: Indiana U.P., 1972), p. 174 and stills 22–35, 35–40.

39. Barry Salt has pointed to the importance of the outdoor-action subject film (notably the Western) historically in this development; 'The Early Development of Film Form', *Film Form*, 1 (Spring 1976): 97–8.

40. *Apprendre le cinéma*, p. 125 ('an orientated empty space is a promise').

41. André Bazin, *What is Cinema?*, vol. I. (Los Angeles and Berkeley: University of California Press, 1967), p. 108.

42. Which is not, of course, to say that deep focus must necessarily be used in this way; for analysis of 'a refusal of perspective within depth of field', see Cl. Bailblé, M. Maire and M.-C. Ropars, *Muriel* (Paris: Galilée, 1974), pp. 128–36.

43. Salt, 'Statistical Style Analysis', p. 20.

44. André Bazin, *Qu'est-ce que le cinéma?*, vol. II (Paris: Cerf, 1959), p. 100.

45. Bazin, *Qu'est-ce que le cinéma?*, vol. IV (Paris: Cerf, 1962), p. 57.

46. Ibid., p. 59. For discussion of Bazin on Neo-Realism, see Christopher Williams's article of that title in *Screen*, **14**: 4 (Winter 1973/4): 61–8.

47. Noël Burch, *Theory of Film Practice* (London: Secker & Warburg, 1973), p. 21.

48. Branigan, art. cit., p. 103.

49. *Apprendre le cinéma*, p. 148.

50. For a detailed analysis of the point-of-view shot, see Edward Branigan, 'Formal Permutations of the Point-of-View Shot', *Screen*, **16**: 3 (Autumn 1975): 54–64.

51. Noël Burch and Jorge Dana, 'Propositions', *Afterimage*, no. 5 (Spring 1974): 45.

52. As summarized by Metz in his 'Current Problems in Film Theory', *Screen*, **14**: 1/2 (Spring/Summer 1973): 49.

53. In fact, and not surprisingly, the less narratively 'metonymical' and the more 'metaphorical' is what is looked at in the pure point-of-view shot (without the marking of image distortion), the nearer such a shot will come to

subjectivizing the image. Released from prison at the beginning of *High Sierra*, Roy Earle is shown walking through a park, breathing the air of freedom; shots of him looking up are followed by shots of tree tops against the sky, with a certain effect of subjectivization in so far as the tree tops against the sky are outside the immediate scope of the movement of the narrative and, objectively useless (unlike Lina's telegram in *Suspicion*), belong only for Roy's character (he was born of a modest farming family and is not the hardened criminal his reputation would have him be).

54. WALTER BENJAMIN, *Illuminations* (London: Fontana, 1970), p. 230; C. METZ, 'Le signifiant imaginaire', p. 35; translation, p. 52.

55. EDWARD BRANIGAN, 'Narration and Subjectivity in Cinema', mimeographed (University of Wisconsin – Madison, 1975), p. 24.

56. Ibid.

57. Discussed by R. BARTHES, 'Diderot, Brecht, Eisenstein', *Screen*, **15**: 2 (Summer 1974): 38; BRANIGAN, 'Formal Permutations', p. 57; and M. NASH, '*Vampyr* and the Fantastic', *Screen*, **17**:3 (Autumn 1976): 32–3, 54–60.

58. BURCH and DANA, art. cit., p. 45.

59. Salt distinguishes three varieties of field/reverse field and assigns an order and approximate dates for their respective appearances: 'It is necessary to distinguish between different varieties of angle – reverse-angle cuts; the cut from a watcher to his point of view was the first to appear; the cut from one long shot of a scene to another more or less oppositely angled long shot, which must have happened somewhat later – the first example that can be quoted is in *Røoverens Brud* (Viggo Larsen, 1907); and the cut between just-off-the-eye-line angle – reverse-angle shots of two people interacting – the earliest example that can be quoted occurs in *The Loafer* (Essanay, 1911).' 'The Early Development of Film Form', p. 98.

60. For details of the introduction and various accounts of suture, see Stephen Heath, 'On suture', *Questions of Cinema* (London: Macmillan, 1981), pp. 86–101.

61. Cf. J. -A. MILLER, 'La suture', *Cahiers pour l'analyse*, 1 (1966): 37–49; translation, 'Suture,' *Screen*, **18**: 4 (Winter 1977/8): 24–34.

62. 'Another characteristic of the film image is its neutrality.' *Encylopaedia Britannica* (Macropaedia), vol. 12 (Chicago, etc., 1974), p. 498.

6 *From* Class and Allegory in Contemporary Mass Culture: *Dog Day Afternoon* as a Political Film*

FREDRIC JAMESON

Fredric Jameson is Professor of Literature at Duke University, North Carolina. His publications include *Marxism and Form* (1971), *The Political Unconscious* (1981) and *Postmodernism, or the Cultural Logic of Late Capitalism*. *Signatures of the Visible*, essays on cinema, appeared in 1991, and *The Geopolitical Aesthetic: Cinema and Space in the World System* in 1992. See 'Introduction', p. 14.

One of the most persistent leitmotivs in liberalism's ideological arsenal, one of the most effective anti-Marxist arguments developed by the rhetoric of liberalism and anticommunism, is the notion of the disappearance of class. The argument is generally conveyed in the form of an empirical observation, but can take a number of different forms, the most important ones for us being either the appeal to the unique development of social life in the United States (so called American exceptionalism), or the notion of a qualitative break, a quantum leap, between the older industrial systems and what now comes to be called 'post-industrial' society. In the first version of the argument, we are told that the existence of the frontier (and, when the real frontier disappeared, the persistence of that 'inner' frontier of a vast continental market unimaginable to Europeans) prevented the formation of the older, strictly European class antagonisms, while the absence from the United States of a classical aristocracy of the European type is said to account for the failure of a classical bourgeoisie to develop in this country – a bourgeoisie which would then, following the continental model, have generated a classical proletariat over against itself. This is what we may call the American mythic explanation, and seems to flourish primarily in those American Studies programs which have a vested interest in preserving

*Reprinted from *Signatures of the Visible* (New York: Routledge, 1991), pp. 35–54; first appearing in *College English*, **38**: 8 (April 1977) the essay was slightly revised for book publication.

the specificity of their object and in preserving the boundaries of their discipline.

The second version is a little less parochial and takes into account what used to be called the Americanization, not only of the older European societies, but also, in our time, that of the Third World as well. It reflects the realities of the transition of monopoly capitalism into a more purely consumer stage on what is for the first time a global scale; and it tries to take advantage of the emergence of this new stage of monopoly capitalism to suggest that classical Marxist economics is no longer applicable. According to this argument, a social homogenization is taking place in which the older class differences are disappearing, and which can be described either as the embourgeoisement of the worker, or better still, the transformation of both bourgeois and worker into that new grey organization person known as the consumer. Meanwhile, although most of the ideologues of a post-industrial stage would hesitate to claim that value as such is no longer being produced in consumer society, they are at least anxious to suggest that ours is becoming a 'service economy' in which production of the classical types occupies an ever dwindling percentage of the work force.

Now if it is so that the Marxian concept of social class is a category of nineteenth-century European conditions, and no longer relevant to our situation today, then it is clear that Marxism may be sent to the museum where it can be dissected by Marxologists (there are an increasing number of those at work all around us today) and can no longer interfere with the development of that streamlined and postmodern legitimation of American economic evolution in the seventies and beyond, which is clearly the most urgent business on the agenda now that the older rhetoric of a classical New Deal type liberalism has succumbed to unplanned obsolescence. On the left, meanwhile, the failure of a theory of class seemed less important practically and politically during the anti-war situation of the 1960s, in which attacks on authoritarianism, racism, and sexism had their own internal justification and logic, and were lent urgency by the existence of the war, and content by the collective practice of social groups, in particular students, blacks, browns, and women. What is becoming clearer today is that the demands for equality and justice projected by such groups are not (unlike the politics of social class) intrinsically subversive. Rather, the slogans of populism and the ideals of racial justice and sexual equality were already themselves part and parcel of the Enlightenment itself, inherent not only in a socialist denunciation of capitalism, but even and also in the bourgeois revolution against the ancien régime. The values of the civil rights movement and the women's movement and the anti-authoritarian egalitarianism of the student's

movement are thus preeminently cooptable because they are already –
as ideals – inscribed in the very ideology of capitalism itself; and we
must take into account the possibility that these ideals are part of the
internal logic of the system, which has a fundamental interest in social
equality to the degree to which it needs to transform as many of its
subjects or its citizens into identical consumers interchangeable with
everybody else. The Marxian position – which includes the ideals of
the Enlightenment but seeks to ground them in a materialist theory of
social evolution – argues on the contrary that the system is structurally
unable to realize such ideals even where it has an economic interest in
doing so.

This is the sense in which the categories of race and sex as well as the
generational ones of the student movement are theoretically
subordinate to the categories of social class, even where they may seem
practically and politically a great deal more relevant. Yet it is not
adequate to argue the importance of class on the basis of an underlying
class reality beneath a relatively more classless appearance. There is,
after all, a reality of the appearance just as much as a reality behind it;
or, to put it more concretely, social class is not merely a structural fact
but also very significantly a function of class consciousness, and the
latter, indeed, ends up producing the former just as surely as it is
produced by it. This is the point at which dialectical thinking becomes
unavoidable, teaching us that we cannot speak of an underlying 'essence'
of things, of a fundamental class structure inherent in a system in which
one group of people produces value for another group, unless we allow
for the dialectical possibility that even this fundamental 'reality', may
be 'realer' at some historical junctures than at others, and that the
underlying object of our thoughts and representations – history and class
structure – is itself as profoundly historical as our own capacity to grasp
it. We may take as the motto for such a process the following still
extremely Hegelian sentence of the early Marx: 'It is not enough that
thought should seek to realize itself; reality must also strive towards
thought.'

In the present context, the 'thought' towards which reality strives is
not only or even not yet class consciousness: it is rather the very
preconditions for such class consciousness in social reality itself, that is
to say, the requirement that, for people to become aware of the class, the
classes be already in some sense perceptible as such. This fundamental
requirement we will call, now borrowing a term from Freud rather than
from Marx, the requirement of *figurability*, the need for social reality and
everyday life to have developed to the point at which its underlying
class structure becomes *representable* in tangible form. The point can be
made in a different way by underscoring the unexpectedly vital role
that culture would be called on to play in such a process, culture not

only as an instrument of self-consciousness but even before that as a symptom and a sign of possible self-consciousness in the first place. The relationship between class consciousness and figurability, in other words, demands something more basic than abstract knowledge, and implies a mode of experience that is more visceral and existential than the abstract certainties of economics and Marxian social science: the latter merely continue to convince us of the information presence, behind daily life, of the logic of capitalist production. To be sure, as Althusser tells us, the concept of sugar does not have to taste sweet. Nonetheless, in order for genuine class consciousness to be possible, we have to begin to sense the abstract truth of class through the tangible medium of daily life in vivid and experiential ways; and to say that class structure is becoming representable means that we have now gone beyond mere abstract understanding and entered that whole area of personal fantasy, collective storytelling, narrative figurability – which is the domain of culture and no longer that of abstract sociology or economic analysis. To become figurable – that is to say, visible in the first place, accessible to our imaginations – the classes have to be able to become in some sense characters in their own right: this is the sense in which the term allegory in our title is to be taken as a working hypothesis.

We will have thereby also already begun to justify an approach to commercial film, as that medium where, if at all, some change in the class character of social reality ought to be detectable, since social reality and the stereotypes of our experience of everyday social reality are the raw material with which commercial film and television are inevitably forced to work. This is my answer, in advance, to critics who object *a priori* that the immense costs of commercial films, which inevitably place their production under the control of multinational corporations, make any genuinely political content in them unlikely, and on the contrary ensure commercial film's vocation as a vehicle for ideological manipulation. No doubt this is so, if we remain on the level of the intention of the filmmaker who is bound to be limited consciously or unconsciously by the objective situation. But it is to fail to reckon with the political content of daily life, with the political logic which is already inherent in the raw material with which the filmmaker must work: such political logic will then not manifest itself as an overt political message, nor will it transform the film into an unambiguous political statement. But it will certainly make for the emergence of profound formal contradictions to which the public cannot not be sensitive, whether or not it yet possesses the conceptual instruments to understand what those contradictions mean.

In any case, *Dog Day Afternoon* (1975), would seem to have a great deal more overt political content than we would normally expect to find in a Hollywood production. In fact, we have only to think of the

CIA-type espionage thriller, or the police show on television, to realize that overt political content of that kind is so omnipresent as to be inescapable in the entertainment industry. It is indeed as though the major legacy of the sixties was to furnish a whole new code, a whole new set of thematics – that of the political – with which, after that of sex, the entertainment industry could reinvest its tired paradigms without any danger to itself or to the system; and we should take into account the possibility that is it the overtly political or contestatory parts of *Dog Day Afternoon* which will prove the least functional from a class point of view ...

It is evident that a Marxian theory of classes involves the restructuring of the fragmentary and unrelated data of empirical bourgeois sociology in a holistic way: in terms, Lukács would say, of the social totality, or, as his antagonist Althusser would have it, of a 'pre-given complex hierarchical structure of dominant and subordinate elements'. In either case, the random sub-groupings of academic sociology would find their place in determinate, although sometimes ambivalent, structural positions with respect to the dichotomous opposition of the two fundamental social classes themselves, about which innovative recent work – I'm thinking, for the bourgeoisie, of Sartre's Flaubert trilogy; for the proletariat has demonstrated the mechanisms by which each class defines itself in terms of the other and constitutes a virtual anti-class with respect to the other, and this, from overt ideological values all the way down to the most apparently non-political, 'merely' cultural features of everyday life.

The difference between the Marxian view of structurally dichotomous classes and the academic sociological picture of independent strata is however more than a merely intellectual one: once again, consciousness of social reality, or on the other hand the repression of the awareness of such reality, is itself 'determined by social being' in Marx's phrase and is therefore a function of the social and historical situation. A remarkable sociological investigation by Ralf Dahrendorf has indeed confirmed the view that these two approaches to the social classes – the academic and the Marxist – are themselves class-conditioned and reflect the structural perspectives of the two fundamental class positions themselves. Thus it is those on the higher rungs of the social ladder who tend to formulate their view of the social order, looking down at it, as separate strata; while those on the bottom looking up tend to map their social experience in terms of the stark opposition of 'them' and 'us'.[1]

But if this is so, then the representation of victimized classes in isolation – whether in the person of Sonny himself as a marginal, or the bank's clerical workers as an exploited group – is not enough to constitute a class system, let alone to precipitate a beginning consciousness of class in its viewing public. Nor are the repeated references to the absent bank management sufficient to transform the situation into a genuine class relationship, since this term does not find concrete representation – or *figuration*, to return to our earlier term – within the filmic narrative itself. Yet such representation is present in *Dog Day Afternoon*, and it is this unexpected appearance, in a part of the film where one would not normally look for it, that constitutes its greatest interest in the present context – our possibility of focusing it being as we have argued directly proportional to our ability to let go of the Sonny story and to relinquish those older narrative habits that program us to follow the individual experiences of a hero or an anti-hero, rather than the explosion of the text and the operation of meaning in other, random narrative fragments.

If we can do this – and we have begun to do so when we are willing to reverse the robbery itself, and read Sonny's role as that of a mere pretext for the revelation of that colonized space which is the branch bank, with its peripheralized or marginalized work force – then what slowly comes to occupy the film's center of gravity is the action outside the bank itself, and in particular the struggle for precedence between the local police and the FBI officials. Now there are various ways of explaining this shift of focus, none of them wrong: for one thing, we can observe that, once Sonny has been effectively barricaded inside the bank, he can no longer initiate events, the center of gravity of the narrative as such then passing to the outside. More pertinently still, since the operative paradox of the film – underscored by Al Pacino's acting – is the fundamental likability of Sonny, this external displacement of the acting can be understood as the narrative attempt to generate an authority figure who can deal directly with him without succumbing to his charm. But this is not just a matter of narrative dynamics; it also involves an ideological answer to the fundamental question: how to imagine authority today, how to conceive imaginatively – that is in non-abstract, non-conceptual form – of a principle of authority that can express the essential impersonality and post-individualistic structure of the power structure of our society while still operating among real people, in the tangible necessities of daily life and individual situations of repression?

It is clear that the figure of the FBI agent (James Broderick) represents a narrative solution to this ideological contradiction, and the nature of the solution is underscored by the characterological styles of the FBI agents and the local police chief, Maretti (Charles Durning), whose impotent rages and passionate incompetence are there, not so much to humanize him, as rather to set off the cool and technocratic expertise of his rival. In one sense, of course, this contrast is what has nowadays come to be called an intertextual one: this is not really the encounter of two characters, who represent two 'individuals', but rather the encounter of two narrative paradigms, indeed, of two narrative stereotypes: the clean-cut Efrem Zimbalist-type FBI agents, with their fifties haircuts, and the earthy urban cop whose television embodiments are so multiple as to be embarrassing: FBI meets Kojak! Yet one of the most effective things in the film, and the most haunting impression left by *Dog Day Afternoon* in the area of performance, is surely not so much the febrile heroics of Al Pacino as rather their stylistic opposite, the starkly blank and emotionless, expressionless, coolness of the FBI man himself. This gazing face, behind which decision-making is reduced to (or developed into) pure technique, yet whose judgments and assessments are utterly inaccessible to spectators either within or without the filmic frame, is one of the most alarming achievements of recent American moviemaking, and may be said to embody something like the truth of a rather different but equally actual genre, the espionage thriller, where it has tended to remain obfuscated by the cumbersome theological apparatus of a dialectic of Good and Evil.

Meanwhile, the more existential and private-tragic visions of this kind of figure – I'm thinking of the lawman (Denver Pyle) in Arthur Penn's *Bonnie and Clyde* (1967) – project a nemesis which is still motivated by personal vindictiveness, so that the process of tracking the victim down retains a kind of passion of a still recognizable human type; Penn's more recent *The Missouri Breaks* (1976) tried to make an advance on this personalized dramatization of the implacability of social institutions by endowing its enforcer with a generalized paranoia (and, incidentally, furnishing Marlon Brando with the occasion of one of his supreme bravura performances); but it is not really much of an improvement and the vision remains locked in the pathos of a self-pitying and individualistic vision of history.

In *Dog Day Afternoon*, however, the organization man is neither vindictive nor paranoid; he is in the sense quite beyond the good and evil of conventional melodrama, and inaccessible to any of the psychologizing stereotypes that are indulged in most of the commercial representations of the power of institutions; his anonymous features mark a chilling and unexpected insertion of the real into the otherwise relatively predictable framework of the fiction film – and this, not, as we have pointed out earlier, by traditional documentary or montage techniques, but rather through a kind of dialectic of connotations on the level of the style of acting, a kind of silence or charged absence in a sign-system in which the other modes of performance have programmed us for a different kind of expressiveness.

Now the basic contrast, that between the police chief and the FBI agent, dramatizes a social and historical change which was once an important theme of our literature but to which we have today become so accustomed as to have lost our sensitivity to it: in their very different ways, the novels of John O'Hara and the sociological investigations of C. Wright Mills documented a gradual but irreversible erosion of local and state-wide power structures and leadership or authority networks by national, and, in our own time, multinational ones. Think of the social hierarchy of Gibbsville coming into disillusioning contact with the new wealth and the new political hierarchies of the New Deal era; think – even more relevantly for our present purposes – of the crisis of figurability implied by this shift of power from the face-to-face small-town life situations of the older communities to the abstraction of nation-wide power (a crisis already suggested by the literary representation of 'politics' as a specialized theme in itself).

The police lieutenant thus comes to incarnate the very helplessness and impotent agitation of the local power structure; and with this inflection of our reading, with this interpretive operation, the whole allegorical structure of *Dog Day Afternoon* suddenly emerges in the light of day. The FBI agent – now that we have succeeded in identifying what he supersedes – comes to occupy the place of that immense and decentralized power network which marks the present multinational stage of monopoly capitalism. The very absence in his features becomes a sign and an expression of the presence/absence of corporate power in our daily lives, all-shaping and omnipotent and yet rarely accessible in figurable terms, that is to say, in the representable form of individual actors or agents. The FBI man is thus the structural opposite of the secretarial staff of the branch bank: the latter present in all their existential individuality, but inessential and utterly marginalized, the former so depersonalized as to be little more than a marker – in the empirical world of everyday life, of *fait divers* and newspaper articles – of the place of ultimate power and control.

Yet with even this shadowy embodiment of the forces of those multinational corporate structures that are the subject of present-day world history, the possibility of genuine figuration, and with it, the possibility of a kind of beginning adequate class consciousness itself, is given. Now the class structure of the film becomes articulated in three tiers: the first, that newly atomized petty bourgeoisie of the cities whose 'proletarianization' and marginalization is expressed both by the women employees on the one hand, and by the lumpens on the other (Sonny and his accomplice, Sal [John Cazale], but also the crowd itself, an embodiment of the logic of marginality that runs all the way from the 'normal' deviances of homosexuality and petty crime to the pathologies of Sal's paranoia and Ernie's [Chris Sarandon] transsexuality). A second level is constituted by the impotent power structures of the local neighborhoods, which represent something like the national bourgeoisies of the Third World, colonized and gutted of their older content, left with little more than the hollow shells and external trappings of authority and decision making. Finally, of course, that multinational capitalism into which the older ruling classes of our world have evolved, and whose primacy is inscribed in the spatial trajectory of the film itself as it moves from the ghettoized squalor of the bank interior to that eerie and impersonal science fiction landscape of the airport finale: a corporate space without inhabitants, utterly technologized and functional, a place beyond city and country alike – collective, yet without people, automated and computerized, yet without any of that older utopian or dystopian clamor, without any of those still distinctive qualities that characterized the then still 'modern' and streamlined futuristic vision of the corporate future in our own recent past. Here – as in the blank style of acting of the FBI agents – the film makes a powerful non-conceptual point by destroying its own intrinsic effects and cancelling an already powerful, yet conventional, filmic and performative language.

Two final observations about this work, the one about its ultimate aesthetic and political effects, the other about its historical conditions of possibility. Let us take the second problem first: we have here repeatedly stressed the dependence of a narrative figuration of class consciousness on the historical situation. We have stressed both the dichotomous nature of the class structure, and the dependence of class consciousness itself on the logic of the social and historical conjuncture. Marx's dictum, that consciousness is determined by social being, holds for class consciousness itself no less than for any other form. We must now therefore try to make good our claim, and say why, if some new and renewed possibility of class consciousness seems at least faintly detectable, this should be the case now and today rather than ten or twenty years ago.

But the answer to this question can be given concisely and decisively; it is implicit in the very expression, 'multinational corporation', which – as great a misnomer as it may be (since all of them are in reality expressions of American capitalism) – would not have been invented had not something new suddenly emerged which seemed to demand a new name for itself. It seems to be a fact that after the failure of the Vietnam War, the so-called multinational corporations – what used to be called the 'ruling classes' or later on the 'power elite' of monopoly capitalism – have once again emerged in public from the wings of history to advance their own interests. The failure of the war

> has meant that the advancement of world capitalist revolution now depends more on the initiative of corporations and less on governments. The increasingly political pretensions of the global corporation are thus unavoidable but they inevitably mean more public exposure, and exposure carries with it the risk of increased hostility.[2]

But in our terms, the psychological language of the authors of *Global Reach* may be translated as 'class consciousness', and with this new historical visibility capitalism becomes objectified and dramatized as an actor and as a subject of history with an allegorical intensity and simplicity that had not been the case since the 1930s.

Now a final word about the political implications of the film itself and the complexities of the kind of allegorical structure we have imputed to it. Can *Dog Day Afternoon* be said to be a political film? Surely not, since the class system we have been talking about is merely implicit in it, and can just as easily be ignored or repressed by its viewers as brought to consciousness. What we have been describing is at best something pre-political, the gradual rearticulation of the raw material of a film of this kind in terms and relationships which are once again, after the anti-political and privatizing, 'existential' paradigms of the forties and fifties recognizably those of class.

Yet we should also understand that the use of such material is much more complicated and problematical than the terminology of representation would suggest. Indeed, in the process by which class structure finds expression in the triangular relationship within the film between Sonny, the police chief, and the FBI man, we have left out an essential step. For the whole qualitative and dialectical inequality of this relationship is mediated by the star system itself, and in that sense – far more adequately than in its overt thematics of the media exploitation of Sonny's hold-up – the film can be said to be about itself. Indeed we reach each of the major actors in terms of his distance from the star system: Sonny's relationship to Maretti is that of superstar to character actor, and our reading of this particular narrative is not a direct passage from one character or actant to another, but passes through the mediation of our identification and decoding of the actors' status as such. Even more interesting and complex than this is our decoding of the FBI agent, whose anonymity in the filmic narrative is expressed very precisely through his anonymity within the framework of the Hollywood star system. The face is blank and unreadable precisely because the actor is himself unidentifiable.

In fact, of course, it is only within the coding of a Hollywood system that he is unfamiliar, for the actor in question soon after became a permanent feature of the durable and well-known television series, *Family* (1976–80). But the point is precisely that in this respect television and its system of references is another production, but even more, that television comes itself to figure, with respect to Hollywood films, that new and impersonal multinational system which is coming to supersede the more individualistic one of an older national capitalism and an older commodity culture. Thus, the external, extrinsic sociological fact or system of realities finds itself inscribed within the internal intrinsic experience of the film in what Sartre in a suggestive and too-little known concept in his *Psychology of Imagination* calls the analogon[3]: that structural nexus in our reading or viewing experience, in our operations of decoding or aesthetic reception, which can then do double duty and stand as the substitute and the representative within the aesthetic object of a phenomenon on the outside which cannot in the very nature of things be 'rendered' directly. This complex of intra- and extra-aesthetic relationships might then be schematically represented as follows:

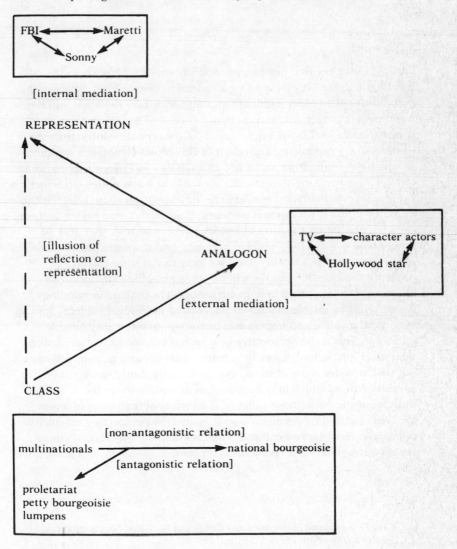

Here then we find an ultimate formal confirmation of our initial hypothesis, that what is bad about the film is what is best about it, and that the work is a paradoxical realization in which qualities and defects form an inextricable dialectical unity. For it is ultimately the star system itself – that commodity phenomenon most stubbornly irreconcilable with any documentary or *ciné-verité* type of exploration of the real – which is thus responsible for even that limited authenticity which *Dog Day Afternoon* is able to achieve.

Afterword

I would today say that this essay is a study in what I have come to call *cognitive mapping*.[4] It presupposes a radical incompatibility between the possibilities of an older national language or culture (which is still the framework in which literature is being produced today) and the transnational, worldwide organization of the economic infrastructure of contemporary capitalism. The result of this contradiction is a situation in which the truth of our social life as a whole – in Lukács's terms, as a totality – is increasingly irreconcilable with the possibilities of aesthetic expression or articulation available to us; a situation about which it can be asserted that if we can make a work of art from our experience, if we can give experience the form of a story that can be told, then it is no longer true, even as individual experience; and if we can grasp the truth about our world as a totality, then we may find it some purely conceptual expression but we will no longer be able to maintain an imaginative relationship to it. In current psychoanalytic terminology, we will thus be unable to insert ourselves, as individual subjects, into an ever more massive and impersonal or transpersonal reality outside ourselves. This is the perspective in which it becomes a matter of more than mere intellectual curiosity to interrogate the artistic production of our own time for signs of some new, so far only dimly conceivable, collective forms which may be expected to replace the older individualistic ones (those either of conventional realism or of a now conventionalized modernism); and it is also the perspective in which an indecisive aesthetic and cultural phenomenon like *Dog Day Afternoon* takes on the values of a revealing symptom.

Notes

1. RALF DAHRENDORF, *Class and Class Conflict in Industrial Society* (Stanford: Stanford University Press, 1959), pp. 280–9.

2. See RICHARD J. BARNET and RONALD E. MULLER, *Global Reach* (New York: Simon and Schuster, 1974), p. 68.

3. JEAN-PAUL SARTRE, *The Psychology of Imagination* (New York: Washington Square Press, 1968), pp. 21–71, where analogon is translated as 'the analogue'.

4. See my *Postmodernism, or, The Cultural Logic of Late Capitalism* (Durham: Duke University Press, 1991), particularly the first and last chapters.

Part Three

Gender And The Gaze

7 Visual Pleasure and Narrative Cinema*

LAURA MULVEY

Laura Mulvey is a freelance writer and film-maker. With Peter Wollen she made *Penthesilia, Queen of the Amazons* (1974), *Riddles of the Sphinx* (1977) and *Amy* (1980). Her writings on cinema have been collected in *Visual and Other Pleasures* (1989). See 'Introduction', pp. 15–16.

I. Introduction

(a) *A political use of psychoanalysis*

This paper intends to use psychoanalysis to discover where and how the fascination of film is reinforced by pre-existing patterns of fascination already at work within the individual subject and the social formations that have moulded him. It takes as its starting-point the way film reflects, reveals and even plays on the straight, socially established interpretation of sexual difference which controls images, erotic ways of looking and spectacle. It is helpful to understand what the cinema has been, how its magic has worked in the past, while attempting a theory and a practice which will challenge this cinema of the past. Psychoanalytic theory is thus appropriated here as a political weapon, demonstrating the way the unconscious of patriarchal society has structured film form.

The paradox of phallocentrism in all its manifestations is that it depends on the image of the castrated woman to give order and meaning to its world. An idea of woman stands as linchpin to the system: it is her lack that produces the phallus as a symbolic presence, it is her desire to make good the lack that the phallus signifies. Recent writing in *Screen* about psychoanalysis and the cinema has not sufficiently brought out the importance of the representation of the

* Reprinted from *Screen*, **16**: 3 (Autumn 1975): 6–18.

female form in a symbolic order in which, in the last resort, it speaks
castration and nothing else. To summarise briefly: the function of
woman in forming the patriarchal unconscious is twofold: she firstly
symbolises the castration threat by her real lack of a penis and secondly
thereby raises her child into the symbolic. Once this has been achieved,
her meaning in the process is at an end. It does not last into the world of
law and language except as a memory, which oscillates between
memory of maternal plenitude and memory of lack. Both are posited on
nature (or on anatomy in Freud's famous phrase). Woman's desire is
subjugated to her image as bearer of the bleeding wound; she can exist
only in relation to castration and cannot transcend it. She turns her child
into the signifier of her own desire to possess a penis (the condition, she
imagines, of entry into the symbolic). Either she must gracefully give
way to the word, the name of the father and the law, or else struggle to
keep her child down with her in the half-light of the imaginary. Woman
then stands in patriarchal culture as a signifier for the male other,
bound by a symbolic order in which man can live out his fantasies and
obsessions through linguistic command by imposing them on the silent
image of woman still tied to her place as bearer, not maker, or of meaning.

There is an obvious interest in this analysis for feminists, a beauty in
its exact rendering of the frustration experienced under the
phallocentric order. It gets us nearer to the roots of our oppression, it
brings closer an articulation of the problem, it faces us with the ultimate
challenge: how to fight the unconscious structured like a language
(formed critically at the moment of arrival of language) while still
caught within the language of the patriarchy? There is no way in which
we can produce an alternative out of the blue, but we can begin to make
a break by examining patriarchy with the tools it provides, of which
psychoanalysis is not the only but an important one. We are still
separated by a great gap from important issues for the female
unconscious which are scarcely relevant to phallocentric theory: the
sexing of the female infant and her relationship to the symbolic, the
sexually mature woman as non-mother, maternity outside the
signification of the phallus, the vagina. But, at this point, psychoanalytic
theory as it now stands can at least advance our understanding of the
status quo, of the patriarchal order in which we are caught.

(b) *Destruction of pleasure as a radical weapon*

As an advanced representation system, the cinema poses questions
about the ways the unconscious (formed by the dominant order)
structures ways of seeing and pleasure in looking. Cinema has changed
over the last few decades. It is no longer the monolithic system based on

large capital investment exemplified at its best by Hollywood in the 1930s, 1940s and 1950s. Technological advances (16mm and so on) have changed the economic conditions of cinematic production, which can now be artisanal as well as capitalist. Thus it has been possible for an alternative cinema to develop. However self-conscious and ironic Hollywood managed to be, it always restricted itself to a formal *mise en scène* reflecting the dominant ideological concept of the cinema. The alternative cinema provides a space for the birth of a cinema which is radical in both a political and an aesthetic sense and challenges the basic assumptions of the mainstream film. This is not to reject the latter moralistically, but to highlight the ways in which its formal preoccupations reflect the psychical obsessions of the society which produced it and, further, to stress that the alternative cinema must start specifically by reacting against these obsessions and assumptions. A politically and aesthetically avant-garde cinema is now possible, but it can still only exist as a counterpoint.

The magic of the Hollywood style at its best (and of all the cinema which fell within its sphere of influence) arose, not exclusively, but in one important aspect, from its skilled and satisfying manipulation of visual pleasure. Unchallenged, mainstream film coded the erotic into the language of the dominant patriarchal order. In the highly developed Hollywood cinema it was only through these codes that the alienated subject, torn in his imaginary memory by a sense of loss, by the terror of potential lack in fantasy, came near to finding a glimpse of satisfaction: through its formal beauty and its play on his own formative obsessions. This article will discuss the interweaving of that erotic pleasure in film, its meaning and, in particular, the central place of the image of woman. It is said that analysing pleasure, or beauty, destroys it. That is the intention of this article. The satisfaction and reinforcement of the ego that represent the high point of film history hitherto must be attacked. Not in favour of a reconstructed new pleasure, which cannot exist in the abstract, nor of intellectualised unpleasure, but to make way for a total negation of the ease and plenitude of the narrative fiction film. The alternative is the thrill that comes from leaving the past behind without simply rejecting it, transcending outworn or oppressive forms, and daring to break with normal pleasurable expectations in order to conceive a new language of desire.

II. Pleasure in looking/fascination with the human form

A The cinema offers a number of possible pleasures. One is scopophilia (pleasure in looking). There are circumstances in which looking itself is a source of pleasure, just as, in the reverse formation, there is pleasure in being looked at. Originally, in his *Three Essays on Sexuality*, Freud isolated scopophilia as one of the component instincts of sexuality which exist as drives quite independently of the erotogenic zones. At this point he associated scopophilia with taking other people as objects, subjecting them to a controlling and curious gaze. His particular examples centre on the voyeuristic activities of children, their desire to see and make sure of the private and forbidden (curiosity about other people's genital and bodily functions, about the presence or absence of the penis and retrospectively, about the primal scene). In this analysis scopophilia is essentially active. (Later, in 'Instincts and Their Vicissitudes', Freud developed his theory of scopophilia further, attaching it initially to pre-genital auto-eroticism, after which, by analogy, the pleasure of the look is transferred to others. There is a close working here of the relationship between the active instinct and its further development in a narcissistic form.) Although the instinct is modified by other factors, in particular the constitution of the ego, it continues to exist as the erotic basis for pleasure in looking at another person as object. At the extreme, it can become fixated into a perversion, producing obsessive voyeurs and Peeping Toms whose only sexual satisfaction can come from watching, in an active controlling sense, an objectified other.

At first glance, the cinema would seem to be remote from the undercover world of the surreptitious observation of an unknowing and unwilling victim. What is seen on the screen is so manifestly shown. But the mass of mainstream film, and the conventions within which it has consciously evolved, portray a hermetically sealed world which unwinds magically, indifferent to the presence of the audience, producing for them a sense of separation and playing on their voyeuristic fantasy. Moreover the extreme contrast between the darkness in the auditorium (which also isolates the spectators from one to another) and the brilliance of the shifting patterns of light and shade on the screen helps to promote the illusion of voyeuristic separation. Although the film is really being shown, is there to be seen, conditions of screening and narrative conventions give the spectator an illusion of looking in on a private world. Among other things, the position of the spectators in the cinema is blatantly one of repression of their exhibitionism and projection of the repressed desire onto the performer.

B The cinema satisfies a primordial wish for pleasurable looking, but it also goes further, developing scopophilia in its narcissistic aspect. The conventions of mainstream film focus attention on the human form. Scale, space, stories are all anthropomorphic. Here, curiosity and the wish to look intermingle with a fascination with likeness and recognition: the human face, the human body, the relationship between the human form and its surroundings, the visible presence of the person in the world. Jacques Lacan has described how the moment when a child recognises its own image in the mirror is crucial for the constitution of the ego. Several aspects of this analysis are relevant here. The mirror phase occurs at a time when children's physical ambitions outstrip their motor capacity, with the result that their recognition of themselves is joyous in that they imagine their mirror image to be more complete, more perfect than they experience in their own body. Recognition is thus overlaid with misrecognition: the image recognised is conceived as the reflected body of the self, but its misrecognition as superior projects this body outside itself as an ideal ego, the alienated subject which, reintrojected as an ego ideal, prepares the way for identification with others in the future. This mirror moment predates language for the child.

Important for this article is the fact that it is an image that constitutes the matrix of the imaginary, of recognition/misrecognition and identification, and hence of the first articulation of the I, of subjectivity. This is a moment when an older fascination with looking (at the mother's face, for an obvious example) collides with the initial inklings of self-awareness. Hence it is the birth of the long love affair/despair between image and self-image which has found such intensity of expression in film and such joyous recognition in the cinema audience. Quite apart from the extraneous similarities between screen and mirror (the framing of the human form in its surroundings, for instance), the cinema has structures of fascination strong enough to allow temporary loss of ego while simultaneously reinforcing it. The sense of forgetting the world as the ego has come to perceive it (I forgot who I am and where I was) is nostalgically reminiscent of that pre-subjective moment of image recognition. While at the same time, the cinema has distinguished itself in the production of ego ideals, through the star system for instance. Stars provide a focus or centre both to screen space and screen story where they act out a complex process of likeness and difference (the glamorous impersonates the ordinary).

C Sections A and B have set out two contradictory aspects of the pleasurable structures of looking in the conventional cinematic situation. The first, scopophilic, arises from pleasure in using another person as an object of sexual stimulation through sight. The second, developed through narcissism and the constitution of the ego, comes from identification with the image seen. Thus, in film terms, one implies a separation of the erotic identity of the subject from the object on the screen (active scopophilia), the other demands identification of the ego with the object on the screen through the spectator's fascination with and recognition of his like. The first is a function of the sexual instincts,

the second of ego libido. This dichotomy was crucial for Freud.
Although he saw the two as interacting and overlaying each other, the
tension between instinctual drives and self-preservation polarises in
terms of pleasure. But both are formative structures, mechanisms
without intrinsic meaning. In themselves they have no signification,
unless attached to an idealisation. Both pursue aims in indifference to
perceptual reality, and motivate eroticised phantasmagoria that affect
the subject's perception of the world to make a mockery of empirical
objectivity.

During its history, the cinema seems to have evolved a particular
illusion of reality in which this contradiction between libido and ego
has found a beautifully complementary fantasy world. In *reality* the
fantasy world of the screen is subject to the law which produces it.
Sexual instincts and identification processes have a meaning within the
symbolic order which articulates desire. Desire, born with language,
allows the possibility of transcending the instinctual and the imaginary,
but its point of reference continually returns to the traumatic moment of
its birth: the castration complex. Hence the look, pleasurable in form,
can be threatening in content, and it is woman as representation/image
that crystallises this paradox.

III. Woman as image, man as bearer of the look

A In a world ordered by sexual imbalance, pleasure in looking has
been split between active/male and passive/female. The determining
male gaze projects its fantasy onto the female figure, which is styled
accordingly. In their traditional exhibitionist role women are
simultaneously looked at and displayed, with their appearance coded
for strong visual and erotic impact so that they can be said to connote
to-be-looked-at-ness. Woman displayed as sexual object is the *leitmotif* of
erotic spectacle: from pin-ups to strip-tease, from Ziegfeld to Busby
Berkeley, she holds the look, and plays to and signifies male desire.
Mainstream film neatly combines spectacle and narrative. (Note,
however, how in the musical song-and-dance numbers interrupt the
flow of the diegesis.) The presence of woman is an indispensable
element of spectacle in normal narrative film, yet her visual presence
tends to work against the development of a story-line, to freeze the flow
of action in moments of erotic contemplation. This alien presence then
has to be integrated into cohesion with the narrative. As Budd
Boetticher has put it:

> What counts is what the heroine provokes, or rather what she
> represents. She is the one, or rather the love or fear she inspires in

the hero, or else the concern he feels for her, who makes him act the way he does. In herself the woman has not the slightest importance.

(A recent tendency in narrative film has been to dispense with this problem altogether; hence the development of what Molly Haskell has called the 'buddy movie', in which the active homosexual eroticism of the central male figures can carry the story without distraction.) Traditionally, the woman displayed has functioned on two levels: as erotic object for the characters within the screen story, and as erotic object for the spectator within the auditorium, with a shifting tension between the looks on either side of the screen. For instance, the device of the show-girl allows the two looks to be unified technically without any apparent break in the diegesis. A woman performs within the narrative; the gaze of the spectator and that of the male characters in the film are neatly combined without breaking narrative verisimilitude. For a moment the sexual impact of the performing woman takes the film into a no man's land outside its own time and space. Thus Marilyn Monroe's first appearance in *The River of No Return* and Lauren Bacall's songs in *To Have and Have Not*. Similarly, conventional close-ups of legs (Dietrich, for instance) or a face (Garbo) integrate into the narrative a different mode of eroticism. One part of a fragmented body destroys the Renaissance space, the illusion of depth demanded by the narrative; it gives flatness, the quality of cut-out or icon, rather than verisimilitude, to the screen.

B An active/passive heterosexual division of labour has similarly controlled narrative structure. According to the principles of the ruling ideology and the psychical structures that back it up, the male figure cannot bear the burden of sexual objectification. Man is reluctant to gaze at his exhibitionist like. Hence the split between spectacle and narrative supports the man's role as the active one of advancing the story, making things happen. The man controls the film fantasy and also emerges as the representative of power in a further sense: as the bearer of the look of the spectator, transferring it behind the screen to neutralise the extra-diegetic tendencies represented by woman as spectacle. This is made possible through the processes set in motion by structuring the film around a main controlling figure with whom the spectator can identify. As the spectator identifies with the main male[1] protagonist, he projects his look onto that of his like, his screen surrogate, so that the power of the male protagonist as he controls events coincides with the active power of the erotic look, both giving a satisfying sense of omnipotence. A male movie star's glamorous characteristics are thus not those of the erotic object of the gaze, but those of the more perfect, more complete, more powerful ideal ego conceived in the original moment of recognition in front of the mirror. The character in the story can make things happen and control events better than the subject/spectator, just as the image in the mirror was more in control of motor co-ordination.

In contrast to woman as icon, the active male figure (the ego ideal of the identification process) demands a three-dimensional space corresponding to that of the mirror recognition, in which the alienated subject internalised his own representation of his imaginary existence. He is a figure in a landscape. Here the function of film is to reproduce as accurately as possible the so-called natural conditions of human perception. Camera technology (as exemplified by deep focus in particular) and camera movements (determined by the action of the protagonist), combined with invisible editing (demanded by realism), all tend to blur the limits of screen space. The male protagonist is free to command the stage, a stage of spatial illusion in which he articulates the look and creates the action. (There are films with a woman as main protagonist, of course. To analyse this phenomenon seriously here would take me too far afield. Pam Cook and Claire Johnston's study of *The Revolt of Mamie Stover* in Phil Hardy (ed.), *Raoul Walsh* (Edinburgh, 1974), shows in a striking case how the strength of this female protagonist is more apparent than real.)

C1 Sections IIIA and B have set out a tension between a mode of representation of woman in film and conventions surrounding the diegesis. Each is associated with a look: that of the spectator in direct scopophilic contact with the female form displayed for his enjoyment (connoting male fantasy) and that of the spectator fascinated with the image of his like set in an illusion of natural space, and through him gaining control and possession of the woman within the diegesis. (This tension and the shift from one pole to the other can structure a single text. Thus both in *Only Angels Have Wings* and *To Have and Have Not*, the film opens with the woman as object of the combined gaze of spectator and all the male protagonists in the film. She is isolated, glamorous, on display, sexualised. But as the narrative progresses she falls in love with the main male protagonist and becomes his property, losing her outward glamorous characteristics, her generalised sexuality, her show-girl connotations; her eroticism is subjected to the male star alone. By means of identification with him, through participation in his power, the spectator can indirectly possess her too.)

But in psychoanalytic terms, the female figure poses a deeper problem. She also connotes something that the look continually circles around but disavows: her lack of a penis, implying a threat of castration and hence unpleasure. Ultimately, the meaning of woman is sexual difference, the visually ascertainable absence of the penis, the material evidence on which is based the castration complex essential for the organisation of entrance to the symbolic order and the law of the father. Thus the woman as icon, displayed for the gaze and enjoyment of men, the active controllers of the look, always threatens to evoke the anxiety it originally signified. The male unconscious has two avenues of escape from this castration anxiety: preoccupation with the re-enactment of the original trauma (investigating the woman, demystifying her mystery), counterbalanced by the devaluation, punishment or saving of the guilty object (an avenue typified by the concerns of the *film noir*); or else complete disavowal of castration by the substitution of a fetish object or turning the represented figure itself into a fetish so that it becomes reassuring rather than dangerous (hence overvaluation, the cult of the female star).

This second avenue, fetishistic scopophilia, builds up the physical beauty of the object, transforming it into something satisfying in itself. The first avenue, voyeurism, on the contrary, has associations with sadism: pleasure lies in ascertaining guilt (immediately associated with castration), asserting control and subjugating the guilty person through punishment or forgiveness. This sadistic side fits in well with narrative. Sadism demands a story, depends on making something happen, forcing a change in another person, a battle of will and strength, victory/defeat, all occurring in a linear time with a beginning and an end. Fetishistic scopophilia, on the other hand, can exist outside linear time as the erotic instinct is focused on the look alone. These contradictions and ambiguities can be illustrated more simply by using works by Hitchcock and Sternberg, both of whom take the look almost as the content or subject matter of many of their films. Hitchcock is the more complex, as he uses both mechanisms. Sternberg's work, on the other hand, provides many pure examples of fetishistic scopophilia.

C2 It is well known that Sternberg once said he would welcome his films being projected upside down so that story and character involvement would not interfere with the spectator's undiluted appreciation of the screen image. This statement is revealing but ingenuous. Ingenuous in that his films do demand that the figure of the woman (Dietrich, in the cycle of films with her, as the ultimate example) should be identifiable. But revealing in that it emphasises the fact that for him the pictorial space enclosed by the frame is paramount rather than narrative or identification processes. While Hitchcock goes into the investigative side of voyeurism, Sternberg produces the ultimate fetish, taking it to the point where the powerful look of the male protagonist (characteristic of traditional narrative film) is broken in favour of the image in direct erotic rapport with the spectator. The beauty of the

woman as object and the screen space coalesce; she is no longer the
bearer of guilt but a perfect product, whose body, stylised and
fragmented by close-ups, is the content of the film and the direct
recipient of the spectator's look. Sternberg plays down the illusion of
screen depth; his screen tends to be one-dimensional, as light and
shade, lace, steam, foliage, net, streamers, etc., reduce the visual field.
There is little or no mediation of the look through the eyes of the main
male protagonist. On the contrary, shadowy presences like La Bessière
in *Morocco* act as surrogates for the director, detached as they are from
audience identification. Despite Sternberg's insistence that his stories
are irrelevant, it is significant that they are concerned with situation,
not suspense, and cyclical rather than linear time, while plot
complications revolve around misunderstanding rather than conflict.
The most important absence is that of the controlling male gaze within
the screen scene. The high point of emotional drama in the most typical
Dietrich films, her supreme moments of erotic meaning, take place in
the absence of the man she loves in the fiction. There are other
witnesses, other spectators watching her on the screen, their gaze is one
with, not standing in for, that of the audience. At the end of *Morocco*,
Tom Brown has already disappeared into the desert when Amy Jolly
kicks off her gold sandals and walks after him. At the end of
Dishonoured, Kranau is indifferent to the fate of Magda. In both cases,
the erotic impact, sanctified by death, is displayed as a spectacle for
the audience. The male hero misunderstands and, above all, does not
see.

In Hitchcock, by contrast, the male hero does see precisely what the
audience sees. However, in the films I shall discuss here, he takes
fascination with an image through scopophilic eroticism as the subject
of the film. Moreover, in these cases the hero portrays the contradictions
and tensions experienced by the spectator. In *Vertigo* in particular, but
also in *Marnie* and *Rear Window*, the look is central to the plot,
oscillating between voyeurism and fetishistic fascination. As a twist, a
further manipulation of the normal viewing process which in some
sense reveals it, Hitchcock uses the process of identification normally
associated with ideological correctness and the recognition of
established morality and shows up its perverted side. Hitchcock has
never concealed his interest in voyeurism, cinematic and non-cinematic.
His heroes are exemplary of the symbolic order and the law – a
policeman (*Vertigo*), a dominant male possessing money and power
(*Marnie*) – but their erotic drives lead them into compromised
situations. The power to subject another person to the will sadistically
or to the gaze voyeuristically is turned on to the woman as the object of
both. Power is backed by a certainty of legal right and the established
guilt of the woman (evoking castration, psychoanalytically speaking).

True perversion is barely concealed under a shallow mask of ideological correctness – the man is on the right side of the law, the woman on the wrong. Hitchcock's skilful use of identification processes and liberal use of subjective camera from the point of view of the male protagonist draw the spectators deeply into his position, making them share his uneasy gaze. The audience is absorbed into a voyeuristic situation within the screen scene and diegesis which parodies his own in the cinema. In his analysis of *Rear Window*, Douchet takes the film as a metaphor for the cinema. Jeffries is the audience, the events in the apartment block opposite correspond to the screen. As he watches, an erotic dimension is added to his look, a central image to the drama. His girlfriend Lisa had been of little sexual interest to him, more or less a drag, so long as she remained on the spectator side. When she crosses the barrier between his room and the block opposite, their relationship is re-born erotically. He does not merely watch her through his lens, as a distant meaningful image, he also sees her as a guilty intruder exposed by a dangerous man threatening her with punishment, and thus finally saves her. Lisa's exhibitionism has already been established by her obsessive interest in dress and style, in being a passive image of visual perfection; Jeffries' voyeurism and activity have also been established through his work as a photo-journalist, a maker of stories and captor of images. However, his enforced inactivity, binding him to his seat as a spectator, puts him squarely in the phantasy position of the cinema audience.

In *Vertigo*, subjective camera predominates. Apart from one flash-back from Judy's point of view, the narrative is woven around what Scottie sees or fails to see. The audience follows the growth of his erotic obsession and subsequent despair precisely from his point of view. Scottie's voyeurism is blatant: he falls in love with a woman he follows and spies on without speaking to. Its sadistic side is equally blatant: he has chosen (and freely chosen, for he had been a successful lawyer) to be a policeman, with all the attendant possibilities of pursuit and investigation. As a result, he follows, watches and falls in love with a perfect image of female beauty and mystery. Once he actually confronts her, his erotic drive is to break her down and force her to tell by persistent cross-questioning. Then, in the second part of the film, he re-enacts his obsessive involvement with the image he loved to watch secretly. He reconstructs Judy as Madeleine, forces her to conform in every detail to the actual physical appearance of his fetish. Her exhibitionism, her masochism, make her an ideal passive counterpart to Scottie's active sadistic voyeurism. She knows her part is to perform, and only by playing it through and then replaying it can she keep Scottie's erotic interest. But in the repetition he does break her down and succeeds in exposing her guilt. His curiosity wins through and she is punished. In *Vertigo*, erotic involvement with the look is disorientating: the spectator's fascination is turned against him as the narrative carries him through and entwines him with the processes that he is himself exercising. The Hitchcock hero here is firmly placed within the symbolic order, in narrative terms. He has all the attributes of the patriachal super-ego. Hence the spectator, lulled into a false sense of security by the apparent legality of his surrogate, sees through his look and finds himself exposed as complicit, caught in the moral ambiguity of looking. Far from being simply an aside on the perversion of the police, *Vertigo* focuses on the implications of the active/looking, passive/looked-at split in terms of sexual difference and the power of the male symbolic encapsulated in the hero. Marnie, too, performs for Mark Rutland's gaze and masquerades as the perfect to-be-looked-at image. He, too, is on the side of the law until, drawn in by obsession with her guilt, her secret, he longs to see her in the act of committing a crime, make her confess and thus save her. So he, too, becomes complicit as he acts out the implications of his power. He controls money and words, he can have his cake and eat it.

IV. Summary

The psychoanalytic background that has been discussed in this article is relevant to the pleasure and unpleasure offered by traditional narrative film. The scopophilic instinct (pleasure in looking at another person as an erotic object) and, in contradistinction, ego libido (forming identification processes) act as formations, mechanisms, which mould this cinema's formal attributes. The actual image of woman as (passive) raw material for the (active) gaze of man takes the argument a step further into the content and structure of representation, adding a further layer of ideological significance demanded by the patriarchal order in its favourite cinematic form – illusionistic narrative film. The argument must return again to the psychoanalytic background: women in representation can signify castration, and activate voyeuristic or fetishistic mechanisms to circumvent this threat. Although none of these interacting layers is intrinsic to film, it is only in the film form that they can reach a perfect and beautiful contradiction, thanks to the possibility in the cinema of shifting the emphasis of the look. The place of the look defines cinema, the possibility of varying it and exposing it. This is what makes cinema quite different in its voyeuristic potential from, say, striptease, theatre, shows and so on. Going far beyond highlighting a woman's to-be-looked-at-ness, cinema builds the way she is to be looked at into the spectacle itself. Playing on the tension between film as controlling the dimension of time (editing, narrative) and film as controlling the dimension of space (changes in distance, editing), cinematic codes create a gaze, a world and an object, thereby producing an illusion cut to the measure of desire. It is these cinematic codes and their relationship to formative external structures that must be broken down before mainstream film and the pleasure it provides can be challenged.

To begin with (as an ending), the voyeuristic-scopophilic look that is a crucial part of traditional filmic pleasure can itself be broken down. There are three different looks associated with cinema: that of the camera as it records the profilmic event, that of the audience as it watches the final product, and that of the characters at each other within the screen illusion. The conventions of narrative film deny the first two and subordinate them to the third, the conscious aim being always to eliminate intrusive camera presence and prevent a distancing awareness in the audience. Without these two absences (the material existence of the recording process, the critical reading of the spectator), fictional drama cannot achieve reality, obviousness and truth. Nevertheless, as this article has argued, the structure of looking in narrative fiction film contains a contradiction in its own premises: the female image as a castration threat constantly endangers the unity of the diegesis and bursts through the world of illusion as an intrusive, static, one-dimentional fetish. Thus the two looks materially present in time and space are obsessively subordinated to the neurotic needs of the male ego. The camera becomes the mechanism for producing an illusion of Renaissance space, flowing movements compatible with the human eye, an ideology of representation that revolves around the perception of the subject; the camera's look is disavowed in order to create a convincing world in which the spectator's surrogate can perform with verisimilitude. Simultaneously, the look of the audience is denied an intrinsic force: as soon as fetishistic representation of the female image threatens to break the spell of illusion, and the erotic image on the screen appears directly (without mediation) to the spectator, the fact of fetishisation, concealing as it does castration fear, freezes the look, fixates the spectator and prevents him from achieving any distance from the image in front of him.

This complex interaction of looks is specific to film. The first blow against the monolithic accumulation of traditional film conventions (already undertaken by radical film-makers) is to free the look of the camera into its materiality in time and space and the look of the audience into dialectics and passionate detachment. There is no doubt that this destroys the satisfaction, pleasure and privilege of the 'invisible guest', and highlights the way film has depended on voyeuristic active/passive mechanisms. Women, whose image has continually been stolen and used for this end, cannot view the decline of the traditional film form with anything much more than sentimental regret.[1]

Note

1. This article is a reworked version of a paper given in the French Department of the University of Wisconsin, Madison, in the Spring of 1973.

8 Afterthoughts on 'Visual Pleasure and Narrative Cinema' inspired by King Vidor's *Duel in the Sun* (1946)*

LAURA MULVEY

See headnote for Essay 7, p. 111 and 'Introduction', pp. 15–16.

So many times over the years since my 'Visual Pleasure and Narrative Cinema' article was published in *Screen*, I have been asked why I only used the *male* third person singular to stand in for the spectator. At the time, I was interested in the relationship between the image of woman on the screen and the 'masculinisation' of the spectator position, regardless of the actual sex (or possible deviance) of any real live movie-goer. In-built patterns of pleasure and identification impose masculinity as 'point of view'; a point of view which is also manifest in the general use of the masculine third person. However, the persistent question 'what about the women in the audience?' and my own love of Hollywood melodrama (equally shelved as an issue in 'Visual Pleasure') combined to convince me that, however ironically it had been intended originally, the male third person closed off avenues of inquiry that should be followed up. Finally, *Duel in the Sun* and its heroine's crisis of sexual identity brought both areas together.

I still stand by my 'Visual Pleasure' argument, but would now like to pursue the other two lines of thought. First (the 'women in the audience' issue), whether the female spectator is carried along, as it were by the scruff of the text, or whether her pleasure can be more deep-rooted and complex. Second (the 'melodrama' issue), how the text and its attendant identifications are affected by a *female* character occupying the centre of the narrative arena. So far as the first issue is concerned, it is always possible that the female spectator may find herself so out of key with the pleasure on offer, with its 'masculinisation', that the spell of fascination is broken. On the other hand, she may not. She may find herself secretly, unconsciously almost, enjoying the freedom of action and control over the diegetic world that

---

* Reprinted from *Framework* **15/16/17** (1981): 12–15.

identification with a hero provides. It is *this* female spectator that I want to consider here. So far as the second issue is concerned, I want to limit the area under consideration in a similar manner. Rather than discussing melodrama in general, I am concentrating on films in which a woman central protagonist is shown to be unable to achieve a stable sexual identity, torn between the deep blue sea of passive femininity and the devil of regressive masculinity.

There is an overlap between the two areas, between the unacknowledged dilemma faced in the auditorium and the dramatic double bind up there on the screen. Generally it is dangerous to elide these two separate worlds. In this case, the emotions of those women accepting 'masculinisation' while watching action movies with a male hero are illuminated by the emotions of a heroine of a melodrama whose resistance to a 'correct' feminine position is the critical issue at stake. Her oscillation, her inability to achieve stable sexual identity, is echoed by the woman spectator's masculine 'point of view'. Both create a sense of the difficulty of sexual difference in cinema that is missing in the undifferentiated spectator of 'Visual Pleasure'. The unstable, oscillating difference is thrown into relief by Freud's theory of femininity.

Freud and femininity

For Freud, femininity is complicated by the fact that it emerges out of a crucial period of parallel development between the sexes; a period he sees as masculine, or phallic, for both boys and girls. The terms he uses to conceive of femininity are the same as those he has mapped out for the male, causing certain problems of language and boundaries to expression. These problems reflect, very accurately, the actual position of women in patriarchal society (suppressed, for instance, under the generalised male third person singular). One term gives rise to a second as its complementary opposite, the male to the female, in that order. Some quotations:

> In females, too, the striving to be masculine is ego-syntonic at a certain period – namely in the phallic phase, before the development of femininity sets in. But it then succumbs to the momentous process of repression, as so often has been shown, that determines the fortunes of a woman's femininity.[1]

> I will only emphasise here that the development of femininity remains exposed to disturbances by the residual phenomena of the early masculine period. Regressions to the pre-Oedipus phase very frequently occur; in the course of some women's lives there is a repeated alternation between periods

in which femininity and masculinity gain the upper hand.[2]

We have called the motive force of sexual life 'the libido'. Sexual life is dominated by the polarity of masculine–feminine; thus the notion suggests itself of considering the relation of the libido to this antithesis. It would not be surprising if it were to turn out that each sexuality had its own special libido appropriated to it, so that one sort of libido would pursue the aims of a masculine sexual life and another sort those of a feminine one. But nothing of the kind is true. There is only one libido, which serves both the masculine and the feminine functions. To it itself we cannot assign any sex; if, following the conventional equation of activity and masculinity, we are inclined to describe it as masculine, we must not forget that it also covers trends with a passive aim. Nevertheless, the juxtaposition 'feminine libido' is without any justification. Furthermore, it is our impression that more constraint has been applied to the libido when it is pressed into the service of the feminine function, and that – to speak teleologically – Nature takes less careful account of its [that function's] demands than in the case of masculinity. And the reason for this may lie – thinking once again teleologically – in the fact that the accomplishment of the aim of biology has been entrusted to the aggressiveness of men and has been made to some extent independent of women's consent.[3]

One particular point of interest in the third passage is Freud's shift from the use of active/masculine as *metaphor* for the function of the libido to an invocation of Nature and biology that appears to leave the metaphoric usage behind. There are two problems here: Freud introduces the use of the word *masculine* as 'conventional', apparently simply following an established social-linguistic practice (but which, once again, confirms the masculine 'point of view'); however, secondly, and constituting a greater intellectual stumbling-block, the feminine cannot be conceptualised as different, but rather only as *opposition* (passivity) in an antinomic sense, or as *similarity* (the phallic phase). This is not to suggest that a hidden, as yet undiscovered femininity exists (as is perhaps implied by Freud's use of the word 'Nature') but that its structural relationship to masculinity under patriarchy cannot be defined or determined within the terms offered. This shifting process, this definition in terms of opposition or similarity, leaves women also shifting between the metaphoric opposition 'active' and 'passive'. The correct road, *femininity*, leads to increasing repression of 'the active' (the 'phallic phase' in Freud's terms). In this sense Hollywood genre films structured around masculine pleasure, offering an identification with the *active* point of view, allow a woman spectator to rediscover that lost aspect of her sexual identity, the never fully repressed bed-rock of feminine neurosis.

Narrative grammar and trans-sex identification

The 'convention' cited by Freud (active/masculine) structures most popular narratives, whether film, folk-tale or myth (as I argued in 'Visual Pleasure'), where his metaphoric usage is acted out literally in the story. Andromeda stays tied to the rock, a victim, in danger, until Perseus slays the monster and saves her. It is not my aim, here, to debate the rights and wrongs of this narrative division of labour or to demand positive heroines, but rather to point out that the 'grammar' of the story places the reader, listener or spectator *with* the hero. The woman spectator in the cinema can make use of an age-old cultural tradition adapting her to this convention, which eases a transition out of her own sex into another. In 'Visual Pleasure' my argument took as its axis a desire to identify a pleasure that was specific to cinema, that is the eroticism and cultural conventions surrounding the look. Now, on the contrary, I would rather emphasise the way that popular cinema inherited traditions of story-telling that are common to other forms of folk and mass culture, with attendant fascinations other than those of the look.

Freud points out that 'masculinity' is, at one stage, ego-syntonic for a woman. Leaving aside, for the moment, problems posed by his use of words, his general remarks on stories and day-dreams provide another angle of approach, this time giving a cultural rather than psychoanalytic insight into the dilemma. He emphasises the relationship between the ego and the narrative concept of the hero:

> It is the true heroic feeling, which one of our best writers has expressed in the inimitable phrase, 'Nothing can happen to me!' It seems, however, that through this revealing characteristic of invulnerability we can immediately recognise His Majesty the Ego, the hero of every day-dream and every story.[4]

Although a boy might know quite well that it is most *unlikely* that he will go out into the world, make his fortune through prowess or the assistance of helpers, and marry a princess, the stories describe the male fantasy of ambition, reflecting something of an experience and expectation of dominance (the active). For a girl, on the other hand, the cultural and social overlap is more confusing. Freud's argument that a young girl's day-dreams concentrate on the erotic ignores his own position on her early masculinity and the active day-dreams necessarily associated with this phase. In fact, all too often, the erotic function of the woman is represented by the passive, the waiting (Andromeda again), acting above all as a formal closure to the narrative structure. Three elements can thus be drawn together: Freud's concept of 'masculinity' in women, the identification triggered by the logic of a narrative grammar, and the ego's desire to fantasise itself in a certain, active, manner. All three suggest that, as desire is given cultural materiality in a text, for women (from childhood onwards) trans-sex identification is a *habit* that very easily becomes *second nature*. However, this Nature does not sit easily and shifts restlessly in its borrowed transvestite clothes.

The Western and Oedipal personifications

Using a concept of character function based on V. Propp's *Morphology of the Folk-tale*, I want to argue for a chain of links and shifts in narrative pattern, showing up the changing function of 'woman'. The Western (allowing, of course, for as many deviations as one cares to enumerate) bears a residual imprint of the primitive narrative structure analysed by Vladimir Propp in folk-tales. Also, in the hero's traditional invulnerability, the Western ties in closely with Freud's remarks on day-dreaming. (As I am interested primarily in character function and narrative pattern, not in genre definition, many issues about the Western as such are being summarily side-stepped.) For present purposes, the Western genre provides a crucial node in a series of transformations that *comment* on the function of 'women' (as opposed to 'man') as a narrative signifier and sexual difference as personification of 'active' or 'passive' elements in a story.

In the Proppian tale, an important aspect of narrative closure is 'marriage', a function characterised by 'princess' or equivalent. This is the only function that is sex-specific, and thus essentially relates to the sex of the hero and his marriageability. This function is very commonly reproduced in the Western, where, once again, 'marriage' makes a crucial contribution to narrative closure. However, in the Western the function's presence has also come to allow a complication in the form of its opposite, 'not marriage'. Thus, while the social integration represented by marriage is an essential aspect of the folk-tale, in the Western it can be accepted ... or not. A hero can gain in stature by refusing the princess and remaining alone (Randolph Scott in the Ranown series of movies). As the resolution of the Proppian tale can be seen to represent the resolution of the Oedipus complex (integration into the symbolic), the rejection of marriage personifies a nostalgic celebration of phallic, narcissistic omnipotence. Just as Freud's comments on the 'phallic' phase in girls seemed to belong in limbo, without a place in the chronology of sexual development, so, too, does this male phenomenon seem to belong to a phase of play and fantasy difficult to integrate exactly into the Oedipal trajectory.

The tension between two points of attraction, the symbolic (social integration and marriage) and nostalgic narcissism, generates a common splitting of the Western hero into two, something unknown in the Proppian tale. Here two functions emerge, one celebrating integration into society through marriage, the other celebrating resistance to social demands and responsibilities, above all those of marriage and the family, the sphere represented by woman. A story such as *The Man Who Shot Liberty Valance* juxtaposes these two points of attraction, and spectator fantasy can have its cake and eat it too. This particular tension between the double hero also brings out the underlying significance of the drama, its relation to the symbolic, with unusual clarity. A folk-tale story revolves around conflict between hero and villain. The flashback narration in *Liberty Valance* seems to follow these lines at first. The narrative is generated by an act of villainy (Liberty rampages, dragon-like, around the countryside). However the development of the story acquires a complication. The issue at stake is no longer how the villain will be defeated, but how the villain's defeat will be inscribed into history, whether the *upholder* of law as a symbolic system (Ranse) will be seen to be victorious or the *personification* of law in a more primitive manifestation (Tom), closer to the good or the right. *Liberty Valance*, as it uses a flashback structure, also brings out the poignancy of this tension. The 'present-tense' story is precipitated by a funeral, so that the story is shot through with nostalgia and sense of loss. Ranse Stoddart mourns Tom Doniphon.

This narrative structure is based on an opposition between two irreconcilables. The two paths cannot cross. On one side there is an encapsulation of power, and phallic attributes, in an individual who has to bow himself out of the way of history; on the other, an individual impotence rewarded by political and financial power, which, *in the long run*, in fact becomes history. Here the function 'marriage' is as crucial as it is in the folk-tale. It plays the same part in creating narrative resolution, but is even more important in that 'marriage' is an integral attribute of the upholder of the law. In this sense Hallie's choice between the two men is predetermined. Hallie equals princess equals Oedipal resolution rewarded, equals repression of narcissistic sexuality in marriage.

Woman as signifier of sexuality

In a Western working within these conventions, the function 'marriage' sublimates the erotic into a final, closing, social ritual. This ritual is, of course, sex-specific, and the main rationale for any female presence in this strand of the genre. This neat *narrative* function restates the propensity for 'woman' to signify 'the erotic' already familiar from *visual* representation (as, for instance, argued in 'Visual Pleasure'). Now I want to discuss the way in which introducing a woman as central to a story shifts its meanings, producing another kind of narrative discourse. *Duel in the Sun* provides the opportunity for this.

While the film remains visibly a 'Western', the generic space seems to shift. The landscape of action, although present, is not the dramatic core of the film's story, rather it is the interior drama of a girl caught between two conflicting desires. The conflicting desires, first of all, correspond closely with Freud's argument about female sexuality quoted above, that is: an oscillation between 'passive' femininity and regressive 'masculinity'. Thus, the symbolic equation, woman = sexuality, still persists, but now rather than being an image or a narrative function, the equation opens out a narrative area previously suppressed or repressed. Woman is no longer the signifier of sexuality (function 'marriage') in the 'Western' type of story. Now the female presence as centre allows the story to be actually, *overtly*, about sexuality: it becomes a melodrama. It is as though the narrational lens had zoomed in and opened up the neat function 'marriage' ('and they lived happily ... ') to ask 'what next?' and to focus on the figure of the princess, waiting in the wings for her one moment of importance, to ask 'what does *she* want?'. Here we find the generic terrain for melodrama, in its woman-orientated strand. The second question ('what does *she* want?') takes on greater significance when the hero function is split, as described above in the case of *Liberty Valance*, where the heroine's choice puts the seal of married grace on the upholder of the law. *Duel in the Sun* opens up this question.

In *Duel in the Sun* the iconographical attributes of the two male (oppositional) characters, Lewt and Jesse, conform very closely to those of Tom and Ranse in *Liberty Valance*. But now the opposition between Ranse and Tom (which represents an abstract and allegorical conflict over Law and history) is given a completely different twist of meaning. As Pearl is at the centre of the story, caught between the two men, their alternative attributes acquire meaning *from* her, and represent different sides of her desire and aspiration. They personify the split in *Pearl*, not a split in the concept of *hero*, as argued previously for *Liberty Valance*.

However, from a psychoanalytic point of view, a strikingly similar pattern emerges. Jesse (attributes: books, dark suit, legal skills, love of learning and culture, destined to be Governor of the State, money, and so on) signposts the 'correct' path for Pearl, towards learning a passive sexuality, learning to 'be a lady', above all sublimation into a concept of the feminine that is socially viable. Lewt (attributes: guns, horses, skill with horses, Western get-up, contempt for culture, destined to die an outlaw, personal strength and personal power) offers sexual passion, not based on maturity but on a regressive, boy/girl mixture of rivalry and play. With Lewt, Pearl can be a tomboy (riding, swimming, shooting). Thus the Oedipal dimension persists, but now illuminates the sexual ambivalence it represents for femininity.

In the last resort, there is no more room for Pearl in Lewt's world of misogynist machismo than there is room for her desires as Jesse's potential fiancée. The film consists of a series of oscillations in her sexual identity, between alternative paths of development, between different desperations. Whereas the regressive phallic male hero (Tom in *Liberty Vallance*) had a place (albeit a doomed one) that was stable and meaningful, Pearl is unable to settle or find a 'femininity' in which she and the male world can meet. In this sense, although the male characters personify Pearl's dilemma, it is their terms that make and finally break her. Once again, however, the narrative drama dooms the phallic, regressive resistance to the symbolic. Lewt, Pearl's masculine side, drops out of the social order. Pearl's masculinity gives her the 'wherewithal' to achieve heroism and kill the villain. The lovers shoot each other and die in each other's arms. Perhaps, in *Duel*, the erotic relationship between Pearl and Lewt also exposes a dyadic interdependence between hero and villain in the primitive tale, now threatened by the splitting of the hero with the coming of the Law.

In *Duel in the Sun*, Pearl's inability to become a 'lady' is highlighted by the fact that the perfect lady appears, like a phantasmagoria of Pearl's failed aspiration, as Jesse's perfect future wife. Pearl recognises her and her rights over Jesse, and sees that she represents the 'correct' road. In an earlier film by King Vidor, *Stella Dallas* (1937), narrative and iconographic structures similar to those outlined above make the dramatic meaning of the film although it is not a Western. Stella, as central character, is flanked on each side by a male personification of her instability, her inability to accept correct, married 'femininity' on the one hand, or find a place in a macho world on the other. Her husband, Stephen, demonstrates all the attributes associated with Jesse, with no problems of generic shift. Ed Munn, representing Stella's regressive 'masculine' side, is considerably emasculated by the loss of the Western's accoutrements and its terrain of violence. (The fact that Stella is a mother, and that her relationship to her child constitutes the central drama, undermines a possible sexual relationship with Ed.) He does retain residual traces of Western iconography. His attributes are mapped through associations with horses and betting, the racing scene. However, more importantly, his relationship with Stella is regressive, based on 'having fun', most explicitly in the episode in which they spread itching powder among the respectable occupants of a train carriage. In *Stella Dallas*, too, a perfect wife appears for Stephen, representing the 'correct' femininity that Stella rejects (very similar to Helen, Jesse's fiancée in *Duel in the Sun*).

I have been trying to suggest a series of transformations in narrative pattern that illuminate, but also show shifts in, Oedipal nostalgia. The 'personifications' and their iconographical attributes do not relate to parental figures or reactivate an actual Oedipal moment. On the contrary, they represent an internal oscillation of desire, which lies dormant, waiting to be 'pleasured' in stories of this kind. Perhaps the fascination of the classic Western, in particular, lies in its rather raw touching on this nerve. However, for the female spectator the situation is more complicated and goes beyond simple mourning for a lost fantasy of omnipotence. The masculine identification, in its phallic aspect, reactivates for her a fantasy of 'action' that correct femininity demands should be repressed. The fantasy 'action' finds expression through a metaphor of masculinity. Both in the language used by Freud and in the male personifications of desire flanking the female protagonist in the melodrama, this metaphor acts as a strait-jacket, becoming itself an indicator, a litmus paper, of the problems inevitably activated by any attempt to represent the feminine in patriarchal society. The memory of the 'masculine' phase has its own romantic attraction, a last-ditch resistance, in which the power of masculinity can be used as postponement against the power of patriarchy. Thus Freud's comments illuminate both the position of the female spectator and the image of oscillation represented by Pearl and Stella:

> ... in the course of some women's lives there is a repeated alternation between periods in which femininity and masculinity gain the upper hand ... (the phallic phase) ... then succumbs to the momentous process of repression as has so often been shown, that determines the fortunes of women's femininity.

I have argued that Pearl's position in *Duel in the Sun* is similar to that of the female spectator as she temporarily accepts 'masculinisation' in memory of her 'active' phase. Rather than dramatising the success of masculine identification, Pearl brings out its sadness. Her 'tomboy' pleasures, her sexuality, are not fully accepted by Lewt, except in death. So, too, is the female spectator's fantasy of masculinisation at cross-purposes with itself, restless in its transvestite clothes.

Notes

1.   S. FREUD, 'Analysis Terminable and Interminable', *Standard Edition*, vol. XXIII (London: Hogarth Press, 1964).

2. S. FREUD, 'Femininity', *Standard Edition*, vol. XXII (London: Hogarth Press, 1964).

3. Ibid.

4. S. FREUD, 'Creative Writers and Day Dreaming', *Standard Edition*, vol. IX (London: Hogarth Press, 1964).

9   Double Indemnity*

CLAIRE JOHNSTON

Claire Johnston, who died in 1987, taught film studies at Middlesex University. She edited *Notes on Women's Cinema* (1973) and *Edinburgh '77 Magazine (History/Production/Memory)*; she co-edited *Jacques Tourneur* (1975), *Dorothy Arzner* (1975) and *Edinburgh '76 Magazine (Psychoanalysis/Cinema/Avant-garde)*. See 'Introduction', p. 16.

Double Indemnity, based on James M. Cain's *roman noir* of the same title, is the story of an insurance agent, Walter Neff, who plots with Phyllis Dietrichson to kill her husband by making it appear that he died falling from a moving train, thus allowing them to claim double the insurance money on his life. In attempting to retain James M. Cain's first person interior monologue Billy Wilder and Raymond Chandler, the scriptwriter, used the narrative device, extremely rare in classic Hollywood cinema in the 1940s, of having Neff recite the past events into a dictaphone, so that the plot resolution is known from the outset, the film taking the form of a memory. Such a device at one level would seem to constitute an attempt to preserve the essence of the *roman noir* as a sub-genre of the detective genre as a whole.

As Todorov notes,[1] while retaining the structure of the enigma, the narrator displaces its centrality and relativises its structuring function within the narrative. In that the narrator does not know whether he will remain alive at the end, he becomes problematic for the reader. The *roman noir* fuses two narrative codes, suppressing the code of the detective story which offers the possibility of sense and believability for the reader in terms of an enigma resolved by the Law, and giving life to the first person narration spoken in the present coinciding with the action in the form of a memory. Essentially the *roman noir* as a sub-genre presents a particular social milieu of immorality and sordid crime in which the narrator risks his life and sanity.

* Reprinted from *Women in Film Noir*, ed. E. Ann Kaplan (London: BFI, 1978), pp. 100–11.

The believability of the detective genre as a whole is a particular one founded on questions relating to the social construction of social reality – it is the character who is not suspected who is, in fact, guilty. Such a systematic process of inversion of social reality within the genre necessitates that social reality be re-affirmed through resolution and closure for the reader in terms of the Law. Far from opening up social contradictions, the genre as a whole, through such a process of naturalisation, performs a profoundly confirmatory function for the reader, both revealing and simultaneously eliminating the problematic aspects of social reality by the assertion of the unproblematic nature of the Law.

The use of the 'novelesque' in *Double Indemnity* as a continuous, first person narrative discourse co-extensive with the image track – semi-diegetic speech[2] – undoubtedly draws the film closer to literary speech, but within the filmic discourse its function within the text is displaced and transformed. While the film poses a first person narrating discourse which takes the form of a memory, the filmic/diegetic image is always in the present. Far from displacing the enigma in revealing the plot resolution at the beginning of the film, the first person narrative discourse, in its play of convergence/divergence with the visible, produces an enigma at another level for the viewer: a split relationship to knowledge. The first person narration presents itself as a 'confession' which reveals the truth of the narrative of events by which we can talk of the various characters in the film – it purports to provide the knowledge of how things really happened. But as the film unfolds, a divergence emerges between the knowledge which the first person narrative discourse provides and that which unfolds at the level of the visible. Finally, it is the visual discourse which serves as the guarantee of truth for the reader: 'the spectator can do no other than identify with the camera'.[3] In filmic discourse the relationship between the viewer and reality – the film – is one of pure specularity, in which the look of the spectator is denied, locking the spectator into a particular sense of identity. Ultimately, classic Hollywood cinema is always in the third person – it is always objective – unless subjectivity is marked in the image itself (e.g., the blurred image of Gutman in *The Maltese Falcon*).[4] The narrative of events at the level of the visible provides the knowledge of how things really are and constitutes the dominant narrating instance.

In *Double Indemnity* the process of articulation between the narrating discourses at play is foregrounded by the 'novelesque' aspect of the genre itself, providing a complex interplay of convergence/divergence – a conflict at the level of the knowledges which the film provides for the viewer, setting in motion its own enigma. As the film progresses the narrator loses control of the narrative to the point where he himself comes under scrutiny. Keyes, the company claims investigator, the 'you' of Neff's first person narration, begins to investigate the case and Neff becomes a witness, subject to Keyes' investigation. It is the articulation of the 'I' and the 'you' of the first person narration (the relationship between the two men) with the narrative of events in the realm of the visible (the objective, third person process of narrativisation) which situates a split relationship to knowledge for the viewer and, with it, the enigma. At the centre of the enigma is the Oedipal trajectory of the hero – the problem of the knowledge of sexual difference in a patriarchal order.

The title sequence sets the film under the mark of castration: the silhouette of a male figure in hat and overcoat looms towards the camera on crutches. In the next sequence we see Walter Neff, injured and bleeding, entering the offices of his insurance company and begin his 'confession' to Keyes on the dictaphone. 'I killed Dietrichson – me, Walter Neff – insurance salesman – thirty five years old, no visible scars – till a while ago, that is … I killed him for money – and for a woman … It all began last May.'

It is to Keyes that Walter Neff's discourse, the 'I' of the voice-over, is addressed; a 'you' which is split between the Symbolic and the Imaginary[5] – a split that insists in the attempted overlapping of the functions of symbolic father and idealised father. Neff's opening 'confession' establishes Keyes as the representative of the Law – the symbolic father: 'you were right, but you got the wrong man'. As symbolic father, Keyes' unshakeable access to the truth, to knowledge, resides in his phallic attribute, his 'little man' which, by a process necessitated by censoring mechanisms, 'ties knots in his stomach', enabling him to spot a phoney claim instantly. His knowledge of the laws of mathematical probability, epitomised in his very name, enables him to chart the social excesses of the world and ensure the stability of property relations in the name of the insurance business. In the first scene in the claims office we see him interrogate a man with a phoney claim and render him an 'honest man' again. He describes his function within the institution as 'doctor', 'bloodhound', 'cop' and 'father confessor'.

As signifier of the patriarchal order, Keyes represents for Neff what it means to be capable of saying 'I am who I am', to be the one who knows; he is transcendent. In order to resolve the positive Oedipus and gain access to the Symbolic, the boy has to accept the threat of castration from the father. As Lacan has indicated, 'Law and repressed desire are one and the same thing'.[6] The Oedipus Complex allows access to desire only through repression: it is through lack that desire is instituted. As Keyes says of Neff: 'you're not smarter, you're just taller'. Neff's belief in Keyes' knowledge is absolute: 'you were right'. At the same time the Law always offers itself for transgression: the desire to 'con the system', to devise a scheme so 'perfect' that it can challenge the father's phallic function, his knowledge, and thus reduplicate the perfection of the system once more. But the symbolic father can only be imperfectly incarnate in the real father. As Neff's symbolic father, Keyes is marked by a lack, a blind spot. In the voice-over in the first scene in the claims office, Neff says (in retrospect) that he 'knew he had a heart as big as a house' – the reason why he 'got the wrong man'. It is the repressed, maternal side of Keyes which constitutes a blind spot for the patriarchal order, and it is this blind spot which for Neff sets in motion the desire for transgression which the son may always attempt against the father: to take his place.

Keyes also represents the idealised father for Neff: the ideal ego founded on narcissistic identifications constitutive of the realm of the Imaginary. As Freud indicated,[7] identifications in the pre-Oedipal phase are associated primarily with one's sexual like. The repressed homosexual desire of Neff for the idealised father rests on narcissistic identification, to 'think with your brains, Keyes', to possess his knowledge. In the all-male universe of the insurance business, women are seen as untrustworthy: as Keyes comments, they 'should be investigated' before any relationship is embarked on. Women represent the possibility of social excess which the insurance business seeks to contain – they 'drink from the bottle' (Keyes). The repressed, homosexual desire between the two men, the negative Oedipus, is symbolised by the visual rhyme, running throughout the film, of Neff's ritual lighting of Keyes' cigar as Keyes fumbles each time for a match. This signifier is underpinned in the first scene in the claims office by Neff's words 'I love you, too' as Keyes jokingly threatens to throw his desk at him. Neff's pre-Oedipal, narcissistic identification with Keyes implies a disavowal rather than an acceptance of castration. Thus the film traces the precariousness of the patriarchal order and its internal contradictions precisely in this split between Symbolic and Imaginary symbolised in the place and function of Keyes in the fiction, and the inscription of castration for men within that order. Neff must both assume castration in a process of testing the Law so that he can take the place of the symbolic father, while, at the same time, disavowing castration in his narcissistic identifications with a father-figure – the idealised father.

As an example of the *film noir*, *Double Indemnity* poses a social reality constructed in the split, the interface, between the Symbolic and the Imaginary of a particular social order – that of the male universe of the insurance business – an order which activates/reactivates the trouble of castration for the male in patriarchy. It is in relation to the woman in the film, to Phyllis Dietrichson/Barbara Stanwyck and her step-daughter Lola, that the internal contradictions of the patriarchal order (the Oedipal trajectory of male desire focused in Neff) are to be played out. The 'woman' is thus produced as the signifier of the lack, of heterogeneity – the 'fault' inherent in patriarchy as an order.

As Laura Mulvey has elaborated,[8] it is the contemplation of the female form which evokes castration anxiety for the male: the original trauma being the discovery that the mother is, in fact, not phallic, but castrated. As locus of lack/castration, as the site where radical difference is marked negatively, 'woman' is the pivot around which the circulation of male desire is played out in the text, and it is this process of circulation of desire which fixes the representation of women in the text. Phyllis Dietrichson/Barbara Stanwyck, celebrated female star and *femme fatale*, represents Neff's attempt to disavow castration in his repressed homosexuality and to test the Law, while Lola functions as the term in relation to which an acceptance of castration and the Symbolic Order is inscribed. As the narrative progresses, Phyllis Dietrichson/Barbara Stanwyck gives way to Lola and the contradictions of the patriarchal order opened up by the film are contained for the next generation. It is Neff's paternal function in relation to Lola which restores her as good object within familial relations. The enigma of the problem of the knowledge of sexual difference is thus resolved by the Law *for* patriarchy.

In the scene immediately following Neff's 'confession' to Keyes, both Phyllis Dietrichson/Barbara Stanwyck and Lola are introduced into the narrative, as Neff goes to renew an insurance policy at the house. His voice-over fixes them as memory, *as already known*, in the 'I' and 'you' discourse between the two men. In a dusty semi-darkened room Phyllis Dietrichson/Barbara Stanwyck, covered in a bath towel, stands at the top of the stairs offered to and held in the mastery of Neff's gaze. Neff jokes that she might not be 'fully covered' by the insurance policy on the car: the hint of social excess. At the same time the voice-over draws our attention to the photograph on the piano of Dietrichson and his daughter by his first marriage, Lola. Visually, the women resemble each other in age and general appearance in a striking way. 'Mother' and 'daughter' are nevertheless, from the beginning, established as inhabiting a different space in the diegesis, Phyllis Dietrichson/Barbara Stanwyck frozen as fetish object in Neff's look, already outside the space of familial relations, and Lola frozen in the family photograph from which Phyllis is excluded.

The initial shots of Neff's encounter with Phyllis Dietrichson/Barbara Stanwyck are marked by a fetishistic fascination: simultaneously the dangerous site of castration and the pleasurable appearance – the object

139

of the look – she is the source of reassuring pleasure in the face of castration anxiety. The 'I' of the voice-over talks of this fascination, converging with the 'I' of the look: (the viewer is thus drawn into a fetishistic split between belief and knowledge. As she begins to come down the stairs of the California-style Spanish house, we see a close-up of her legs and her golden anklet. The camera follows Neff and catches his image in the mirror as he watches her finish buttoning up her dress and putting on her lipstick. She turns from the mirror, leaving him still fixed in his gaze, and moves over to the other side of the room.)

His privileged look at her exhibitionism in the mirror shot, a moment of pure specularity, marks a disjuncture between his look and that of the viewer: imprisoned in his narcissistic identifications, the identity of Neff and viewer is simultaneously doubled, split and recomposed – his gaze becomes uneasy. He must investigate the woman further and discover her guilty secret in his desire to test the Law. The possibility of social excess which she represents, her incongruity as suburban housewife, suggests her as a vehicle for his Oedipal transgression. She asks him about accident insurance for her husband and he flirts with her, continuing the driving metaphor around the car insurance, to discover more. She says he's 'going too fast'. He leaves, making an appointment to call the next day.

The following scene of his visit to the house the next day is dominated by shots of Neff watching her as he tries to discover her guilty secret. We see her descend the stairs to open the door as the voice-over recalls her anklet: the mastery of his gaze is re-presented as a memory image. He asks her to call him Walter and offers to run the vacuum cleaner. As he watches, she tells him about the boredom of her married life and asks him about taking out accident insurance on her husband's life. He interrogates her and asks her why she married her husband. The camera remains on his face as she asks how she could take out the accident insurance without either her husband or the company knowing. He tells her how it could be done and says, as he leaves, she 'can't get away with it'. In the voice-over Neff says, 'I knew I had hold of a red hot poker and it was time to drop it before it burned my hand off'. The images confirm his complicity for the viewer, his sadistic play with the woman.

As Laura Mulvey notes,[9] the disavowal of castration for the male in its fascination and the desire to know her guilty secret is fundamentally sadistic – it must also involve her punishment. Phyllis Dietrichson/Barbara Stanwyck, entombed in the domesticity of the Spanish house, represents the possibility of a libidinal satisfaction which cannot be contained within the Symbolic Order and the structure of familial relations. For the patriarchal order founded on castration, she is a trouble which can be spoken about but not acted upon. As such, she encapsulates the concerns of the film noir itself – that (as Neff says in the voice-over) 'murder can sometimes smell like honeysuckle'. In her very impossibility, she offers herself as a vehicle for Neff to test the Law, but the erotic drives she represents must finally, in the film noir, become subject to the Law – she must be found guilty and punished. These drives can only be destructive and lead to death, in that she represents, precisely, the heterogeneity which must form the outside of the Symbolic Order, the excluded that allows the order to exist as an order.[10]

The love scene necessitates the confession of her guilty secret – that which troubles the order and which will have to be worked through in and by the text: 'it was only the beginning ...' (Neff). The bell rings and she stands in a pool of light, offered to the gaze of Neff and viewer, in the doorway of Neff's darkened apartment. The voice-over suggests an appointment which the image denies: 'it would be eight and she would be there'. She is holding his hat and is returning it. Later they embrace on the sofa and he draws her into confessing her guilty secret – that she would like her husband dead. As they embrace, their love-making is elided by the camera tracking out of the apartment room and, in the next shot, into Neff's office as he tells Keyes on the dictaphone that he always wanted to 'con the system'. The camera then tracks back out of the office and back into the apartment room to find them again on the sofa. Sexual knowledge of the woman and Neff's Oedipal trajectory, *vis-à-vis* Keyes, to test the Law, are held and relocated diegetically for the viewer in this relocation of sex with Phyllis into the verbal interchange with Keyes. As she begins to leave, Neff agrees to help her to get her husband to sign the insurance papers. As we hear the car drive away, Neff's voice-over says 'the machinery had started to move'; he would have to 'think with your brains, Keyes', assume mastery of the Symbolic Order, the system, in order to explore its interstices.

At this point the sexual drives opened up by the woman and the need for narcissistic identification with the father come into contradiction. We return to Neff's office and the 'confession' to Keyes on the dictaphone, as Neff tells him he 'didn't like the witness' to Dietrichson's signature, how he felt 'queer in the belly'. There is a fade to Lola's image sitting in mid-shot playing Chinese chequers. The transition emphasises Lola's position on the side of mastery within the order which Neff is testing for gaps – in this sense, Lola is on the side of Keyes. As witness she represents the social order encapsulated in the persona of Keyes: the containment of social excess and the regulation of property relations. The camera tracks out from Lola to reveal the family scene, and as Dietrichson signs the documents, her image remains central in the frame. Neff's eyes follow her as she goes upstairs.

The threat to Neff which Lola represents is precisely her centrality within the family, her role of daughter, subject to the Law of the Father. As witness, she functions as a reference to, a sign of, the Symbolic Order which he seeks to transgress – she's a 'nice kid'. He leaves the house, and arrives at his car to find her sitting in the front seat. At this point there is a disturbance in the point-of-view structure in the text. She asks him to give her a lift into town, and confides in him that she is secretly going to see her boyfriend, Nino. Neff's attitude is paternal. As he drops her off in town the voice-over comments: 'the father was a dead pigeon'.

In order to simulate Dietrichson's death from a moving train and claim the double indemnity on his life, Neff has to take his place. In so doing he not only becomes Phyllis's 'husband', but Lola's 'father'. In destroying the family unit, in testing the Law, Neff has entered an impossible family, a family explicitly based on a sacrificial murder, and thus socially censored. After murdering Dietrichson and taking his place on the train his desire vanishes: having successfully achieved a replica of the family, he is now in the position of the master in an *other* symbolic order, one that exists alongside and in the face of the social order represented by Keyes. The car fails to start: he and Phyllis part on a reluctant embrace. On the way to the drug store, after establishing his alibi, Neff's voice-over says: 'I couldn't hear my own footsteps ... it was the walk of a dead man.' The impossible family is a nightmare. Neff exists in a no-man's-land.

In committing the 'perfect' crime, he and Phyllis now exist outside the certitude of the Symbolic Order represented in the legality of the insurance contract signed by Dietrichson. They can no longer meet at the house, and have to meet at the supermarket. The libidinal drives which Phyllis represents can only lead to her death: she is guilty and will be punished. Keyes' 'little man' will tell him something is wrong. But Neff can rely on Keyes' blind spot, his maternal side, the 'fault' in the Symbolic Order. Neff knows he has a 'heart as big as a house'. Outside the symbolic, Neff remains, nevertheless, subject to the Law: Keyes' relentless scrutiny of the insurance claim and the look of the camera, this time on Neff, as the investigation proceeds.

At this point in the film, the balance in which Phyllis and Lola are held in relation to Neff begins to change in terms of spatial relationships at the level of the visible. Keyes comes to Neff's apartment to tell him that he suspects Phyllis and that he intends to 'put her through the wringer'. Phyllis has come to see Neff and is hiding behind the door as Keyes leaves to get something to ease his stomach. Before he gets to the elevator, he takes out a cigar and turns to Neff for his ritual light. The shot encapsulates a change in the direction of Neff's Oedipal trajectory, with Phyllis foregrounded behind the door in the darkness and the men in the light of the hallway on the other side of the door. When Keyes leaves, Phyllis complains that Neff is 'going off her'. They embrace and there is a fade and transition (for the first time without the voice-over to signal it) which completes this change in direction, revealing Lola waiting outside Neff's office: 'do you remember me, Mr. Neff? ... look at me, Mr. Neff'. The camera underpins his look at the witness.

Lola says she knows Phyllis is guilty and is going 'to tell': she threatens to interrupt Neff's confessional voice-over to Keyes. She will become the narrator and break the imaginary duality of the Neff/Keyes relationship. She says she has moved out of the house and is living alone: the scene ends on a close-up of her tearful face. As 'father', Neff must return the 'daughter' to the safety of familial relations. As the voice-over tells us how he had decided to take her out to 'keep her quiet', we see a series of two-shots, idyllic images of happiness, as they eat in candlelight at a restaurant and go driving in the countryside. At the discursive level, the voice-over no longer provides the truth with which to read the image. In the transition from Phyllis to Lola, unmarked by Neff's voice-over and visible in terms of spatial relationships, Phyllis gives way to Lola and the Symbolic Order which she represents returns, threatening from within the replica of the family which has been constructed.

From now on the metaphor of the car is replaced by that of the 'trolley ride'. Having established Phyllis's guilt, Keyes is now looking for her accomplice – the 'other person'. As Keyes says: 'they are on a trolley ride together and the last stop is the cemetery'. Desire which cannot be contained within the Symbolic Order (the trouble represented by Phyllis) can only lead to death, in that it represents the outside of that order, that which must be repressed or contained if that order is to continue to exist. As Keyes says, 'They are digging their own graves'. In the supermarket scene, Phyllis continues Keyes' metaphor: 'It's straight down the line for both of us, remember?'

The inexorable link between desire and death is relocated diegetically for the viewer as we return to Neff's office and the dictaphone: 'It was the first time I thought of Phyllis that way – dead, I mean, and how it would be if she were dead'. Continuing, he says how at that moment he thought of Lola, and there is a transition to a series of shots of their trip to the Hollywood Bowl. As they sit in two-shot, Lola's back is to the camera and, in the darkness, the physical resemblance to Phyllis is striking. Phyllis, already as good as dead, is replaced by Lola, restoring 'woman' as good object for the patriarchal order: the trouble is contained in its rightful place.

Having acknowledged the impossibility of his Oedipal trajectory, the narrator loses control of the narrative. The voice-over can no longer hold the narrative of events, and becomes questioning and uncertain. Keyes' investigation, inaugurating a counter-discourse to the narrative discourse of Neff's 'I', structured around the enigma of 'that somebody else', comes to hold the process of narrativisation for the viewer. This resituating of the 'I' and the 'you' of the narrative discourse is underpinned in the scene where Neff, thinking Keyes is double-crossing him, goes to Keyes' office and listens on the dictaphone to Keyes' confidential memo on his investigation of him, to discover that Keyes 'personally vouches for him'. The rhyme of the dictaphone asserts the 'you' at the level of the visible, at the same time confirming Keyes' blind spot: he doesn't see Neff's culpability. Having come to occupy the place of the father against the Symbolic Order, and discovered its impossibility, Neff must 'get rid of the whole mess' – Phyllis. 'Woman', locus of castration, of anxiety, the source of the 'whole mess', must be punished: he must 'get off the trolley car' before its logical end.

The rhyme of Phyllis's legs descending the stairs, now no longer caught in the mastery of his gaze, introduces the final flashback scene at the house. We see her descend, holding a gun wrapped in a chiffon scarf, unlock the door and put the gun under a cushion. She pursues her function in relation to the order whose excess she is and reaffirms her guilt still further. She says she is 'rotten to the heart' and that she is trying to persuade Lola's boyfriend, Nino, to 'take care of Lola'. Neff circles round her as she speaks. He walks to the window to shut it and she shoots him. He staggers towards her telling her to try again. The camera is held on her as she drops the gun and moves into a close-up as they embrace. She confesses that she never loved him but that she couldn't fire the second shot. As they remain locked in their embrace, he shoots her: she looks surprised. The eroticisation of death in the final scene of the flashback confirms a universe where access to desire is only through repression: the impossibility of a radical heterogeneity represented by the feminine.

Mortally wounded, Neff leaves the house; he meets Nino and gives him a nickel to ring Lola and make it up with her, restoring, symbolically, the *status quo ante*. The flashback ends and we return to Neff's office and the dictaphone. He ends his message to Keyes by asking him to take care of Lola and Nino. The 'father' restores the 'daughter' to the Symbolic Order and familial relations. 'Woman' as good object is reinstated for the next generation. The patriarchal order is now reaffirmed, and with it the internal contradictions for the male universe of the insurance business. The trouble of castration for the male in patriarchy as it insists in the disjunction between the Symbolic and the Imaginary fathers is reactivated. As Neff finishes his message to Keyes, the camera angle suggests a subjective look. It is the look of the 'you' to whom the 'I' has been addressed. Neff turns and acknowledges Keyes' presence. When asked why he couldn't 'figure it out', Keyes acknowledges his blind spot: 'You can't figure them all, Walter.' Neff asks for four hours' grace to cross 'the border'. Keyes replies that he won't even reach the elevator: he's 'all washed up'.

The split between the Symbolic and the Imaginary which structures the text insists in Keyes' overlapping function as symbolic and idealised father, driving the film towards resolution and closure. As symbolic father Keyes must represent the Law and hand Neff over to the police. As idealised father there remains the problem of narcissistic identification, and with it, repressed homosexuality – 'the border'.

The camera holds the two men in frame and follows Neff as he staggers towards the glass doors of his office while Keyes, now out of frame, speaks on the telephone: 'It's a police job.' Keyes then walks into frame as Neff lies slumped against the door and kneels beside him. Neff says: 'I know why you couldn't figure this one ... because the guy you were looking for was too close ... right across the desk from you.' Keyes replies: 'Closer than that, Walter', to which Neff gives his customary ironic reply: 'I love you, too.' As Neff lies dying he gets out a cigarette and the rhyme completes the mutual confession: Keyes returns Neff's ritual gesture and lights the cigarette. Having handed over his function as symbolic father to the police, Keyes can now acknowledge and return Neff's love in the signifier of repressed desire. The challenge to the patriarchal order eliminated and the internal contradictions of that order contained, a sublimated homosexuality between the men can now be signified. But there can be no more words – only The End.

Notes

1. *The Poetics of Prose* Oxford: Blackwell, 1977, pp. 42–52.

2. CHRISTIAN METZ, 'Current Problems of Film Theory', *Screen*, **14**: 1/2 (Spring/Summer 1973): p. 69.

3. CHRISTIAN METZ, 'History/Discourse: Note on two Voyeurisms', *Edinburgh '76 Magazine*, p. 23.

4. STEPHEN HEATH, 'Narrative Space', see above, p. 84.

5. For an account of the psychoanalytic framework to which these terms belong, see ROSALIND COWARD , 'Lacan and Signification: an Introduction', *Edinburgh '76 Magazine*.

6. JACQUES LACAN, *Ecrits* (Paris: *Editions du Seuil* 1966), p. 782; a selection from *Ecrits* has been translated by Tavistock Press, London, 1977.

7. 'Instincts and their Vicissitudes', *Collected Papers* (London: Hogarth Press, 1951), p. 65.

8. 'Visual Pleasure and Narrative Cinema', see above, p. 118.

9. Ibid., p. 119.

10. See JULIA KRISTEVA, 'Signifying Practice and Mode of Production', *Edinburgh '76 Magazine*.

10 *From* Fantasia*

ELIZABETH COWIE

Elizabeth Cowie is Senior Lecturer in Film Studies at the University
of Kent. Besides a number of articles, she has edited (with Parveen
Adams) *The Woman in Question* (1990). See 'Introduction', pp. 16–17.

This article will seek to elaborate some distinctions in relation to the
concept of fantasy[1] and to suggest some connections between feminist
debates, the field of psychoanalytic theory, and the analysis of films –
that is, to bring together fantasy as a political problem, psychoanalysis's
specific conceptualization of fantasy, and the film as a particular site of
the representation of fantasy. While the problem of fantasy in feminist
politics is the starting point, it will not be the focus of this article.
Rather, by elaborating its mechanisms and illustrating the functioning
of fantasy in film, it is hoped that some of the problems in current
feminist argument in this area will be illuminated, and some directions
for future work suggested. In particular two points will be argued: one,
that the opposition real/not real is wholly inappropriate to a
consideration of fantasy, whether it is used to 'save' fantasy – because
of course one wouldn't want it to *happen* – or is part of a dismissal of
fantasy as unimportant because it isn't real. Two, that, while on the one
hand fantasy can be characterized as a series of wishes presented
through imaginary happenings, on the other hand it is also a structure:
fantasy as the *mise-en-scène* of desire, the putting into a scene, a staging,
of desire. The emphasis of this article will thus be on fantasy as
structure, a structuring of the diverse contents, wishes, scenarios of
wishing, and it will draw on psychoanalysis for this description of
fantasy. While fantasy has been directly addressed within feminist
debates and is a key concept in psychoanalysis, in relation to film the
concept has been used either peripherally or pejoratively – pejoratively,

---

* Reprinted from *The Woman in Question*, ed. Parveen Adams and Elizabeth
Cowie (London: Verso, 1990), pp. 149–96; this is a corrected version of an article
first published in *m/f*, **9** (1984).

in the dismissal of cinema, or at least American cinema, as escapist fantasy; peripherally in that the term is used to describe a genre – the fantasy film – but in which the term simply marks those films that present either the supernatural or an imaginary world unknown to us as yet, for example, science fiction.

Nor is fantasy as such addressed in current studies of film involving psychoanalytic concepts. Rather, in the work of Raymond Bellour, Stephen Heath, or Mary Ann Doane, for example, the analysis involves uncovering the trajectory of desire constituted by the film text, a trajectory that is shown to position and fix the spectator as subject for its enunciation, an enunciation concerning a masculine Oedipal problem. Fantasy as a concept is then invoked to support analyses that center on the problem of *identity*, of the male subject, whether it is a director like Hitchcock, or a character, neurotic or psychotic.[2] In giving attention to fantasy my discussion will be askance from such studies; the difference opened up will I hope offer another way to considering the fixity, or not, of the sexual positions of cinema-subjects.

As noted earlier, fantasies are wishful; however they are not about a wish to have some determinate object, making it present for the subject. Lacan writes that

> The phantasy is the support of desire, it is not the object that is the support of desire. The subject sustains himself as desiring in relation to an ever-more complex signifying ensemble. This is apparent enough in the form of the scenario it assumes, in which the subject, more or less recognisable, is somewhere, split, divided, generally double, in his relation to the object, which usually does not show its true face either.
>
> (*Four Fundamental Concepts*, p. 185)

Similarly, Moustafa Safouan notes 'instead of being co-opted to an object, desire is first co-opted to a phantasy' (*m/f*, no. 9, 1984).

Fantasy involves, is characterized by, not the achievement of desired objects, but the arranging of, a setting out of, desire; a veritable *mise-en-scène* of desire. For of course, Lacan says, desire is unsatisfiable, much as Freud commented that there is something in the nature of sexuality that is resistant to satisfaction. The fantasy depends not on particular objects, but on their setting out; and the pleasure of fantasy lies in the setting out, not in the having of the objects. Within the daydream and more especially in fictional stories, the demands of narrative may obscure this, for the typical ending will be a resolution of the problems, the wars, feuds, etc., the achievement of union in marriage by the hero and heroine, etc. Yet inevitably the story will fall prey to diverse diversions, delays, obstacles and other means to postponing the ending. For though we all want the couple to be united, and the obstacles heroically overcome, we don't want the story to end. And marriage is one of the most definitive endings. The pleasure is in how to bring about the consummation, is in the happening and continuing to happen; in how it will come about, and *not* in the moment of *having happened*, when it will fall back into loss, the past. This can extend into producing endings that remain murky, ill-defined, uncertain even. It is thus not modesty that veils the endings of romantic fiction but wise caution. Sternberg's film *Morocco* is perhaps an extreme example in cinema of the refusal to narrate an ending, to consummate the narrative, for it concludes with another repetition of the setting out of a lack to be fulfilled, which has already been played twice over and more, namely, of Dietrich leaving an anguished Adolphe Menjou for an unknowing Gary Cooper. Fantasy as a *mise-en-scène* of desire is more a setting out of lack, of what is absent, than a presentation of a having, a being present. Desire itself coming into existence in the representation of lack, in the production of a fantasy of its becoming present.

It can be seen, then, that fantasy is not the object of desire, but its setting. As a result

> In fantasy the subject does not pursue the object or its sign: he appears caught up himself in the sequence of images. He forms no representation of the desired object, but is himself represented as participating in the scene although, in the earliest forms of fantasy, he cannot be assigned any fixed place in it ... . As a result, the subject, although always present in the fantasy, may be so in a de-subjectivised form, that is to say, in the very syntax of the sequence in question.
>
> (ibid., p. 17)

The subject is present or presented through the very form of organization, composition, of the scene. It is perhaps only the most reworked, conscious daydream that is able to impose the stabilization of the ego, so that the subject's position is clear and invariable as the 'I' of the story, which the subject as it were 'lives out'. Nevertheless it will be argued later with regard to the fiction film that it is not only in these 'original' fantasies that this desubjectivization takes place. Both the daydream 'thoughtlessly' composed and the more complex fictional narrative join with the 'original' fantasies in visualizing the subject in the scene, and in presenting a varying of subject positions so that the subject takes up more than one position and thus is not fixed.

In Freud's analysis of the fantasy in 'A Child is Being Beaten: A Contribution to the Study of the Origin of Sexual Perversions' he shows three phases in this fantasy, each involving a different subject-position.

In the first phase, the fantasy is 'my father is beating a child, whom I hate'; thus, 'my father loves me since he is beating the other child' but also 'I am making my father beat the other child to show he loves me' in which the subject erases the other, rival child from the father's affections. It is thus egoistic, identifying both father/self-love and father/self as beater of the other child. For this to become transposed into 'A child is being beaten' with its third-person syntax, Freud proposed a second phase 'I am being beaten by my father'; while the first phase may be remembered through analysis, this second phase is wholly unconscious and can only be inferred from analysis. However, it produces the move from sadism to masochism. (Though the first phase is not yet properly sadistic, or erotic, inasmuch as it is pre-genital.) The implicit incestuous desire of the first phase is subject to repression in the second phase, to produce a reversal: 'No, my father does not love me (you), for he is beating me (you).' The beating is not only the punishment for the incestuous wish but is also the 'regressive substitute for that relation, and from this latter source it derives the libidinal excitation which is from this time forward attached to it'. Guiltiness and punishment are thus attached to the sexual desire; to be punished is to have had the forbidden sexual relation, for why else would you be punished? In the third phase, the consciously remembered fantasy 'A child is being beaten', once more appears sadistic

> but it is so only in form; the satisfaction which is derived from it is masochistic. Its significance lies in the fact that it has taken over the libidinal cathexis of the repressed portion and at the same time the sense of guilt which is attached to the content of that portion. All the many unspecified children who are being beaten by the teacher are, after all, nothing more than substitutes for the child itself.
>
> (p. 191)

The fantasy escapes repression by a further distortion, the disguise of the third-person syntax. Out there, there are children being beaten (like I should be, for my forbidden wishes). Apparently sadistic, inasmuch as it represses the parenthesis. The stake, the effectiveness, of this third phase of the fantasy is the interchangeability of the subject and the other children being beaten.

Laplanche and Pontalis give the seduction fantasy as a similar example, which they summarise as 'A father seduces a daughter', emphasising the 'peculiar character of the structure, in that it is a scenario with multiple entries, in which nothing shows whether the subject will be immediately located as *daughter*; it can as well be fixed as *father*, or even in the term *seduces*' (p. 14).

It is however precisely to the extent that desire is articulated in fantasy that the latter is also thereby the locus of defensive operations – it facilitates and can become the site of the most primitive defensive processes, such as turning around upon the subject's own self, reversal into its opposite, projection and negation. Fantasies provide satisfaction, then, not only by presenting a wish but also by presenting the failure of a wish if the latter has undergone repression. This has been seen in the example of 'A child is being beaten'. Defences are inseparably bound up with the work of fantasy, namely, the *mise-en-scène* of desire, a *mise-en-scène* in which what is prohibited is always present in the actual formation of the wish. (Walsh's film *Pursued* can be cited as a filmic example of this.[3]) It is also interesting to consider here Freud's example in his essay on hysterical fantasies (1908); he cites as an involuntary irruption of fantasy, a day-dream which was produced by one of his women patients. She recounts that on one occasion she had suddenly found herself in tears in the street and that, rapidly considering what it was she was actually crying about, she had got hold of a fantasy to the following effect: in her imagination she had formed a tender attachment to a pianist who was well known in the town (though she was not personally acquainted with him); she had had a child by him (she was in fact childless); and he had then deserted her and her child and left them in poverty. It was at this point in her 'romance', Freud says, that she burst into tears.

Freud does not give any analysis of the fantasy himself, but I would like to suggest it as an example of a fantasy subject to defensive processes. Consider the moment of the tears; narratively appropriate, tears of self-pity at her imagined loss. But why has she produced a story to make herself cry, and may not the tears be a response not to the pathos of the story but to its satisfactions? The crying thus acting as a defense, brings the fantasy to an end in the same way Freud speaks of waking oneself up from a dream. This becomes even more plausible if the possibility of multiple subject positions in the story is considered. It commences with a pleasant and typical erotic wish in relation to the pianist, together with its happy consummation. But the fruit of the affair, a child, places the fantasy into an Oedipal context, for the child is the one wished for with the father. A forbidden desire has found expression in the fantasy, that it is forbidden is marked by the punishment immediately meted out – not only that the man deserts her and the child, but more importantly they are left in poverty. More importantly, for it marks that it was not enough punishment for the man to desert her, another hardship must be given to her. But even this is not enough, tears intervene to halt the fantasy. This might suggest that the man's desertion is *not* the punishment, but part of the wish, that is, for the eviction of the father, so that the child has the mother to herself, and it is *this* wish that provokes the final censorship of tears.

(The outline of the daydream bears an astonishing resemblance to Max Ophuls's *Letter From An Unknown Woman*.) It is in the same essay that Freud presents a series of formulas on the nature of hysterical symptoms, in which he suggests that 'Hysterical symptoms are the realisation of an unconscious phantasy which serves the fulfilment of a wish', and: 'Hysterical symptoms are the expression on the one hand of a masculine unconscious sexual phantasy, and on the other hand of a feminine one.' He restates here the innate bisexual disposition of the human made so visible in the analysis of psychoneurotics. But what is thereby emphasized is that this is not a mixing of the masculine and feminine but the juxtaposition, side by side, of both the feminine and masculine as distinct sexual positions of desire ...

The Reckless Moment

This film presents a rather different example of the workings of fantasy in film. It most closely approximates Laplanche and Pontalis's thesis that

> Fantasy is not the object of desire but its setting. In fantasy the subject does not pursue the object or its sign: he appears caught up himself in the sequence of images. He forms no representation of the desired object but is himself represented as participating in the scene

('Fantasy and the Origins of Sexuality', p. 17)

For the film as fantasy, the subject is at one and the same time Lucia, Donnelly (the film's principal characters), and the spectator. The following discussion of *The Reckless Moment* will seek to exemplify this.

The Reckless Moment (made by Columbia and released in 1949, in Britain with an A certificate) was directed by Max Ophuls, or Opuls as he was styled on his American films, from a screenplay by Henry Garson and Robert W. Sodeberg, based on a *Ladies Home Journal* story, 'The Blank Wall', by Elisabeth Sanxay Holding, adapted by Mel Dinelli and Robert E. Kent. The film concerns an American family, white, middle-class, and living in a seaside suburb of Los Angeles. The film opens with a man's voiceover (which does not recur in the film) describing the town and its inhabitants and speculating on how little it might take to shatter the peace of a family. The scene cuts from shots of boats to a boy fishing, he looks up and calls 'Mother, Mother, where are you going?'. The mother is Lucia Harper and she is driving to Los Angeles to see Ted Darby, a man of dubious character, to persuade him to stop seeing her daughter Bea. She is unsuccessful. On returning home she is greeted by her son David, the grandfather, and Sybil the maid in turn, each of whom asks her where she has been. She goes upstairs to tell Bea of her meeting with Darby, to forbid her to see him again, saying that he had asked for money as payment for not seeing her anymore. Bea disbelieves her mother, and has indeed already arranged to meet with Darby that night in the adjacent boathouse. But Darby shows himself to be the no-good that Lucia portrayed him as and Bea, horrified, rejects him. He struggles with her but she hits him with her flashlight and runs out. He stumbles after her, stunned by the blow, and clutching at the rail of the stairway, which we see is broken, he falls to the beach below.

The hysterical Bea is met by Lucia, who goes out to check if Darby is still in the boathouse. Finding no one, she returns to put Bea to bed. Very early the next morning, Lucia goes for a walk and discovers Darby's body speared by their boat anchor. She drags his body to their boat and takes it to marshes some way away. Having covered up the killing, she is visited later that day by Donnelly, who blackmails her over loveletters Bea had sent Darby and which came into his hands as collateral on a loan to Darby. Donnelly falls in love with Lucia, however, but he cannot withdraw the blackmail because of his partner Nagle. Lucia tries to raise the $5,000 demanded but cannot do so without her husband's signature. He is away and she adamantly refuses to contact him. When she meets Donnelly again he tells her that her problems are over since Darby's killer has been arrested. Conscience-stricken, Lucia tells Donnelly that the man couldn't have done it, and, taking the blame herself, confesses that she killed Darby. Donnelly, disbelieving, tells her that it doesn't matter and that she should let the man take the rap since he might have done it anyway. Later Donnelly finds out that the man had an alibi after all, and that Nagle has gone to see Lucia himself. Donnelly goes after Nagle, finds him in the boathouse with Lucia and after an argument strangles him in a struggle. Lucia finally believes in the now-wounded Donnelly and wants to clear him by going to the police and taking the blame. Donnelly, out of love for her, refuses to let her do so and drives off with Nagle's body, but crashes his car. Lucia has followed him but he demands she leave him to await the police alone or else his sacrifice will have been for nothing. She returns home. Crying on her bed, she is called down by the family to receive a phone call from her husband Tom, while Bea tells her that Donnelly was found by the police and died after confessing to killing Darby and Nagle.

A synopsis such as this, of the main elements of the action, elides the narrative drive of the film, which I shall summarize as: extraordinary events intervene into an ordinary family's life as the result of transgressive sexuality on the part of the women of the family. Bea's transgression, her liaison with the no-good Ted Darby, puts Lucia 'out-of-place' – viz. her son David's urgent calling as she drives off to Los Angeles at the beginning of the film. Lucia seeks to confront Darby and takes on the role of the father, in seeking to be the keeper of her daughter's sexuality. But Darby flirts with her, commenting on how like Bea she is, how young she is to be Bea's mother, and Lucia's endeavors to warn Darby off appear impotent.

Later, arguing with Bea, Lucia shifts between acting as the stern father who nevertheless wants to talk things over reasonably, and playing the irrational mother who hysterically demands that Bea obey her without question in one breath as she instructs her to tidy her room in the next. And in addition mother and daughter are identified as she laments that 'I've been stupid and indulgent, your father wanted you to go to college and I took your side and persuaded him to let you go to art school ... [shot changes from Lucia to Bea].... He was right, and I was wrong. You'd never have met Darby if we'd have listened to him.' And later she says 'I probably would have felt the same way at your age.' The moment of identification is interrupted by Tom's phone call giving her the news that he will be in Germany for Christmas, involved in building bridges for the Marshall Plan. He is not told of Bea's misdemeanors.

That evening Lucia writes to Tom (interrupted by her son David, she hides his Christmas presents, then asks him why he isn't wearing slippers – this reference to his clothing is an invariable element at each encounter of mother and son until the end of the film when Lucia is most out of control, and David proudly informs her, as he is about to go to a movie, that he is properly dressed; it is an example of the economic way in which the film narrates Lucia as mother and housekeeper). Lucia begins to write that she wishes David were older, or Tom's father younger, or that Tom were there to deal with Darby himself. The signifying of the lack of the father here is intercut with shots of Bea leaving the house to meet Darby – the cause of Lucia's 'need' for the father. Lucia tears up her letter and writes another, anodyne, one, thus the father's absence is underscored at the same time as he is *excluded* by Lucia's keeping him in ignorance.

Lucia takes charge of Bea, hysterical after her meeting with Darby; firmly reassuring her, she goes to find another flashlight to go out to check the boathouse in an action that precisely mimes that of Bea minutes earlier. Lucia is authoritative after her investigation – 'He's gone' (which she will later find is not the case) – and motherly in putting Bea to bed, and also identified with Bea through the repetition of their actions. The next day, by concealing Darby's body, Lucia assumes the responsibility for his death. This is her *reckless moment*. And the import of sexual transgression that originated with Bea is transferred to Lucia. Bea drops out of the narrative, which has always in any case been centered on Lucia. Meeting Bea on the stairs, Lucia orders her to forget about Darby after first ascertaining that Bea had not told anyone of the relationship. Bea, unaware of his death, is mortified at the thought of him, but Lucia tells her, 'Stop it Bea, I know how you feel but you mustn't talk against him or about him to anyone. You mustn't even mention his name. Do you understand?' Lucia asks if there was anything else, Bea after a pause replies No, and Lucia continues on upstairs as Bea goes to her breakfast. For Bea, but not for Lucia, it is over.

Later that day, at the post office mailing her letter to Tom, Lucia hears that Darby's body has been found. The scene economically narrates both events of the thriller narrative and the melodrama-detail of Lucia's role as 'Mrs. Harper' (distractedly, she buys the family's Christmas tree). Arriving home, a man has been waiting for her. Donnelly is initially presented as a threat, with a deep-focus shot of him in the darkened, shadow-filled room. Lucia is helpless – shown first in her attempts to deny the significance of the letters and then, after her talk with Bea in the kitchen, she slumps defeated into a chair. She feels she must accept the blackmail in order to protect Bea from the possible sexual scandal. But, given the identification I have suggested above, Lucia is equally guilty and thus she is also protecting herself, and this is the motivation for her adamant refusals to contact Tom. The family and the home come to appear as a prison for Lucia, a *mise-en-scène* of containment in the interconnecting tracking shots and framings that always place Lucia within her family, which prevents her from taking decisive and independent action against the external threat.

Meanwhile Donnelly is drawn into the family by the same means that Lucia is shown as entrapped. Lucia leaves Donnelly (introduced as a friend of Tom's) talking to the grandfather, framed together; as she returns from talking to Bea, the camera follows her, revealing Donnelly in big close-up next to the grandfather as she joins them. By this camera movement Donnelly has been included into the family, a portent of later events. (Donnelly also gives the grandfather a racing tip as he leaves and the latter subsequently repeats his request for Lucia to 'invite that nice man' to dinner. At the end of the film Sybil reiterates how nice Donnelly had been, in contrast to her comment – ignorant of who he is – of Nagle as a nasty man.)

Seeing Donnelly off outside the house, Lucia tries to stall for time (a sign of her weak position), refuses to contact Tom, and says that she cannot act precipitously for fear of worrying the family. These elements are replayed in their meeting the next day, adding the further element of Lucia as the site of morality when she berates Donnelly for his way of earning a living, comparing it to David's honest work (for a pittance)

during his vacation. 'You'd never know about that,' she says. He replies
'Do you never get away from your family?' 'No.' The external threat
represented by Donnelly and Nagle's blackmail is split into good and
bad as Donnelly falls in love with Lucia, but it will ultimately be shown
that he does so precisely in terms of her role in the family, as mother
and wife. The following scene at the drugstore, for example, vividly
shows Donnelly in the part of husband as Lucia rushes up to him from
the phone booth (*not* calling Tom) and takes change from him. He buys
her a cigarette holder to save her health, having commented that her
chain smoking was bad for her.

Driving back, the theme of Lucia's entrapment by her family is
repeated, she also again refuses to contact Tom, and the *new* position of
Donnelly is represented when he tries to assure her that but for his
partner he'd not pursue the blackmail, but he has his Nagle just as she
has her family. Lucia angrily denies the comparison, refusing to
believe him. Donnelly comments that Bea is lucky to have a mother like
Lucia, but she retorts, 'Everyone has a mother like me. You probably
had one.'

In this abbreviated gloss of the film I am forced to emphasize
dialogue over the staging of the scenes. But staging, camera movement,
the image track as a whole, etc., are crucial to the film's narration,
producing fore-pleasure; for example in Donnelly's subsequent phone
call to Lucia. Having promised her more time, he phones to tell her
Nagle won't agree. We see Lucia take the phone from the grandfather
who has answered the phone, and cut to Donnelly in a phone
booth saying he understands, that she can't talk because her family is
there. As a result he *alone* talks, and there is no cut back to Lucia, and
Donnelly repeats his wish that she believe him, *in* him: 'I wish things
could have been different in many ways. Only one good thing came of
it. I met you.' Donnelly leaves and goes to join Nagle; thus Donnelly's
good faith is proven to the spectator before it is to Lucia.

Lucia's meeting with Donnelly at the bus station (after failing to raise
any money except for $800 by pawning some jewels) presents her
repositioning in relation to Donnelly, as he tells her that Darby's killer
has been arrested. The scene is orchestrated by alternating tracking
shots and reverse-field close-ups as they go to get a coffee, sit down as
Lucia 'confesses', and finally Lucia leaves to catch her bus. Donnelly has
been accepted by Lucia in the role of 'protector', surrogate father as
Lucia had been to Bea. He takes charge morally and practically, telling
Lucia in words that echo her own to Bea, 'Forget about him [the
arrested man]. What's the use of sacrificing your family for a man that's
no good, that deserves what's coming to him? … It's the right thing to
do Lucy, the right thing. Just you forget this … I'll have it out with
Nagle, I'll have the letters back and bring them to the house.' 'No,

please. No please mail them, I'm sorry but.' Lucia accepts his help but denies him as part of her world. Donnelly has filled the place of the absent father but the place of the absent husband remains empty. Her denial is a delay, and sets up the audience to expect its retraction, desiring Lucia to recognize Donnelly as worthwhile, as we have done!

This is brought about in the scene following the killing of Nagle (the boathouse is the repeated site of death). To Donnelly's declaration of love ('I never did a decent thing in my life, never even wanted to until you came along'), Lucia responds with a corresponding offer of sacrifice: 'I can't let you take this on yourself and be hounded for murder the rest of your life. I got you into this. It was my way of doing something that made everything wrong.' Lucia is lover and mother to Donnelly at the end of the film, trying to tend his wound; he had spoken of his love for her immediately after referring to his mother's unconditional love for him ('she would never learn that I was the bad one'), and he has finally done something she could be proud of. In dying, he has the mother.

Rather than pointing to the various fantasy themes at work (for example, the nullifying of external threat by sexual seduction), I wish to emphasize the way in which the film clearly presents a series of positions through pairings and equivalences, the terms of which are successively taken up by Lucia and Donnelly, the two main protagonists. This not as a manifest narrative content, but a narrated signified. Thus

- Bea is to Darby as Lucia comes to be to Donnelly (lovers)
- Lucia is to Bea as Donnelly comes to be to Lucia (father)

Donnelly is the helpful father to David, showing him how to fix the car horn, and he is the helpful son to the grandfather with his racing tips. But Donnelly is not shown with Bea, this exception tending to confirm the system insofar as Bea and Lucia are identified as interchangeable. Thus

- Donnelly is to the family as Tom is to the family (father)
- Donnelly is to Lucia as Tom is to Lucia (husband/lover)
- Lucia is mother to Bea (and her family) as she comes to be to Donnelly

But the sliding of positions is unstoppable, and Donnelly's gestures of 'caring' for Lucia, his concern over her smoking, as well as the formal motivation of inverted parallelism, bring him too into the position of mother. The work of the film is to transform Donnelly from being 'bad' insofar as he substitutes for the no-good Darby in the first set of equivalences, into being 'good' as the father and husband/lover. This is clearly a typical fantasy, in which censorship renders the adulterous love-object bad, and the fantasy reverses this, but with a cost – death. The perversity of the fantasy is suggested obliquely, in a way which the film does not underline as such. That is, the opposition and pairing of Nagle and Donnelly, which the latter himself compares to Lucia's relation with her family, and he does so in terms of it being a *constraint*. The pressure of the film's working, its drive, centers on such equivalences, so that though there is no other reference to this equivalence, and Nagle dies at the hands of Donnelly in order to save the family, the film system as a whole supports such an inference – an inference that is an attack on the family as imprisoning, as marked by the film's closing image of Lucia.

In *The Reckless Moment* the hermeneutic, the problem of Bea's letters to Darby and the blackmail, is displaced by the other hermeneutic, of the story of Donnelly and Lucia. At the end, Lucia has the letters back, on behalf of her daughter, but is crying over a new lack – Donnelly we presume. And the ostensible lack that 'causes' the narrative, that is, the absence of the father, is only ironically made good, filled by the final phone call from Tom Harper. The staging of desire emerges through the series of figures, the exchanges and equivalences set up, produced, by the narrative.

The discussion of *The Reckless Moment* has sought to show the particular shifts of positioning in that film, so that it comes to seem that the film is *about* these, and Donnelly's death only halts this exchange, it does not resolve it. This is made clear by the irony of the closing shot. The 'proper' father makes himself heard as the third term, putting an end to the imaginary play of dyadic relations, pairings. However, he is only heard by Lucia, the cinematic audience receive no aural or visual signification of the father except through Lucia's declaration of how much she loves him! The possibility of the imaginary play continuing thus remains. Further, the repositionings are not simply the substitution of Tom by Donnelly, but involve the diverse positions father, mother, child, lover, wife, husband, each of which are never finally contained by any one character. And any position only has meaning by its relation to the others (this can be seen in the sliding of 'meaning' of the role 'mother').

The film thus illustrates the way in which at its most radical, that is in the original fantasies, the staging of desire has multiple entries, where the subject is both present *in* the scene and interchangeable with any other character. Narrative in the film, just like secondary elaboration of the dream, organizes the material, restoring a minimum of order and coherence to the raw material and imposing on this heterogeneous assortment a facade, a scenario, which gives it relative coherence and continuity. A holding down, fixing, is performed in the production of a coherence, a continuity; the narrative seeks to *find* (produce) a proper place for the subject. What is interesting in the analysis of *Now Voyager* and *The Reckless Moment* is that, though in different ways, in each film the subject-positions shift across the boundary of sexual difference but do so always in terms of sexual difference. Thus while subject-positions are variable, the terms of sexual difference are fixed. It is the form of tension and play between the fixing of narrative – the secondary elaboration – and the lack of fixity of the subject in the original fantasies that would seem to be important, and not any already-given privileging of one over the other.

Furthermore the 'fixing' produced by the narrative may not reproduce the fixed positions of sexual difference. In *Now Voyager*, Charlotte achieves a transgressive feminine position. *The Reckless Moment* presents a closure that replaces Lucia in the feminine position as wife and mother, but the irony of the final image and its figuring of Lucia framed behind the bannisters of the stairs, restates a wish presented in the film for the eviction of the Father, in his symbolic function. While the terms of sexual difference are fixed, the places of characters and spectators in relation to those terms are not.

Notes

1. The decision in this article (apart from in quotations where the term is given as it occurs in the original) to use the spelling 'fantasy' rather than 'phantasy' has been adopted inasmuch as the former spelling is normally used in discussions of film and literature, and the intention of this article is to show that fantasy in film can be understood to work in the same way as fantasy in the daydream and in the unconscious. The 'ph' spelling used within the English translation of Freud's works in the *Standard Edition* is sometimes also used to distinguish between conscious and unconscious fantasies. However, the French psychoanalysts Laplanche and Pontalis make a congent argument for rejecting this distinction in the translating of Freud's work. 'It betrays little respect for the text to render words such as *Phantasie* or *Phantasieren*, which Freud invariably employed, by different terms according to the context. Our opposition to this terminological and conceptual innovation rests on three grounds: (i) the distinction should not be introduced into translations of Freud's work, even if the interpretation of his thought were correct; (ii) this interpretation of Freud's thought is incorrect; (iii) this distinction contributes less to the study of the problem than Freud's concept' ('Fantasy and the Origins of Sexuality,' p. 11, footnote 24).

    The usage of 'fantasy' here follows the practice adopted by Elisabeth Lyon in 'The Cinema of Lol V. Stein', and this article is indebted to her discussion there of fantasy as the circulation among positions of subject and object, the look and looked-at, which she notes are characteristic of the structure of the fantasy where the subject is at once included in the scene and excluded from it. While her discussion concerns Marguerite Duras's *India Song*, this article will seek to consider similar questions in relation to two Hollywood films.

2. See here Raymond Bellour's discussion of *Psycho* in 'Psychosis, Neurosis, Perversion'.

3. See Paul Willemen's discussion, which concerns the role of fantasy and repression in *Pursued*.

References

R. Barthes, *The Pleasure of the Text*, trans. R. Miller (New York: Hill & Wang, 1974 (1973)).

R. Bellour, 'Le blocage symbolique', *Psychanalyse et Cinèma, Communications*, 23 (1974) (on *North by Northwest*).

R. Bellour, 'Hitchcock the Enunciator', *Camera Obscura,* 2 (1977) *(on Marnie)*.

R. Bellour, 'Psychosis, Neurosis, Perversion', *Camera Obscura*, 3–4 (1979).

P. Califia, 'Feminism and Sado-Masochism', in *Heresies*, 3: 4 (1981).

M. A. Doane, 'Film and the Masquerade' – Theorising the Female Spectator', *Screen,* 23: 3–4 (1982).

S. Freud, *The Interpretation of Dreams* (1900) *The Standard Edition of the Complete Psychological Works of Sigmund Freud*, vol. V.

S. Freud, *Three Essays on the Theory of Sexuality* (1905), *SE*, vol. VII.

S. Freud, *Jokes and Their Relation to the Unconscious* (1905), *SE*, vol. VIII.

S. Freud, 'Creative Writers and Day-Dreaming' (1908), *SE*, vol. IX.

S. Freud, 'Hysterical Phantasies and their Relation to Bisexuality' (1908), *SE*, vol. IX.

S. Freud, 'Family Romances' (1908), *SE*, vol. IX.

S. Freud, 'A Case of Paranoia Running Counter to the Psycho-Analytic Theory of the Disease' (1915), *SE*, vol. XIV.

S. Freud, 'A Child is Being Beaten: A Contribution to the Study of the Origin of the Perversions' (1919), *SE*, vol. XVII.

N. Friday, *My Secret Garden*, Pocket Books (1974).

G. Genette, 'Vraisemblance et motivation', *Figures II* (Paris: Seuil, 1969).

M. Haskell, *From Reverence to Rape* (London: New English Library, 1974).

H. Hawks, 'Interview', *Movie,* 5 (1962).

S. Heath, 'Difference', *Screen*, 19: 3 (1978).

S. Heath, 'Film and System, Terms of Analysis', *Screen*, 16: 1 and 16: 2 (1975; *Heresies*, 3: 4 (1981).

L. Jacobs, '*Now Voyager*: Some Problems of Enunciation and Sexual Difference', *Camera Obscura,* 7 (1981).

R. Jakobson, 'On Realism in Art', *Readings in Russian Poetics*, ed. L. Matejka and K. Pomorska (Cambridge, Mass.: MIT Press) 1971.

J. LACAN, *The Four Fundamental Concepts of Psychoanalysis*, trans. A Sheridan (London: Hogarth Press, 1977).

J. LAPLANCHE and J. B. PONTALIS, 'Fantasy and the Origins of Sexuality', *International Journal of Psychoanalysis*, **49** (1968).

J. LAPLANCHE and J. B. PONTALIS, *The Language of Psycho-Analysis*, trans. D. Nicholson-Smith (London: Hogarth Press, 1973).

E. LYON, 'The Cinema of Lol V. Stein', *Camera Obscura*, **6** (1980).

C. METZ, *Psychoanalysis and Cinema: The Imaginary Signifier*, trans. C. Britton, A. Williams, B. Brewster and A. Guzzetti (London: Macmillan, 1982).

L. SEGAL, 'Sensual Uncertainty, or Why the Clitoris is Not Enough', *Sex and Love*, ed. S. Cartledge and J. Ryan (London: The Women's Press, 1983).

H. THORNING, 'The Mother-Daughter Relationship and Sexual Ambivalence', *Heresies*, **3**: 2 (1981).

P. WILLEMAN, 'The Fugitive Subject', *Raoul Walsh* (Edinburgh: Edinburgh Festival, 1974).

This article derives from a paper presented in July 1982 as one of a series of *m/f* workshops called *Re-opening the Case: Feminism and Psychoanalysis*. Some of the ideas in that paper were prompted by and drew upon lectures and discussions with Ben Brewster. This article has benefited from subsequent discussions with colleagues, friends, and students. I would especially like to acknowledge the invaluable intellectual and editorial help of Parveen Adams.

11 Subjectivity and Desire: An(other) Way of Looking*

MARY ANN DOANE

Mary Ann Doane is Professor of Film and Semiotic Theory at Brown University, Rhode Island. Besides writing *The Desire to Desire* (1987) she is co-editor with Linda Williams of *Re-vision: Essays in Feminist Film Criticism* (1984). See 'Introduction', p. 17.

Toward the end of Woody Allen's *The Purple Rose of Cairo* (1985), there is a close-up of some duration of Mia Farrow in spectatorial ecstasy, enraptured by the image, her face glowing (both figuratively and literally through its reflection of light from the movie screen). This rapture persists despite the rather tawdry surroundings of a lower-class movie theater. What the shot signifies, in part, is the peculiar susceptibility to the image – to the cinematic spectacle in general – attributed to the woman in our culture. Her pleasure in viewing is somehow more *intense*. The woman's spectatorship is yet another clearly delineated mark of her excess. This hyperbolically intimate relation with the screen is assumed by the plot of *Purple Rose*. In the course of Mia Farrow's fifth or sixth viewing of the film of the same name, she actually catches the gaze of the male romantic lead who notices her, turns, and, drawn by her fascination, steps down off the screen to join her in the 'real world'. He rapidly falls in love with her, fulfilling her spectatorial dreams. What strikes me about this scenario is that, given culturally (over)determined structures of seeing, this narrative could work most convincingly only by positing a female spectator. For there is a certain naiveté assigned to women in relation to systems of signification – a tendency to deny the processes of representation, to collapse the opposition between the sign (the image) and the real. To 'misplace' desire by attaching it too securely to a representation. The figure of the woman repeatedly viewing the same film (despite the principle that Hollywood movies are made to be 'consumed' once) or becoming an avid reader of fan magazines is the

---

* Reprinted from *The Desire to Desire* (Indiana University Press, 1987), pp. 1–13.

condition of possibility of narratives based on her purportedly excessive collusion with the cinematic imaginary.

It is also critically important that *Purple Rose* is a historical film, set in the 1930s, at the beginning of a period in which the Hollywood cinema perfected its language and reached the height of its power. In the midst of the depression, Mia Farrow is clearly a member of the lower class, watching a typical '30s glossy sophisticated comedy detailing the foibles of the upper classes. For her, at least a part of the scopophiliac power of the image is that it represents money and the style associated with it. She is encouraged to align her gaze with that of the consumer.

I have lingered on this film because it demonstrates the extent to which the image of the longing, overinvolved female spectator is still with us. While it may be argued that, as a historical film, *The Purple Rose* introduces a distance between its own spectator and its represented spectator, the image retains a great deal of its effect – certainly its recognizability and even familiarity. The idea that the cinematic image functions as a lure, so forcefully elaborated in contemporary film theory, seems to apply even more insistently in the case of the female spectator who, in the popular imagination, repeatedly 'gives in' to its fascination. Proximity rather than distance, passivity, overinvolvement and overidentification (the use of the term 'weepies' to indicate women's pictures is symptomatic here) – these are the tropes which enable the woman's assumption of the position of 'subject' of the gaze. It is, of course, a peculiarly ironic assumption of subjectivity. For, although spectatorship is thus conceptualized in terms which appear to preeminently feminize it, feminist film criticism has consistently demonstrated that, in the classical Hollywood cinema, the woman is deprived of a gaze, deprived of subjectivity and repeatedly transformed into the object of a masculine scopophiliac desire.

Yet, women would seem to be perfect spectators, culturally positioned as they are outside the arena of history, politics, production – 'looking on'. The iconography is quite insistent: women and waiting are intimately linked, and the scenario of the woman gazing out of a window usually streaked by a persistent rain has become a well-worn figure of the classical cinematic text. And, indeed, the rise of the novel as the most popular vehicle for the formulation of narrative is usually linked explicitly with a female reading public.[1] The greater amount of leisure time associated with the woman authorized an analysis of the 'feminization' of the process of reading. Yet, although the cinema is often theorized as the extension and elaboration of the narrative mechanisms of the nineteenth-century novel, its spectator is almost always conceptualized in the masculine mode. It is as though the historical threat of a potential feminization of the spectatorial position required an elaborate work of generic containment. In this respect, the very fact that there is a specific genre allocated to the female spectator – the 'woman's film' – is revealing. As Pam Cook notes,

> One question insists: why does the women's picture exist? There is no such thing as 'the men's picture', specifically addressed to men; there is only 'cinema', and 'the women's picture', a sub-group or category specially for women, excluding men; a separate, private space designed for more than half the population, relegating them to the margins of cinema proper. The existence of the women's picture both recognises the importance of women, and marginalises them. By constructing this different space for women (Haskell's 'wet, wasted afternoons') it performs a vital function in society's ordering of sexual difference.[2]

The cinema in general, outside of the genre of the woman's picture, constructs its spectator as the generic 'he' of language. The masculine norm is purportedly asexual while sexually defined seeing is relegated to the woman. Access to the gaze is hence very carefully regulated through the specification of generic boundaries.

The woman's film is therefore in many ways a privileged site for the analysis of the given terms of female spectatorship and the inscription of subjectivity precisely because its address to a female viewer is particularly strongly marked. The label 'woman's film' refers to a genre of Hollywood films produced from the silent era through the 1950s and early '60s but most heavily concentrated and most popular in the 1930s and '40s.[3] The films deal with a female protagonist and often appear to allow her significant access to point of view structures and the enunciative level of the filmic discourse. They treat problems defined as 'female' (problems revolving around domestic life, the family, children, self-sacrifice, and the relationship between women and production vs. that between women and reproduction), and, most crucially, are directed toward a female audience.

There is something extremely compelling about women's films – with their constantly recurring figures of the unwed mother, the waiting wife, the abandoned mistress, the frightened newlywed or the anguished mother. And this is so even today, when their images are experienced more readily as a historical memory, no longer completely culturally negotiable since they are, in an era which believes itself to be post-feminist, so strongly marked as belonging to the recent past. As Roland Barthes notes, History is 'the time when my mother was alive *before me*', and, for many of us, these are the films of our mothers' time.[4] And although their images inevitably infiltrate or perhaps contaminate our cultural memories, they are already a bit defamiliarized, somewhat strange. But not strange enough. For these mythemes of femininity trade on their very familiarity and recognizability. The scenarios of the woman's film somehow seem immediately accessible in their presentation of the 'obvious truths' of femininity with which we are all overly acquainted.

It is crucial to remember, then, that the genre is the outcome of Hollywood's analysis of its own market, its own grouping of films along the lines of a sexual address. Filmic narratives and *mise-en-scène* are organized in the service of the production of female fantasy. Thus, we have the nomenclature by means of which certain films of the '30s and '40s are situated and sold as 'women's pictures', a label which stipulates that the films are in some sense the 'possession' of women and that their terms of address are dictated by the anticipated presence of the female spectator. Yet, it is the precise meaning of this notion of 'possession' which must be isolated and interrogated. In what sense are these films 'ours'? Or should they be, somewhat forcefully, reclaimed and reoccupied by a contemporary feminist analysis? There is an extremely strong temptation to find in these films a viable alternative to the unrelenting objectification and oppression of the figure of the woman in mainstream Hollywood cinema.[5] The recent focus on issues surrounding female spectatorship and the woman's film is determined by a desire to shift the terms of an analysis of fantasy and history in favor of the woman and away from a paternal reference point. Yet, the woman's film does not provide us with an access to a pure and authentic female subjectivity, much as we might like it to do so. It provides us instead with an image repertoire of poses – classical feminine poses and assumptions about the female appropriation of the gaze. Hollywood women's films of the 1940s document a crisis in subjectivity around the figure of the woman – although it is not always clear whose subjectivity is at stake.

I have chosen to focus on the films of the 1940s (a subset of the woman's film as a genre) for a number of reasons. In the first half of the decade, due to the war and the enlistment of large numbers of young men in the armed forces, film producers assumed that cinema audiences would be predominantly female. Despite the fact that statistical analyses of audiences during the 1940s suggest that this was not ultimately the case, the anticipation of a female audience resulted in a situation wherein female stars and films addressed to women became more central to the industry.[6] Therefore, not only generic but specifically historical considerations dictate that the terms of address and the inscription of female subjectivity become more crucial in this particular group of films. Furthermore, there is an intensity and an aberrant quality in the '40s films which is linked to the ideological upheaval signaled by a redefinition of sexual roles and the reorganization of the family during the war years. The very speed of moving women into and out of the work force (the 'Rosie the Riveter' phenomenon) creates ideological imperatives which are quite explicit in the films. The intensity and interest of these films is also associated with a kind of generic intertextuality which seems to characterize the period. The woman's film is frequently combined with other genres – the film noir and the gothic or horror film, even the musical. This strategy tends to expand the boundaries of what is known as the 'woman's film' (which is often thought of primarily in relation to its seemingly most exemplary subgroup, the maternal melodrama).

Nevertheless, although the isolation of films from the 1940s enables an examination of not only the sexually specific but the historically specific terms of spectatorship, my interest in the films is primarily inspired by certain issues and theoretical blockages in contemporary feminist work. The insistence of their address and the forcefulness of their tropes make the women's films of the 1940s an appropriate textual field for the investigation of issues surrounding the concepts of subjectivity and spectatorship and the ability or inability of feminist theorists to align these concepts with sexual specificity. Feminist film theory has convincingly demonstrated the extent to which the woman in the cinema is imaged as deficient or lacking in her 'object-hood'.[7] But it is becoming increasingly evident that the construction of her 'subject-hood' poses difficulties as well. One can readily trace, in the women's films of the 1940s, recurrent suggestions of deficiency, inadequacy, and failure in the woman's appropriation of the gaze. It is the very concept of subjectivity and its place in feminist theory which is in question. The predicament is specified most succinctly in the question posed by Ann Kaplan, 'Is the gaze male?'.[8]

Much of this important work in feminist film theory delineates a scenario which would seem to indicate the very impossibility of a genre such as the woman's film. For the figure of the woman is aligned with spectacle, space, or the image, often in opposition to the linear flow of the plot. From this point of view, there is something about the representation of the woman which is resistant to narrative or narrativization. The problematic status of a genre which purports to produce women's 'stories' thereby becomes apparent. In Laura Mulvey's now classic article, 'Visual Pleasure and Narrative Cinema', the woman is the object of the fixation and obsession associated with male spectatorial desires – preeminently voyeurism and fetishism.[9] The transfixing or immobilizing aspects of the spectacle constituted by the woman work against the forward pull of the narrative. While all the resources of the cinematic apparatus – including framing, lighting, camera movement, and angle – are brought to bear in the alignment of the woman with the surface of the image, the male character is allowed to inhabit and actively control its illusory depths, its constructed three-dimensional space. Similarly, Linda Williams demonstrates how, in Muybridge's contributions to the prehistory of the cinema, the male figure seems more compatible with processes of narrativization than the female figure.[10] While the man comfortably adopts 'natural' poses of activity and agency, the 'plotting' of the female body is more difficult. Williams outlines the lengths to which Muybridge goes in constructing narrative situations for the woman which are marked by their very lack of familiarity. With respect to a narrativization of the woman, the apparatus strains; but the transformation of the woman into spectacle is easy. Through her forced affinity with the iconic, imagistic aspects of cinema, the woman is constituted as a resistance or impedance to narrativization.

This scenario is, perhaps, most forcefully elaborated in Teresa de Lauretis's analysis of the articulation of feminism, semiotics, and cinema. In the course of a discussion of Jurÿ Lotman's semiotics of plot construction, de Lauretis claims that his description is predicated

> on the *single* figure of the hero who crosses the boundary and penetrates the other space. In so doing the hero, the mythical subject, is constructed as human being and as male; he is the active principle of culture, the establisher of distinction, the creator of differences. Female is what is not susceptible to transformation, to life or death; she (it) is an element of plot-space, a topos, a resistance, matrix and matter.[11]

The male is the mover of narrative while the female's association with space or matter deprives her of subjectivity. This has particularly problematic consequences for the notion of female spectatorship. As de Lauretis goes on to explain, '... each reader – male or female – is constrained and defined within the two positions of a sexual difference thus conceived: male-hero-human, on the side of the subject; and female-obstacle-boundary-space, on the other'.[12] Although de Lauretis is careful to point out that Lotman himself is unaware of the sexual politics informing his theory of narrative, she does not explicitly contest the relevance of its sexual divisions.

This delineation of the a-subjectivity of the represented woman goes some way toward explaining the convolutions and complexities of the attempt to theorize female spectatorship. A sometimes confusing array of concepts – transvestism, masochism, masquerade, double identification – is mobilized in the effort to think the relation between female spectator and screen.[13] Laura Mulvey, for instance, has recourse to the notion of an 'uncomfortable' transvestism in her delineation of female spectatorship as an oscillation between a passive feminine position and a regressive but active masculine position that enables the female spectator's engagement with narrative mechanisms. Identification with an active protagonist or with the linear movement of narrative is specified as masculine: 'The phantasy "action" can only find expression, its only *signifier* for a woman is through the metaphor of masculinity.'[14] De Lauretis attempts to move beyond Mulvey's formulation by specifying a way in which the woman's identification with narrative process can be conceptualized outside of masculine parameters (or at least by reducing these parameters as much as possible). She refers to this operation as 'double identification' or 'a surplus of pleasure':

> If women spectators are 'related as subject' in the film's images and movement, as Heath puts it, it is insofar as they are engaged in a twofold process of identification sustaining two distinct sets of identifying relations. The first set is well known in film theory: the masculine, active, identification with the gaze (the looks of the camera and of the male characters) and the passive, feminine identification with the image (body, landscape). The second set, which has received much less attention, is implicit in the first as its effect and specification, for it is produced by the apparatus which is the very condition of vision (that is to say, the condition under which what is visible acquires meaning). It consists of the double identification with the figure of narrative movement, the mythical subject, and with the figure of narrative closure, the narrative image. Were it not for the possibility of this second, figural identification, the woman spectator would be stranded between two incommensurable entities, the gaze and the image. Identification, that is, would be either impossible, split beyond any act of suture, or entirely masculine.[15]

In other words, identifications associated with narrative as a process overlay those associated with the more cinematically specific concepts of the gaze and the image. This is consistent with de Lauretis's contention that it is the Oedipal logic of narrative which decisively inflects any reading of the image. Yet, several questions remain, indicating the extreme complexity of the issues at hand. De Lauretis substantially complicates the notion of female spectatorship by activating two different sets of terms and by making the figural identifications simultaneous (rather than alternating or oscillating as in Mulvey's description). And, somehow, the second set of terms, unlike the first (active-gaze/passive-image) becomes disengendered. Is the mythical subject no longer male? More importantly, I am struck by the sheer multiplicity and dispersal of subject positions activated in the description. While it is certainly true that spectatorship is a complex and multi-faceted process, why should it be the case that processes of identification and spectatorial engagement are more complicated (if not convoluted) for the female spectator than for the male? And why does it seem essential that a masculine position appear somewhere in the delineation of female spectatorship (in Mulvey's, de Lauretis's, and, for that matter, my own formulations)?

My contention is that this apparent blockage at the level of theory (the seemingly insurmountable difficulties in conceptualizing the female gaze) does not simply indicate a disagreement among various feminist critics but a series of contradictions which are active at the level of the social/psychological construction of female spectatorship. Perhaps the female spectator – or, more accurately, the projected image of the female spectator – *is* that of a being stranded between incommensurable entities. Elsewhere in her analysis, de Lauretis refers to the association of the feminine with a masochist position defined as 'the (impossible) place of a purely *passive* desire'.[16] This formulation would seem to designate more accurately the appeal made to the female spectator by genres which are specifically *addressed* to her.

From this point of view it is important to specify precisely what is meant by the 'female spectator' or 'female spectatorship'. Clearly, these terms are not meant to refer directly to the woman who buys her ticket and enters the movie theater as the member of an audience, sharing a social identity but retaining a unique psychical history. Frequently, they do not even refer to the spectator as a social subject but, rather, as a psychical subject, as the effect of signifying structures. Historically, the emphasis on issues of spectatorship in film theory derives from a psychoanalytically informed linguistics, not from a sociologically based analysis. It has been the task of feminist theory to point out that this spectator has been consistently posited and delineated as masculine. Feminist theory therefore necessarily introduces the question of the social subject, but unfortunately, it frequently and overhastily collapses the opposition between social and psychical subjects, closing the gap prematurely. There has never been, to my mind, an adequate articulation of the two subjects in theory (which is another way of saying that psychoanalysis and a Marxist analysis have never successfully collaborated in the theorization of subjectivity).

There seems to be general agreement, however, that the terms *femininity* and *masculinity, female spectatorship* and *male spectatorship*, do not refer to actual members of cinema audiences or do so only in a highly mediated fashion. Women spectators oscillate or alternate between masculine and feminine positions (as de Lauretis points out, identification is a process not a state), and men are capable of this alternation as well. This is simply to emphasize once again that feminine and masculine positions are not fully coincident with actual men and women. Nevertheless, men and women enter the movie theater as social subjects who have been compelled to align themselves in some way with respect to one of the reigning binary oppositions (that of sexual difference) which order the social field. Men will be more likely to occupy the positions delineated as masculine, women those specified as feminine. What is interesting, from this point of view, is that masculinity is consistently theorized as a *pure*, unified, and self-sufficient position. The male spectator, assuming the psychical positions of the voyeur and the fetishist, can easily and comfortably identify with his like on the screen. But theories of female spectatorship constantly have recourse, at some level, to notions of *bisexuality* – Mulvey's transvestism or de Lauretis's double identification. It is as though masculinity were required to effectively conceptualize access to activity or agency (whether illusory or not).

What I am interested in in this study are the ramifications of this idea, in the exploration of the specifically feminine aspects of spectatorship, acknowledging all the while that this notion of female spectatorship may be specified only by its lapses or failures, in what de Lauretis refers to as the impossible place of a 'non-subject effect'.[17] I hope to analyze what is, above all, a certain *representation* of female spectatorship, produced as both image and position as an effect of certain discourses specified as 'belonging' to the woman. De Lauretis is careful to differentiate between her own analysis of female spectatorship and the 'prevailing notion of woman's narcissistic overidentification with the image'.[18] The idea of feminine overidentification 'prevails' nowhere if not in the popular imagination, in the signifying structures which ground genres labeled 'weepies' and 'tearjerkers' and which enable the image of Mia Farrow submitting to the lure of the screen. The tropes of female spectatorship are not empowering. But we need to understand the terms of their psychical appeal more fully before we can produce an effective alternative cinema.

The female spectator (the spectator singled out and defined entirely by her sex) exists nowhere but as an effect of discourse, the focal point of an address. Sexual differentiation in spectatorship is not something to be sought after and applauded as an end in itself. In the same way, one would not necessarily embrace and applaud the conceptualization of the male spectator as voyeur or fetishist. One would hope, instead, that spectatorship could one day be theorized outside the pincers of sexual difference as a binary opposition. On the other hand, the shift in focus from the male spectator to the female spectator in contemporary film theory is a political gesture of some significance in itself. The blockage is similar to one experienced by literary theorists concerned to include women in the traditional canon. After Barthes and Foucault have proclaimed the death of the author,[19] is it feasible or desirable to isolate, identify, and honor women authors? As literary theorists ask – is it possible for the woman to relinquish the idea of the author before she has had a chance to become one?[20] In an era which is post-author, post-Cartesian subject, in which the ego is seen above all as illusory in its mastery, what is the status of a search for feminine identity?

It is for these very reasons, I believe, that we must continue to investigate the representation of female subjectivity or its failure in a variety of discourses – film, psychoanalysis, literature, law. The aim of this study is to outline the terms in which a female spectator is conceptualized – that is, the terms in which she is simultaneously projected and assumed as an image (the focal point of an address) by the genre of the woman's film. And that image is a troubled one. Here, the representations of the cinema and the representations provided by psychoanalysis of female subjectivity coincide. For each system specifies that the woman's relation to desire is difficult if not impossible. Paradoxically, her only access is to the desire to desire.

The notions of the 'subject' and 'subjectivity' which I have been referring to are categories of a linguistically based psychoanalysis. The subject is not synonymous with the 'self', still less is it compatible with any notion of agency. The crucial role of the 'I' in language has been systematically delineated by Émile Benveniste, who holds that ' "subjectivity", whether it is placed in phenomenology or in psychology, as one may wish, is only the emergence in the being of a fundamental property of language. "Ego" is he who *says* "ego". '[21] The sense of uniqueness, identity, and unity which we tend to associate with subjectivity are the effects of the ability to say 'I' and to thereby appropriate language as one's own. But the dependence is reciprocal. Language is only possible because it is infused with subjectivity. The personal pronouns 'I' and 'you' enable the 'conversion of language into discourse', in other words, the situation or instance of speech whereby language is actualized and becomes an event. The peculiarity of the cinema as a signifying system composed of heterogeneous materials (image, dialogue, music, etc.), is that it cannot produce a coherent 'I'. An 'I' may occur in the dialogue but it is not the 'I' of the film, properly speaking. Subjectivity is inscribed in the cinema in various ways – through voice-over, point of view structures, etc. – but it is always localized. This condition of the medium has led theorists such as Christian Metz to align the cinema with Benveniste's concept of history (a form of statement which conceals the source of its enunciation) rather than his concept of discourse (a statement which exhibits or foregrounds its 'I').[22] Subjectivity in the cinema (the inscription of the 'I') is hence displaced from the producer of the discourse to its receiver. In film, there is a curious operation by means of which the 'I' and the 'you' of discourse are collapsed in the figure of the spectator.

171

Analyses of language which have stressed the role of subjectivity as its privileged ground and effect have also strongly asserted that the major mechanism of language is difference. Following the Saussurean dictum that language is composed of differences rather than positive terms, these analyses emphasize the extent to which loss or lack (of the referent) is the condition of possibility of linguistic systems. And since a linguistically based psychoanalysis, Lacanian psychoanalysis, makes the phallus the master representative of the lack which structures language, sexual difference is mapped onto linguistic difference – and this is not to the advantage of the woman. The woman, whose access to that signifier is problematic, finds herself in a kind of signifying limbo.[23] For the logical consequence of the Lacanian alignment of the phallus with the symbolic order and the field of language is the exclusion of the woman or, at the very least, the assumption of her different or deficient relation to language and its assurance of subjectivity. The French feminists who are repeatedly accused of situating the woman in an impossible place, outside language, are simply elaborating on the implications of such a theory.[24]

Subjectivity can, therefore, only be attributed to the woman with some difficulty. Luce Irigaray goes even further when she claims that 'any theory of the subject has always been appropriated by the "masculine"'. She specifies the a-subjectivity of the woman as an inability to maintain the gap between subject and object by posing the somewhat sarcastic question: 'A "subject" that would re-search itself as lost (maternal-feminine) "object"?'[25] Because the feminine is the ground, the foundation of phallocentric philosophical systems, the woman must be described as 'the non-subjective sub-jectum'.[26]

But it is still necessary to ask what this linguistic/psychical subjectivity (which the woman is denied) amounts to beyond the ability, first and foremost, to say 'I'. The subject of a psychoanalytic semiotics is not endowed with the attributes of agency, identity, and coherency usually associated with, for instance, the Cartesian 'I'. Indeed, any notion of mastery is greatly reduced, and, as Kaja Silverman extensively demonstrates, the subject is more accurately understood as 'subject to' rather than 'subject of': the subject 'has no meaning of its "own", and is entirely subordinated to the field of social meaning and desire.'[27] Similarly, Jacqueline Rose problematizes the concept of subjectivity by defining it as the constant failure of identity: '… the division and precariousness of human subjectivity itself … was, for Lacan, central to psychoanalysis' most radical insights.'[28] Subjectivity is characterized by the division and splitting effected by the operations of that 'other scene', the unconscious. In short, the subject is no authority on its own activities. From this point of view one might be led to believe that it is, in fact, disadvantageous to be a subject.

However, this description is somewhat misleading. The attributes of agency, identity, and coherence are not absent from the definition of subjectivity but, instead, constantly referred to as fictions or illusions. The 'ego' is the term which most precisely specifies the psychical locus of this illusion of mastery, and the mistake of ego psychology is its misrecognition of the unity of the ego as a reality. The function of the ego is to foster such a belief. Jean Laplanche speaks of the ego as 'indeed an object, but a kind of relay object, capable of passing itself off, in a more or less deceptive and usurpatory manner, as a desiring and wishing subject'.[29] It is this *illusion* of a coherent and controlling identity which becomes most important at the level of social subjectivity. And the woman does not even possess the same access to the *fiction* as the man.

Furthermore, subjectivity in its psychoanalytic formulation is always a desiring subjectivity. Desire is a form of disengagement – from need, from the referent, from the object – which is crucial to the assumption of the position of speaking subject. As Julia Kristeva points out, '... by overestimating the subject's having been the slave of language since before his birth, one avoids noting the two moods, active and passive, according to which the subject is constituted in the signifier ... '.[30] It is with the Oedipal complex, the intervention of a third term (the father) in the mother – child relation and the resulting series of displacements which reformulate the relation to the mother as a desire for a perpetually lost object, that the subject accedes to the active use of the signifier. Distance from the 'origin' (the maternal) is the prerequisite to desire; and insofar as desire is defined as the excess of demand over a need aligned with the maternal figure, the woman is left behind. Voyeurism, according to Christian Metz, is a perfect type of desire insofar as it presupposes and activates as its fundamental condition a spatial distance between subject and object.[31] The necessity of such a disengagement is explicitly delineated by Lacan when he distinguishes between the human and animal relations to the fascination of the lure. 'Only the subject – the human subject, the subject of the desire that is the essence of man – is not, unlike the animal, entirely caught up in this imaginary capture. He maps himself in it. How? In so far as he isolates the function of the screen and plays with it.'[32] The terms 'man' and 'he' in this description of the desiring subject should be taken literally as denoting a specifically masculine subject, while the woman is situated within the realm of the animal. Desire may be insatiable, it may entail the constantly renewed pursuit for a perpetually lost object, but at least the male has desire.

The woman's relation to desire, on the other hand, is at best a mediated one. Lacan defines the hysteric's desire as 'the desire for an unsatisfied desire'.[33] In a discussion of the 'framework of perversions in the woman', Lacan attempts to delineate her different relation to desire and ultimately specifies it as the 'envy of desire': 'Far from its being the case that the passivity of the act corresponds to this desire, feminine sexuality appears as the effort of a *jouissance* wrapped in its own contiguity (for which all circumcision might represent the symbolic rupture) to be *realised in the envy* of desire, which castration releases in the male by giving him its signifier in the phallus.'[34] The image of the woman 'wrapped' in contiguity, deprived of the phallus as signifier of desire, has been taken up by French theorists such as Irigaray, Cixous, Montrelay, and Kofman in a sometimes hyperbolic celebration of the only picture of feminine 'subjectivity' available from psychoanalysis. These theorists activate the tropes of proximity, overpresence or excessive closeness to the body, and contiguity in the construction of a kind of 'ghetto politics' which maintains and applauds woman's exclusion from language and the symbolic order. In Montrelay's analysis, what the woman lacks is lack, the ability to represent for herself a distance from the body which is the prerequisite for desire. The description by these theorists of a body wrapped up in itself, too close, is effectively political only in its hyperbole or excess, for what they delineate is not a desirable place. In fact, it is a nonplace.

Nevertheless, it is the position allotted to the female 'subject' both by psychoanalytic scenarios and by the cinema. A distance from the image is less negotiable for the female spectator than for the male because the woman is so forcefully linked with the iconic and spectacle or, in Mulvey's terms, 'to-be-looked-at-ness'. Voyeurism, the desire most fully exploited by the classical cinema, is the property of the masculine spectator. Fetishism – the ability to balance knowledge and belief and hence to maintain a distance from the lure of the image – is also inaccessible to the woman, who has no need of the fetish as a defense against a castration which has always already taken place. Female spectatorship, because it is conceived of temporally as immediacy (in the reading of the image – the result of the very absence of fetishism) and spatially as proximity (the distance between subject and object, spectator and image is collapsed), can only be understood as the confounding of desire. Similarly, the increasing appeal in the twentieth century to the woman's role as perfect consumer (of commodities as well as images) is indissociable from her positioning *as* a commodity and results in the blurring of the subject/object dichotomy (the relation between the woman, consumerism, and the commodity form will be discussed more fully later in this chapter). Situating the woman in relation to a desiring subjectivity seems to effect a perversion of the very notion of agency. Insofar as the woman is constructed culturally as the perfect spectator – outside the realm of events and actions – it is important to note that spectating is not the same as seeing. And consuming is certainly not synonymous with controlling the means of production.

The woman's film, in its insistent address to the female spectator-consumer, confronts all the difficulties and blockages outlined so far in the attempt to conceptualize female subjectivity: the woman's positioning as the very resistance to narrative, her problematic relation to language and the signifier *par excellence* (the phallus) of its major mechanism (difference), and her purportedly deficient and highly mediated access to desire. The woman's film is in many respects formally no different from other instances of the classical Hollywood cinema; its narrative structure and conventions reiterate many of the factors which have contributed to a theorization of the cinema spectator largely in terms of masculine psychical mechanisms. Nevertheless, because the woman's film insistently and sometimes obsessively attempts to trace the contours of female subjectivity and desire within the traditional forms and conventions of Hollywood narrative – forms which cannot sustain such an exploration – certain contradictions within patriarchal ideology become more apparent. This makes the films particularly valuable for a feminist analysis of the way in which the 'woman's story' is told. The formal resistances to the elaboration of female subjectivity produce perturbations and contradictions within the narrative economy. The analyses in this study emphasize the symptoms of ideological stress which accompany the concerted effort to engage female subjectivity within conventional narrative forms. These stress points and perturbations can then, hopefully, be activated as a kind of lever to facilitate the production of a desiring subjectivity for the woman – in another cinematic practice.

Notes

1. See, for example, IAN WATT, *The Rise of the Novel* (Berkeley and Los Angeles: University of California Press, 1957), pp. 43–7.

2. PAM COOK, 'Melodrama and the Women's Picture', *Gainsborough Melodrama*, ed. Sue Aspinall and Sue Harper, British Film Institute Dossier 18 (London: British Film Institute, 1983), p. 17.

3. There is also a group of British 'women's pictures' (see Pam Cook), and Christian Viviani refers to French and Italian instances of the maternal melodrama. ('Who is Without Sin? The Maternal Melodrama in American Film, 1930–39', *Wide Angle*, 4: 2 (1980): 4–17.) However, I have confined this study to the extensive field of American women's films.

4. ROLAND BARTHES, *Camera Lucida: Reflections on Photography*, trans. Richard Howard (New York: Hill and Wang, 1981), p. 65.

5.   Some of the most compelling examples of this type of analysis include: TANIA MODLESKI, ' "Never to be thirty-six years old": *Rebecca* as Female Oedipal Drama', *Wide Angle* 5: 1 (1982): 34–41; LINDA WILLIAMS, ' "Something Else Besides a Mother": *Stella Dallas* and the Maternal Melodrama', *Cinema Journal*, **24**: 1 (Fall 1984): 2–27; MARIA LA PLACE, 'Bette Davis and the Ideal of Consumption', *Wide Angle*, **6**: 4 (1985): 34–43. La Place's article is an analysis of the star as a potential site of the assertion of female control over representation.

6.   LEO A. HANDEL, *Hollywood Looks at Its Audience: A Report of Film Audience Research* (Urbana: The University of Illinois Press, 1950), p. 99.

7.   The major texts in the area of feminist film criticism (along with important articles too numerous to detail) include: *Camera Obscura: A Journal of Feminism and Film Theory*; TERESA DE LAURETIS, *Alice Doesn't: Feminism, Semiotics, Cinema* (Bloomington: Indiana University Press, 1984); E. ANN KAPLAN, *Women and Film: Both Sides of the Camera* (New York: Methuen, 1983); ANNETTE KUHN, *Women's Pictures: Feminism and Cinema* (London: Routledge and Kegan Paul, 1982); and MARY ANN DOANE, PATRICIA MELLENCAMP, and LINDA WILLIAMS,(eds) *Re-vision: Essays in Feminist Film Criticism* (Frederick, Md.: University Publications of America and the American Film Institute, 1984). KAJA SILVERMAN's *The Subject of Semiotics* (New York: Oxford University Press, 1983) is primarily intended as an introduction to semiotic theory but uses films extensively to illustrate that theory and to reflect on the condition of the female subject. Special issues of journals such as *Screen, Wide Angle*, and *Film Reader* have also contributed strongly to the elaboration of feminist film criticism.

8.   This is the title of the first chapter of Kaplan's book *Women and Film*.

9.   LAURA MULVEY, 'Visual Pleasure and Narrative Cinema', *Screen* ,**16**: 3 (Autumn 1975): 6–18.

10. LINDA WILLIAMS, 'Film Body: An Implantation of Perversions', *Ciné-tracts*, **3**: 4 (Winter 1981): 19–35.

11. DE LAURETIS, *Alice Doesn't*, p. 119.

12. Ibid., p. 121.

13. The relevant texts here are LAURA MULVEY, 'Afterthoughts on "Visual Pleasure and Narrative Cinema" Inspired by *Duel in the Sun*', *Framework*, **15, 16, 17** (1981): 12–15; DE LAURETIS, *Alice Doesn't*, especially the chapter 'Desire in Narrative'; E. ANN KAPLAN,*Women and Film*, chapter one, 'Is the Gaze Male?', and my article, 'Film and the Masquerade: 'Theorising the Female Spectator', *Screen*, **23**: 3, 4 (September, October 1982): 74–88.

14. MULVEY, 'Afterthoughts', p. 15.

15. DE LAURETIS, *Alice Doesn't*, pp. 143–4.

16. Ibid., p. 151.

17. DE LAURETIS, 'Oedipus Interruptus', *Wide Angle*, **7**: 1, 2 (1985): 36.

18. Ibid., p. 38.

19. See ROLAND BARTHES, 'The Death of the Author', in *Image/Music/Text*, trans. Stephen Heath (New York: Hill and Wang, 1977), pp. 142–8; and MICHEL FOUCAULT, 'What is an Author?' in *Language, Counter-memory, Practice*, trans.

Donald F. Bouchard and Sherry Simon (Ithaca: Cornell University Press, 1977), pp. 113–38.

20. See the dialogue in *Diacritics* (Summer 1982) on this issue: PEGGY KAMUF, 'Replacing Feminist Criticism', pp. 42–7 and NANCY K. MILLER, 'The Text's Heroine: A Feminist Critic and Her Fictions', pp. 48–53.

21. ÉMILE BENVENISTE, *Problems in General Linguistics*, trans. Mary Elizabeth Meek (Coral Gables: University of Miami Press, 1971), p. 224.

22. See CHRISTIAN METZ, 'History/Discourse: Note on Two Voyeurisms', trans. Susan Bennett, *Edinburgh '76 Magazine*, 1 (1976): 21–5.

23. For a fuller discussion of these issues, see my article 'Woman's Stake: Filming the Female Body', *October*, 17 (Summer 1981): 23–36.

24. See LUCE IRIGARAY, *This Sex Which Is Not One*, trans. Catherine Porter (Ithaca: Cornell University Press, 1985); HÉLÈNE CIXOUS, 'The Laugh of the Medusa', *New French Feminisms*, ed. Elaine Marks and Isabelle de Courtivron (Amherst: The University of Massachusetts Press, 1980), pp. 245–64; SARAH KOFMAN, 'Ex: The Woman's Enigma', *Enclitic*, 4: 2 (Fall 1980): 17–28; and MICHÈLE MONTRELAY, 'Inquiry into Femininity', *m/f*, 1 (1978): 83–102.

25. IRIGARAY, *Speculum of the Other Woman*, trans. Gillian C. Gill (Ithaca: Cornell University Press, 1985), p. 133.

26. Ibid., p. 165.

27. SILVERMAN, *Subject of Semiotics*, p. 173.

28. *Feminine Sexuality: Jacques Lacan and the École Freudienne*, ed. Juliet Mitchell and Jacqueline Rose (New York: W.W. Norton, 1982), p. 29.

29. JEAN LAPLANCHE, *Life and Death in Psychoanalysis*, trans. Jeffrey Mehlman (Baltimore: The Johns Hopkins University Press, 1976), p. 66.

30. JULIA KRISTEVA, *Powers of Horror: An Essay on Abjection*, trans. Leon S. Roudiez (New York: Columbia University Press, 1982), pp. 62–3.

31. CHRISTIAN METZ, 'The Imaginary Signifier', *Screen*, **16**: 2 (Summer 1975): 61.

32. JACQUES LACAN, *The Four Fundamental Concepts of Psycho-Analysis*, trans. Alan Sheridan (Middlesex: Penguin Books, 1979), p. 107. Something should be added here about one of Lacan's most famous formulations, 'man's desire is the desire of the Other', which would seem, once again, to diminish any notion of agency associated with the subject. The 'Other' here refers to the locus of speech, discourse, language, the unconscious. Desire may be the effect of a condition imposed on the subject by which he must 'make his need pass through the defiles of the signifier', but a desiring subject is one who can be conceptualized as residing within the realm of language and who attains an active relation to the signifier. The formulation 'man's desire is the desire of the Other' thus indicates 'man's' privileged relation to language. See JACQUES LACAN, 'The Direction of the Treatment and the Principles of Its Power', *Ecrits: A Selection*, trans. Alan Sheridan (New York: W.W. Norton, 1977), p. 264. Compare, 'There is woman only as excluded by the nature of things which is the nature of words, and it has to be said that if there is one thing they themselves are complaining about enough at the moment it is well and truly that – only they don't know what they are

saying, which is all the difference between them and me.' 'God and the *Jouissance* of The Woman', *Feminine Sexuality*, p. 144.

33. LACAN, *Ecrits*, p. 257. In reference to Freud's analysis of a hysteric who dreams of another woman's desire, Lacan states, 'One should try and count the number of substitutions that operate here to bring desire to a geometrically increasing power.' 'The hysteric's desire, precisely because it is so displaced and convoluted – so distanced from any 'real' object – becomes representative of all desire, and this is why the Freudian exploration of the unconscious begins with the hysteric. But curiously, because the hysteric comes to represent and exemplify desire, she loses access to it. For Lacan later in this same analysis claims, 'To be the phallus, if only a somewhat thin one. Was not that the ultimate identification with the signifier of desire?' (p. 202). The woman's goal is to *be* the phallus (*the* signifier of desire) rather than to *have* it.

34. LACAN, 'Guiding Remarks for a Congress on Feminine Sexuality' in *Feminine Sexuality*, p. 97.

12 From *Casablanca* to *Pretty Woman*: the Politics of Romance*

Rob Lapsley and Michael Westlake

Rob Lapsley and Michael Westlake are the co-authors of *Film Theory: An Introduction* (1988). Rob Lapsley teaches in Manchester while Michael Westlake lives in Paris, and is the author of a number of novels, including *Imaginary Women* (1987), *The Utopian* (1989) and *51 Soko to the Islands on the Other Side of the World* (1990). See 'Introduction', pp. 17–18.

> Entre l'homme et l'amour,
> Il y a la femme.
> Entre l'homme et la femme,
> Il y a un monde.
> Entre l'homme et le monde,
> Il y a un mur.
>
> Antoine Tudel

> *God took a rib from Adam and made Eve. Now maybe men chase women to get the rib back. When God took the rib he left a big hole there. A place where there used to be something, and the women have that. Now maybe a man is not complete as a man without a woman.*
>
> Johnny (Nicholas Cage) in *Moonstruck* (1987)

The myth of romance

Between the final embrace in *Pretty Woman* (1990) and the credit sequence the camera pans away from the romantically united couple and tracks alongside a street person chanting 'This is Hollywood, the land of dreams. Some dreams come true, some don't, but keep on dreaming ...'. The effect of this framing reprise is retrospectively to introduce a measure of irony into an otherwise traditional form. Termed

* Reprinted from *Screen*, **33**: 1 (Spring 1992) 27–49.

'double coding' by Umberto Eco, it permits expression that would otherwise be risible in an age of lost innocence, as when – to use Eco's example – the lover declares, 'As Barbara Cartland would put it, I love you madly.'[1] By deliberately announcing itself as a fairy tale, *Pretty Woman* succeeds in bridging the contradiction faced by the spectator who is no longer able to believe in romance (especially in a film so beset with implausibility and inconsistency), yet at the same time wishes to do so.

For there can be little doubt our culture does want romance and the promise of happiness it brings. Romantic films with their basic structure of boy meets girl, boy loses girl, boy gets girl; pop songs whose I/you address envelops the listener in the dream of fulfilment; romantic literature; even television-serial advertisements where the unfolding narrative poses the 'will they? won't they?' question over cups of instant coffee – all testify to the saturation of contemporary culture with the myth of romance. People do not fantasize about what they have got; the omnipresence of romance points to the absence of the sexual relation. The notion of an intrinsic absence pertaining to human sexuality was signalled by Freud, but only with Lacan did it become an inescapable consequence of the construction of subjectivity through language: '… in the case of the speaking being the relation between the sexes does not take place'.[2]

If there is one thematically dominant strain within American narrative cinema, it lies precisely in the denial of this: the sexes are complementary, and this harmony is nowhere more perfectly figured than in romantic love. In short, Hollywood is the pretence that the sexual relation exists. Clearly not every Hollywood film makes such an assertion and equally there are many films made outside Hollywood that share its romantic view of sexuality, but given this thematic dominance we shall limit our examples to romance within American popular cinema. Romance does not deny that there is a lack, but it claims that it can be made good. In *Pretty Woman*, Edward (Richard Gere), with his failed relationships and his parasitical business, is transformed by Vivien (Julia Roberts) into a decent human being who is able to 'make things', while she acquires from him the culture, status, wealth and love which are notably absent from her life as a prostitute and which the film's moral economy makes evident that someone as fundamentally nice as her deserves.

Absence of sexual relation

The possibility of such reciprocal completion is precisely what Lacan denies: relations of non-reciprocity are 'co-extensive with the formation of the subject'[3]; more bleakly still, 'love is impossible'.[4] Only within the imaginary can lack be made good; the real for Lacan is this hole around which human life is organized and which can never be filled, even – or least of all – by romantic love.

Shocking though such a stance may seem, it is less contrary to common sense than may be at first supposed. It is consistent with everyday observation, in that romantic love seen from the outside is fraught with illusion, that lovers' estimation of what their life together will be like is deeply unrealistic, that their mutual valuation is absurdly inflated, and that in representing their love they are pretending something exists that really does not. Equally it has been the concern of much western art, of which two well-known twentieth-century paintings may serve as examples. Duchamp's *The Bride Stripped Bare by her Bachelors, Even* depicts the woman and her several suitors in two unconnected spaces, each with its own apparatus and activities, unable to communicate, with the only unity being the imaginary one of their dreams. Again, in a recent analysis by Rosine and Robert Lefort of *Les Demoiselles d'Avignon*, it is argued that the painting is an attempt to represent the unrepresentable – the real as impossibility (not least of sexual rapport) – and that the horror evoked by the painting in Picasso's circle was due to his metonymic imagery of fundamental lack in the Other represented by the prostitutes.[5] The nose of the female figure crouching on the right of the canvas is, on this reading, 'a pacifying signifier', a means of exorcizing the horror of lack by representing it within the imaginary of the painting.

The absence of sexual relation has also been a recurrent theme in cinema, of which Godard's later films provide an instance. Whereas in Godard's early work sexual rapport is absent not because of its intrinsic impossibility but because of the failings of the man (*Le Mépris* [1963]) or more usually the woman (*Breathless* [1959], *Pierrot le Fou* [1965]), by the time of *Sauve Qui Peut* (1980) any confidence in the contingency of this absence has evaporated. While a certain mystery may remain around the woman, it is a mystery to which men have no access; otherwise, the emblematic way men relate to women is by hitting them, while women relate to men by leaving them. Popular as well as high culture is equally cognizant of this absence, as evidenced by comedians whose stock in trade are jokes about failed relationships (Woody Allen, for instance) or Rita Rudner's comment that the secret of a successful relationship is to let him be himself and to pretend he's someone else – a line that echoes Sophia Loren's remark that sex appeal is fifty per cent what you've got and fifty per cent what he thinks you've got. As a corollary to such widely shared scepticism about the possibility of sexual relationship is the disbelief or unease experienced at implausible happy endings (*Mildred Pierce* [1945], *White Palace* [1991]) or many scenes purportedly depicting sexual harmony (Steve MacQueen driving Faye Dunawaye around in his beach buggy in *The Thomas Crown Affair* [1968], Bruce Willis serenading Kim Basinger on his guitar in *Blind Date* [1987]).

Lacan's pessimistic conclusion was drawn not from clinical experience (although this could hardly fail to have confirmed and quite possibly inspired his thinking on the topic), but was rather the outcome of his rereading of Freud. The proposition that 'there is no sexual relation' was first stated in the seminar La Logique du Fantasme (1966–7) and was a central point of reference from then until Les Non-dupes Errent (1973–4).[6] It was, however, implicit in his work from a much earlier stage, in his thinking on the formation of the human subject, three moments of which are relevant here, all of them centrally concerned with lack.

Misrecognition

In the first of these Lacan elaborated the so-called mirror phase, which is so well known as to require only the briefest of recapitulations. Prior to achieving motor control, the entirely dependent human infant anticipates the control and unity it has not yet attained (and indeed never will) by assuming an image of itself. But to do so is to be caught up in misrecognition; the image is a mirage; the subject in becoming captured by its image is alienated. For there is always a discordance between the body and the assumed image, an absence that Lacan would later term *objet a*. Although at this stage Lacan made little reference to the question of the sexual relation, the state of being in love was seen as involving the misrecognition and narcissism of the mirror phase. Like the infant's anticipated yet never attained unity, the lovers' dream of harmonious wholeness belongs to the imaginary, is nothing more than 'a reciprocal mutually agreeable self-deception'.[7] (When in *Henry: Portrait of a Serial Killer* [1985] Becky (Tracy Arnold) looks into the eyes of the man who will inevitably kill her and murmurs how she feels she has always known him, her tragedy is that her misrecognition means that she never will.) One further aspect of Lacan's thinking in this moment, which prefigures his later ideas, concerns the role of the Other in determining the subject's self-image. For it is the signifiers of the parent holding the child in front of the mirror which determines its identification with the alienating image. In assuming an identity assigned by the Other, the child both sees the world from its own subjective viewpoint while being denied the viewpoint of the gaze of the constituting Other. Thus to be a subject is to be looked at from somewhere other than the position from which one sees. What is red in love is to be seen by the Other as one wishes to be seen, to overcome the split between the eye of the subject and the gaze of the Other. But this can be achieved only in the Imaginary. Insofar as it is a bid to determine what is determining, it is impossible.

Aphanisis

Subsequently Lacan was to recast his conception of the Other that pre-exists and determines the subject in terms of language: it was now the symbolic order inscribing the laws of society. In shifting the emphasis onto the subject's relation to the signifier and the signifying chain. Lacan also reconceived castration as the effect of language upon the subject, rather than as a threat emanating from the father. Thus conceived, castration has two dimensions: alienation and separation.

The first of these stems from the fact that the subject does not control his or her representation in the signifying chain, since the signifier S_1 representing the subject is given its value by another signifier S_2. Divided between the signifiers S_1 and S_2, the subject therefore emerges in the signifying chain only to fade. Although dependent on the signifier the subject is not a signifier, hence is at once included and excluded from language, endlessly displaced along the signifying chain in pursuit of the (nonexistent) signifier that would fully represent it. Just as the subject is unable to coincide with its image, so the subject of the enounced is unable to coincide with the subject of the enunciation. This disappearance of the subject was termed aphanisis by Lacan.

Castration entails not only that the subject is divided and alienated but also that it is separated from its living being, something vital is lost in entering language. This was described at one stage of Lacan's thinking in terms of an evacuation of *jouissance* from the subject's body. What remains, what cannot be inscribed in the signifying chain is *objet a*; which has led Jacques-Alain Miller to posit an equivalence between it and the subject.[8] Developing this idea, Michel Sylvestre has proposed that the subject 'is either a lack, a hole in the signifier (- 1) or an object. In both cases it is real, that is to say excluded from the symbolic.'[9]

Thus this moment in Lacan's thinking can be understood in terms of the three registers, symbolic, real and imaginary. In being represented within the symbolic, something of the subject is missing and this can be equated with the *objet a*, which in turn is the real of the subject, that which cannot be symbolized. The imaginary consists in the forever elusive objects that the subject believes will make good the lack. There is in other words a necessarily failed dialectic in entering the symbolic, in becoming a subject: once divided there can be no return to the lost unity; 'sublation is one of those sweet dreams of philosophy'.[10] None of which prevents the subject from trying, indeed the *manque à être* expressive of the subject's lack acts as a spur to search for *objet a*. Such a search, whose guidelines are framed by fantasy, always fails, indeed must do so since otherwise 'it would end the division of the subject from the object and bring about the death of the subject'.[11] Every encounter with *objet a* is therefore a failed encounter: which is another way of saying there is no sexual relation.

The recasting of the concept of the Other has profound implications for the relations between the sexes. Whereas for the earlier Lacan the Other was the other person and the problem was the illusions entertained about that person, in the later formulation the Other is language. The lack in the Other produces a barred subject $, who has no recourse but to pursue the lost *objet a* in its imaginary mode within another person. Because this object is always already lost, the other person is encountered as lacking; man and woman are 'one for the other the Other'.[12] Sexual relation exists therefore only in the imaginary and only insofar as each pretends to be what will make good the lack in the Other. Any semblance of sexual rapport thus hinges on the phallus, the pretence that the *objet a* exists in a form capable of making good the lack: the man must appear to have it, the woman must engage in the masquerade that she is it. (We shall return to the evident asymmetry involved here in the concluding section.) Consequently, for both the man and the woman, Lacan can say, loving is giving what they do not have; and the manifestations of it 'are entirely propelled into comedy'.[13]

La chose

A third moment in Lacanian theory turns on the concept of *la chose*, which was introduced in his seminar on ethics and which since his death has become the focus for increasing attention, in particular from Bernard Baas and Alain Juranville. *La chose* may be defined preliminarily in terms of the primordial mother, not as a plenitude that is subsequently lost with the intervention of the father, but rather the desiring mother, the mother as lacking, the real Other. Here Lacan breaks with both Freud and Melanie Klein, who in their different ways held that the child experiences satisfaction through the mother and will therefore subsequently seek objects that are in the last analysis substitutes for the mother's body. For Lacan, the encounter with *la chose* is the encounter with an originary and fundamental lack, the experience of which, however, paradoxically gives rise to the myth of lost plenitude, because 'the loss is anterior to what is lost'.[14] That is to say, it is the original experience of loss that accounts both for desire and for the myth of the lost paradise where desire was unknown. Belonging to the real, *la chose* may be elaborated as both the promise of an absolute plenitude and, when encountered, the experience of its lack.

Insofar as the mother is lacking, she is a signifier, and the subject who will emerge – and is always already in the signifying chain – is confronted with the question of what it is she wants, of what is the signified of the desire of the maternal signifier. This can only be what she lacks, namely the phallus, which is defined as the signifier with no signified (because as that which will make good the lack in the Other, it signifies what does not exist). By posing him or herself as the phallus, the subject becomes a signifier in relation to the signifier of the mother, but only from the perspective of the Other. And the subject no more coincides with this signifier than with any other; subjection to this signifier too involves castration. 'The subject is the phallus for the Other, but for himself he is castrated.'[15] Thus the experience of *la chose* results in castration. On entering the signifying chain the subject is separated from *objet a* (which remains as the trace of *la chose*), and the fiction is born of the lost object that will make good the lack. For by taking the place of *la chose*, *objet a* both masks the absence of absolute *jouissance* and makes it possible to believe it exists. Unreconciled to the imaginary lack, the subject pursues a unity that never was – once again there is no sexual relation. Equally without lack there would be no subject: *la chose* is thus the void around which the subject is structured. Hence the man approaches the woman demanding she be *la chose* as plenitude but experiences only *la chose* as pure lack in encountering the real Other.

History

Before leaving this exposition of Lacan we shall address a possible objection to this paper, that the theory of the subject we are using is ahistorical. While it is true that all human subjects are divided and experience *manque à être*, it is not the case that lack always manifests itself in the same way. Indeed, since desire is the desire of the Other and since there are many Others, there can only be a diversity of responses to castration among individuals (whose experience of the Other is always unique). Psychoanalysis is 'the science of the particular'. At the same time there is a measure of generalization possible, insofar as individuals share a culture or cultures. Indeed it is not every culture that seeks to make good the lack through romance. In a recent radio broadcast Geoffrey Hawthorn pointed out that only in western culture are relations of love between individuals held to be the supreme form of self-expression, an idea that would be ludicrous to non-western cultures.[16] Even in the West the fantasy about romance is historically a relatively recent phenomenon that until this century was confined to certain frequently privileged social groups. In fact it seems reasonable to suppose that for most people, lacking adequate food, shelter, health and rest, the satisfaction of these basic needs functioned as a lure for the imagined abolition of lack. Only in the twentieth century did mass culture, notably cinema and popular music, extend the myth of romance to all social classes. But whatever the historical context, for Lacan any turn to romantic love is culturally determined – hence his approving citation as 'an authentic recognition of what love owes to the symbol' of La Rochefoucauld's remark that there are people who would never have been in love if they had not heard talk of it.[17]

Idealization

Given the lack in the Other, the Lacanian subject is at once divided as the effect of language ($\cancel{S}$) and the remainder left over from the division (*objet a*). The bid to overcome division can only occur in fantasy (since division is the condition of the subject's existence) – the formula for which $\cancel{S} \Diamond a$, puts the two elements into relation. Thus fantasy seeks to mask the lack in the Other by supposing that subject and object can be united. Out of the many fantasies offered by Hollywood, our specific concern is with the fantasy of sexual rapport, which itself is implemented by a variety of strategies. We shall limit our analysis to a discussion of just two of such elements: the establishment of figures that function to mask the lack in the Other, and romantic narrative structures.

Among figures disguising the lack in the Other, a first category comprises strong, self-sufficient characters, who are predominantly male – roles typically played by such actors as John Wayne, Clint Eastwood and Arnold Schwarzenegger. Because they are seemingly complete and lack nothing, they do not address demands to the Other, they do not desire (and as such mask the very condition of human subjectivity). Such completeness is, of course, illusory: it exists only in the imaginary unity and mastery of the mirror phase, and therefore depends upon the Other and can be achieved only at the cost of division and lack. The corollary of narcissism is thus aggression; either against any otherness that comes between the subject and his desired image of unity, or against the Other as affording unity at the cost of division. It is no accident therefore that films centred on such figures are replete with violence.

At stake there is always a relation to the Other: violence is precisely a
 of dealing with the lack in the Other; but the relation to the Other
 as the following examples will indicate. One kind of violence

seeks to complete the Other by extirpating the villain who is the obstacle to social harmony. It typically occurs in those movies where a murderous psychopath is on the rampage, necessitating the cop – who usually has a history of failed relationships or is flawed in some other way – going out onto the streets after him. The implication is that were it not for the villain all would be well socially and sexually; by eliminating him the hero would be fulfilled and society restored to harmony. Thus the villain functions to hide the impossibility of such a state of affairs: he masks the lack in the Other.

Another kind of violence, typically that directed against women, occurs as the corollary of identification with the Other. Here the Other is portrayed as lacking, no sexual relation is possible. But, instead of accepting this inescapable condition of subjectivity, men have traditionally situated this lack in women rather than in language. In so doing lack is transformed into women's deficiency – and hence in many films women as the embodiment of lack are threatened, attacked and killed. As in Freud's account of the fantasy 'a child is being beaten', the subject moves from the position of beaten (by the signifier that divides him) to beater (of women), and thereby becomes, though only in the imaginary, the Other. The muted verbal violence of Rhett's 'Frankly, my dear, I don't give a damn' at the end of *Gone with the Wind* (1939) mistakenly involves the fantasy that he can be done with the lack and the desire that in Hollywood is figured by women.

A third strategy involving violence attempts not to fill the hole in the Other but to abolish the Other altogether – and hence be free of the signifying chain, of desire, of the burden of existence. It can take a number of forms. One is the murder of the counterpart, which in different contexts can be either the ideal image of the mirror phase or the lost object. What these very different counterparts have in common is that the subject exists only by virtue of being separated from them. By directing violence at the counterpart the aim is to end that separation; but since the subject cannot exist without separation, such violence is suicidal. When at the end of Peckinpah's film Pat Garrett shoots Billy he is actually destroying himself, which the film subsequently makes explicit by having him turn and shoot his own image in the mirror. Another variant is the destruction of the Other as that which refuses to recognize you as you wish to be recognized. *The Long Goodbye* (1973) ends with Terry Lennox saying 'You always were a loser, Marlowe'; to which Marlowe responds by shooting him. Finally there is the destruction of the Other because it permits the subject no more than lack and desire. Weary of the empty promises of plenitude, the subject wants to abolish the Other so as to begin again. This is what occurs at the end of *The Wild Bunch* (1969) when Pike Bishop chooses death preference to an existence that has become intolerable. His attack

Mexicans is an attack on the castrating Other; but the end of lack and the end of desire is the death of the subject. (We return to the topic of the death wish, which this invokes, later in the paper.) In all of these instances, it is no accident that the violence occurs at the end of the film. For the subject depends upon the Other, and without it ceases to exist. While resolution occurs, it is at the cost of closing down rather than opening up the future.

La femme

The second category of figures masking the lack in the Other are those idealized figures who make good the lack in the protagonists. Although there are many Hollywood films where the idealized figure is a male making good the lack in the woman's life – for instance, Kris Kristofferson in *Alice Doesn't Live Here Anymore* (1974), or Alan Bates in *An Unmarried Woman* (1977) (films that were purportedly feminist in their allegiance) – more typically the idealized figure is a woman. Indeed the recurrence in countless films of women representing the current ideal of beauty has been a major concern of recent film theory.

Following Mulvey (who, though never using the concept of *la femme*, pointed to the idealization of women) and other commentators, we would suggest that these supposedly perfect beings are so many versions of *la femme*, the nonexistent figuration of the *objet a*, that by concealing castration can within the male fantasy make good the lack. It is because of this that Lacan could say that a beautiful woman is a perfect incarnation of man's castration [18] and that beauty is 'a barrier so extreme as to forbid access to a fundamental horror'. [19] From the countless instances of the attempt to figure *la femme*, we will cite just four, together with independent critical comment. Thus, Greta Garbo in *Camille* (1936), the woman of mystery, of whom Serge André commented that 'the enigma of woman functions as a fog covering the absence of sexual rapport'[20] ; Tippi Hedren in *Marnie* (1963) (at least in the opening sequence of the film), who as Raymond Bellour has pointed out,[21] is established in a relay of looks of the male gaze, and as such is a signifier without a referent in that, according to Zdenko Urdlouec, 'her only link with reality is fantasy'[22] ; Kim Novak as Madeleine in *Vertigo* (1958), a film that more than any other perhaps, is concerned with the fundamental absence and impossibility of *la femme*; Faye Dunàway as Evelyn Mulwray in *Chinatown* (1974), whose fall from the position of elusive mystery in the early part of the film, like Madeleine's in *Vertigo*, makes her into the reject, *le dechet*, already dead when she dies. Behind the masquerade there is nothing; all these beautiful women are simulacra.

Our analysis, like others before it, implies that in Hollywood women appear largely on the terms dictated by male fantasy: those women deemed beautiful function to mask the lack in the Other and support the illusion of sexual rapport, while those considered unattractive become the objects of the male aggression resulting from disappointment at the lack in the Other. This is not to say that female stars function only as objects for the male gaze – spectators' relation to fantasy is more complex than that. Male and female spectators do not identify with characters as such or simply in terms of their respective genders; rather they identify with figures in particular fantasy scenarios. For instance, spectators identify with Robocop not because they wish to be automata but because of his effective way of dealing with troublesome people. Similarly an actress figuring *la femme* can also be a point of identification for both female and male spectators. When Vivien in *Pretty Woman* passes through the hotel lobby past the admiring hotel staff on the way to the opera, she is at once the object of the voyeuristic gaze (itself by no means limited to male spectators) and a point of identification for spectators of both sexes in that in the fantasy scenario she is looked at from the position she would like to be looked at from, and thus overcomes castration. For being a subject, to recall the mirror phase, involves being seen, and that in terms which are given by the Other; and one desires to be seen by the Other as one sees oneself in one's narcissism; one wishes to be recognized by the Other; or rather, misrecognized (since the mirror identification with one's image is misrecognition). When characters in a film (or for that matter in reality) ask to be loved for themselves they mean for the ideal they narcissistically take themselves to be. Being so seen never occurs except in the imaginary, which points precisely to the source of the pleasure of scenes such as the one we have referred to from *Pretty Woman*: in the imaginary of the text Vivien, with whom the spectator identifies, is seen in terms of her narcissistic ideal.

We thus follow a number of writers, among them David Rodowick, Elizabeth Cowie and Cora Kaplan[23] in arguing that identification in cinema is multiple and dispersed, with both sexes identifying across gender boundaries. In the present context we would propose further that the dispersed identification with both partners of the couple is, by avoiding sexual difference, a way of also avoiding taking up a position from which sexual rapport is impossible. More speculatively we would suggest too that there might in some instances by a hysterical dimension to such identifications. According to classical psychoanalytic theory the hysteric is a woman asking what it is to be a woman; or, more precisely, and given the determination of female roles by male-dominated society, what it is to be a woman for a man. Hysteria then may be seen as a questioning of and protest against the positions assigned to the female subject; its way of doing so is precisely through a relay of cross-gender identifications, which in turn characterizes the identificatory behaviour of the spectator.

Rapport deferred

Out of a sample of one hundred Hollywood films David Bordwell discovered that ninety-five of these contained a romantic element and that in no fewer than eighty-five romance was the principal line of action, figures that confirm the rule of thumb that a 'love interest' is good box office.[24] In film after film a heterosexual couple is united in perfect rapport, thereby implying that far from there being a lack in the Other, it on the contrary contains both a signifier that will finally name the subject and the *objet a*, hence the possibility of *jouissance*. But as obvious as this promise of sexual rapport is the fact that very little of such films' running time is given over to the depiction of it. Instead romantic narratives are almost invariably concerned with the obstacles in the way of its realization. The question then is, why if what is wanted is sexual relation should films not celebrate it rather than concern themselves with problems preventing it occurring? Why in *Pretty Woman* do Edward and Vivien not simply unproblematically fall in love and spend the remainder of the film in a state of bliss? Why in so many films does an initial erotic encounter precipitate a crisis that is only resolved at the end of the film, if at all? Why should films swerve away from what is desired at the very point when satisfaction could be given?

By way of answers to these questions we would point to a number of possible lines of research. A first step towards an explanation could lie in the concept of the dialectic of the subject, which we have outlined elsewhere.[25] A central debate during the 1970s and early 1980s turned on the question of the relation of the spectator to the text. On the one hand a structuralist approach (particularly associated with *Screen*) proposed that the text itself determined the way in which it was read and thus constituted the spectator; on the other hand ethnographic criticism stressed the constitutive role of the spectator, pointing to the empirical evidence of varied responses among spectators to the same text. Those emphasizing the constitutive role of the text saw texts as essentially the same for all spectators, while those emphasizing the constitutive role of the spectator saw them as essentially different. Against this polarity we argued that the relation between text and subject is better comprehended as a dialectic. On the one hand the spectator constitutes the text, augmenting his or her competence in reading (shared by other members of the interpretive community) with a unique set of associations, memories or points of fascination (in this sense no two spectators see the same film). On the other hand the spectator is constituted by the text, in that its shared meaning and in particular the affective states deriving from an understanding of that meaning are determined by its narrative and other structures and would not otherwise exist for the spectator. The dialectic is analogous to that between a lover and the love object, in which the lover simultaneously constitutes the object through overvaluation and projection of fantasy and is constituted in that the affective state is dependent upon the existence of the particular individual who is the love object. Here, as in relation to the text, the subject is both transforming and transformed.

All this concerns the question of sexual relation in that cinema does not simply provide fantasies to satisfy spectators' already existing desires – though it can do so, with spectators extracting episodes from films and integrating them into their own personal fantasy scenarios. Also and more importantly cinema promises to answer the desire it constitutes through the scenarios it enacts. Before entering the cinema the spectator does not care whether or not ET calls home, or the towering inferno is extinguished, or Roger Thornhill clears his name, or Vivien remains a prostitute. But in the course of constituting the text the spectator is in turn constituted by it, and comes to care. Desire, in the cinema as elsewhere is the desire of the Other; the obstacles and delays of the Other of the text produce a lack that in turn gives rise to a desire. And equally the text produces the imaginary objects that will satisfy this desire.

It is here, we would argue, that the power and success of cinema lies. In everyday reality there is, in Lacan's terms, always a failed dialectic, in which the encounter with the Other produces not a unified but a divided subject: demand can only find expression through signifiers within the signifying system of the Other, but because the signifier that would adequately represent the subject's wish does not exist there is always something left to desire. In the cinema, however, there are times (perhaps infrequently) when it seems that there is nothing left to desire, when everything demanded of the text seems to have been gratified. That this can be so is because the text itself has determined the nature of that demand in such a way that the desires that emerge can apparently be satisfied. In returning time and again to the cinema in the expectation of pleasure, spectators are not so much seeking to possess a lost object as to become the subjects who in the imaginary of the text can possess the lost object it constructs. Just as in the Hollywood romance the couple seem made for one another, so too the film and the spectator.

Therefore, to return to the questions we have posed, a first reason for the difficulties in the way of romantic fulfilment is that this is a means of evoking desire. A second reason is that they keep the object at a distance. On the one hand the exchange between spectator and film produces a subject who lacks and hence desires, and on the other hand objects that will apparently satisfy those desires. But it does so in specific ways. In the case of romance the constitution of the subject typically takes the form of an identification with a character who is lacking – Scarlett (Vivien Leigh) in *Gone with the Wind* seeking fulfilment, Bronte (Andie MacDowell) in *Green Card* (1990) whose passion for her garden is a metaphor for her putting order before life. Spectators identify not solely with idealized figures, but with those who lack, and they do so in order to have fantasy organize desire. At the same time an object is constituted, Rhett for Scarlett, Georges for Bronte, that will apparently make good the lack. But as we have already shown, such an object exists in the real, as the cause of desire (in that separation from it produces a lack), and in the imaginary, as the lure promising to make good the lack, but it crucially does not exist within the symbolic (for if it did the subject would cease to be a subject). The form it takes within the imaginary masks a void, and fantasies are constructions which function to hide this void behind what seems to be *objet a*. As in courtly love on Lacan's reading, narrative functions to maintain a distance, lending enchantment to the object, guarding against exposure of the void behind it. Through the narrative economy of the text any object can be made to appear to be the *objet a*, any woman *la femme*, so long as they are not approached too closely.

The presence of obstacles can therefore be explained as a means of both making the object desirable and of preventing its exposure as nothing. Just as in courtly love where the barrier permits the lover to believe in sexual relation, so fantasy in film (as elsewhere) engenders representations of the ultimately unrepresentable object in order to screen off the real of castration, *la chose* and the experience of lack.

This can be also described, appositely, in optical terms, through the concept of anamorphosis invoked by Lacan in his discussion of Holbein's painting *The Ambassadors*. In the foreground of the painting there is a mark or patch that viewed frontally on is impossible to decipher; only when seen from a foreshortening sideways perspective does this reveal itself to be a skull. Narrative has a similarly anamorphic function, in that the obstacles constituting it place the object in a particular perspective that renders it desirable. The positions occupied by the spectator through identifications determine what can be perceived and desired: by identifying with Fred Astaire in *Top Hat* (1935) the spectator finds Ginger Rogers desirable, with Celia Johnson in *Brief Encounter* (1945), Trevor Howard. All these are signifiers, whose desirability derives only from the point of view of another signifier; by identifying with one signifier the spectator finds another signifier desirable. In practice, of course, as we have already explained, the spectator's identifications are multiple and fractured, they are not limited to any one character on screen. As in Freud's analysis of the fantasy 'a child is being beaten', the spectator is able to switch identifications in the course of a narrative. For example, when the spectator identifies with Edward in *Pretty Woman*, Vivien, onwards from the moment in the film when romantic music first occurs and he sees her asleep, is *la femme*. But she is not necessarily *la femme* when the spectator identifies with her. At times she is – as when she is seen as she would wish to be seen; while at other times she is lacking, as when during the first shopping expedition she is humiliated by the hostile saleswoman.

At which point we can specify a final reason for the need of obstacles, that is implicit in the preceding passage. It is this: by keeping the object of desire at a distance and masking the lack in the Other, narrative is able to sustain desire rather than, as is generally supposed, to fulfil it. As such, narrative is on the side of desire and opposed to the death drive. For as Alain Juranville has explained, the death drive is the turning against desire itself and 'its partial truth', as a result of the discovery that there is no ultimate satisfaction, that *la chose* does not exist.[26] But there is an evident problem here. If narrative is that which lures us forward, desiring that which does not exist, then how is it to be resolved? If sexual rapport means bringing object and subject together, how is the death implicit in this to be avoided? The contradiction may be summarized as that between the impossibility of attaining the real object and the requirement of the myth of sexual rapport that this is effected. Hollywood faces the problem of how to represent what is finally unrepresentable.

Representing the unrepresentable

The most obvious solution is to construct the semblance of sexual relation by showing the couple in perfect harmony, but as we have already indicated such attempts are usually fraught with discomfort for the spectator. Jack Nicholson and Susan Sarandon romping together amidst pink balloons (in *The Witches of Eastwick* [1987]), or Jonathan Switcher (Andrew McCarthy) in *Mannequin* (1987) kissing his 'living doll' atop a mound of teddy bears, are less than utterly convincing as representations of sexual rapport. Nor do metaphors from nature fare much better, still less when as in *Dances with Wolves* (1990) the voice-over narration draws the audience's attention to what is already self-evident, namely the unity of hero and heroine in the idyllic prairie setting. Sometimes, however, such attempts are successful, as arguably in the scene from *Klute* (1971) where Bree Daniels (Jane Fonda) and

Klute (Donald Sutherland) walk together through a street market. A number of factors contribute to the success of this scene, among them the aura produced by the couple (possibly an effect of the stars having an affair at the time), the ease and seeming unscriptedness of the occasion, the displacement of the personal onto the social setting of the market and the diegetic presence of the signifier fruit (rather more resonant than balloons or dolls) as a metaphor for desire and sexual pleasure. Above all though, it is the romantic music on the soundtrack that transfigures the everyday activity of shopping.

For Hegel the effect of music is to articulate through the dialectic of conflict and resolution something of the unity that underlies the subject's own thought and consciousness. The effect of the process that can be discerned beneath the discrete phrases is to transform time from an infinite succession of nows into a unified whole. Just such an experience is afforded romantic music on the soundtrack. But what for Hegel is a process of recognition, from a Lacanian perspective can only be one of misrecognition. For Lacan the dialectic always fails, because in a chain of signifiers $S_1 \ldots S_2$ something is always lost, the *objet a* falls out. It is for this reason that Juranville calls time the primordial place of the real. The gap between the signifiers is 'the time of pure suffering', since what is desired does not occur there.[27] In this real time S_1 and S_2 emerge only as lures and the gap between them becomes a nothingness where they are abolished. However, romantic music sutures this gap; instead of real time there is the time of the imaginary and what is anticipated arrives. Whereas in the ordinary run of events what occurs is never identical with what is anticipated, both because the image of unity in the mirror is never achieved and because the desired object once attained is found to be lacking, with music nothing appears to be lost between the signifiers. As in Hegel's account the notes seem to relate to a larger process with an underlying unity. Instead of there being 'no whole without a hole' absences exist only to become presence, holes open up only to be filled.[28] When Rogers and Astaire dance, when in *Ghost* (1990) Sam (Patrick Swayze) and Molly (Demi Moore) come together for the last time to the strains of *Unchained Melody*, it seems that the harmony extends beyond the music to envelop the couple.

If something is lost in entering the signifying chain, then meaning and being never coincide. Divided by the signifier, the subject can never achieve self-expression and there is always an impossible-to-say. One of the functions of analysis is to bring out the existence of this impossibility and to thereby free the subject from the illusion that he or she can ever be other than divided. With romantic music the impossible-to-say is if not enunciated at any rate rendered present, an effect further accomplished by music's semantic component. But even when there are lyrics the meaning can never fully be captured; its sense is present but cannot be stated. Such presence of the impossible-to-say tames the unconscious, changes it from a threatening otherness to a comforting closeness through which the subject can imagine him or herself to be whole and undivided, the man and the woman proceed in step with the signifier, and meaning and being coincide. (Of course not all music functions in this way: the Leforts cite Beethoven's *Grosse Fugue* and we would also mention Barraqué's *Piano Sonata* as examples of works where the real as impossible to say is only too evident.)

More usually Hollywood prefers a solution that enables it to avoid having to attempt any explicit representation of sexual rapport, and it does so by adopting a tense other than the present. The three principal options are to say that the sexual relation will exist, that it has existed, or that it would exist but for a particular set of circumstances. In each case the resolution is deferred to an imaginary time outside the text.

Of the three, the solution of setting the sexual relation in the text's future is by far and away the most common, in that this is the standard happy ending in which the lovers come together all set to live happily ever after. Since the time of the imaginary is time anticipated, as when in the mirror phase the child anticipates its future unity, this solution remains wholly within the imaginary, by deferring the need to put the sexual relation to the test of the symbolic. As the credits roll over the terminal kiss, the spectator is screened from the real impossibility of what is proposed. *North by Northwest* (1959) ends like this, and *Pretty Woman*, and hundreds of other films.

Another solution is to set the sexual relation in the past. At the end of *Walkabout* (1970) Jenny Agutter imagines a lost plenitude, but as the film has already shown this never happened; she rejected the aboriginal boy's advances, he killed himself; *la chose* as plenitude does not exist. Hollywood romance, in contrast, has tended to suggest that *la chose* can exist as plenitude. In *Casablanca* (1942), for example, the sexual rapport between Rick (Humphrey Bogart) and Ilsa (Ingrid Bergman) is suggested not by the scenes where they are shown together in Paris but in those where they realize that their idyll is lost forever. When Rick says, 'We'll always have Paris', it is not the Paris depicted in the flashbacks but the one retroactively created by the tears in Ilsa's eyes that is the emblem of sexual rapport. A similar retroactive traversal of the text to convert what has just been seen into the overcoming of lack occurs at the end of *Pretty Woman*, when Roy Orbison's title song, repeated over the credits, is able to suggest that the spectator has witnessed something altogether more magical than a red dress, a plane flight to San Francisco and an opera.

The third strategy is to imply that the sexual relation would have existed were it not for the existence of some insurmountable obstacle. The emblematic phrase here is 'if only': if only they had met earlier; if

only they had understood each other better; if only she hadn't died... .
Thus in *Gone with the Wind* the sexual relation is presented as failing
through the inability at certain crucial moments of Scarlett and Rhett to
express their true emotions, with the result that there is a breakdown in
communication between them. In *Letter from an Unknown Woman* (1947)
a failure to appreciate the depth of the other's feelings until too late
ruins the romance. Similarly in *Dangerous Liaisons* (1988), Valmont (John
Malkovich) discovers too late, when she is already dying, that he really
loved Madame de Tourvel (Michelle Pfeiffer) rather than the Marquise
de Merteuil (Glenn Close) he spurned her for. Death by itself without
the complication of belated self-discovery may also figure as the
obstacle, as in *Love Story* (1970), *Camille, Bobby Deerfield* (1977) and, most
recently, *Ghost*, where but for the fact that Sam is dead and Molly alive
they would form a perfect couple. Perhaps the most striking example is
Dr Zhivago (1965), in which it is made clear that were it not for the
tragedy of Russian history Lara (Julie Christie) and Zhivago (Omar
Sharif) would have lived happily ever after. Another type of obstacle
consists of character flaws, as in *Five Easy Pieces* (1970), *The Way We
Were* (1973), *McCabe and Mrs Miller* (1971) and *Sophie's Choice* (1982),
where, because of what happened to her in Auschwitz, Sophie (Meryl
Streep) is trapped in a self-destructive relationship and cannot therefore
break away into a genuinely fulfilling one. Moral prohibition also can
function to keep the lovers apart – for example, *Brief Encounter, Someone
to Watch Over Me* (1987) and *Now Voyager* (1942). Of course, as we have
already indicated, films can combine two or more of these elements: *The
Reckless Moment* (1944) brings together moral prohibition and death;
Casablanca, the circumstances of Ilsa's having met Laszlo before Rick
and the requirements of duty.

One key 'if only' narrative we have not so far mentioned is that of
Oedipus, the obstacle of course being the taboo against incest. During
the 1970s a number of critics, among them most notably Raymond
Bellour, argued for the centrality of the Oedipus complex as an
organizing principle both for the nineteenth-century novel and for
narrative cinema. Bellour proposed that American cinema constantly
re-enacts and is fundamentally shaped by the kind of subjectivity and
its scenarization whose logic was first established by psychoanalysis. A
propos of his study of *North by Northwest*, he notes his constant surprise
at the extent to which 'everything was organized according to a classic
Oedipal scenario'.[29] Recent readings of Freud, however, suggest that
this confidence in the ur-text of Oedipus is misplaced. Rather than
expressing a fundamental reality of desire and the possibility of its
fulfilment, that recurs as a consequence across a spectrum of texts, it has
been suggested that the Oedipus is itself a way of masking off
something that does not exist. Thus Lacan in his Seminar XVII describes

the Oedipus as 'a dream of Freud's', a comment that Juranville and Baas have taken to mean that while the castration complex really exists, the presumed Oedipus complex is a myth, a 'symptom' of Freud's.[30] According to Juranville desire is not initially Oedipal, but is rather a desire for *la chose*, which as we have already seen, is absent but nonetheless gives rise to the myth of plenitude. In the words of Mireille Ardrès, 'Castration is not the effect of the myth, rather the myth is an effect of castration.'[31] The Oedipus functions to suggest that plenitude is not innately impossible but is merely forbidden: were it not for the law of the father there could be a return to the original satisfaction associated with the mother's body. What it does is erroneously substitute paternal interdiction for the castration that is the inevitable consequence of the signifier. Hence Oedipus is a neurotic perspective on castration, a flight from the desire to which castration gives rise. The mother mistakenly comes to occupy the place of *la chose* and is desirable only because of the attribution to her of *objet a*, the trace of *la chose*. Oedipus is a way of dissimulating the absence of *la chose* and of repressing castration.

On this reading, such obviously Oedipal dramas as *The Postman Always Rings Twice* (1981), *Double Indemnity* (1944), *Shane* (1952) and *Body Heat* (1981), serve to mask the impossibility of absolute *jouissance*. Thus when Shane (Alan Ladd) rides out of the valley at the end of the film there is no implication that absolute *jouissance* is impossible, rather the spectator is left with the fantasy that it is merely prohibited. Because Marion (Jean Arthur) is already married and they are both too honest to transgress the law, Shane has to settle for her handshake and renounce the *jouissance* that could otherwise have been his. Although *Body Heat* has been characterized by Frederic Jameson as a postmodern text, by reason of its supposed depthlessness and evacuation of affect, it can more convincingly be seen as a traditional Oedipal drama. The fact that Ned (William Hurt) does not achieve the sexual rapport he seeks nevertheless leads the audience to believe in principle that it exists, since Matty (Kathleen Turner) in remaining a mystery to the end represents *la femme*, terminus of male desire. Here as in other examples we have discussed, the allocation of *jouissance* to a hypothetical beyond of the text enables *la chose* as the irreducible absence of plenitude to remain undisclosed.

During the 1970s the emphasis within film theory shifted from the texts themselves to the exchange between texts and spectators and to the meanings thereby produced. Studies such a those by Baudry and Metz on the effect of the apparatus on the spectator and by Heath on the suturing effects of certain narrative procedures typified the new approach. Despite subsequent criticism of many aspects of such thinking, the central thesis in our opinion still remains valid, to the effect that in reading a text the subject is taken up and changed, and that such reconstitution permits meanings to become available that would not otherwise exist. Such we would argue is the case with romance. The subject is taken up by the narrative and other textual strategies of the genre and is placed at the appropriate distance so that the mirage of sexual rapport can be sustained.

The politics of romance

Our initial assumption in thinking about romance was that the politics of it were unproblematic: it seemed a straightforward instance of a discursive regime producing both a characteristic mode of subjectivity – the assignation of roles – and a domain of objects – one reality constituted at the expense of others, and so instituting relations of power. As a discourse produced within and bearing the marks of male dominated culture, and typically 'authored' by men, romance would be acted out differently by male and female spectators. Our intention was to write a preliminary outline sketch of the issues, while leaving to one side mutations within the genre during its history and the varying relationships of different audiences to it over time. What seemed clear was that the roles assigned in spectating would be shaped by its authorial dominance by men and that historically these roles were those indicated by the lower portion of Lacan's formulas of sexuation.

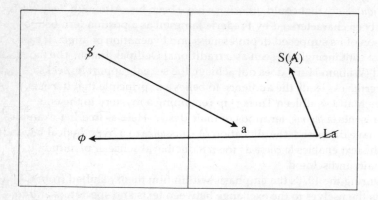

While men (Ş) relate directly to the cause of desire (a) and seek ways of fulfilling it by developing such stratagems as courtly love, women (Ła) are forced to seek fulfilment from a position assigned by men, relating firstly to the phallus (ϕ) men claim to have but in fact do not and secondly to S($\cancel{A}$) which is at once the lack in the Other and the putative site of another mode of *jouissance*. That is to say, men relate to the lost object and seek to overcome its loss by imagining certain women to incarnate it, whereas women have to desire within a situation where men demand they play out particular roles. The political implications of this asymmetry are that women have to pretend they are something they are not (or indeed anyone ever could be) on the masquerade of *la femme*. It is not so much that male fantasy wilfully misrepresents women as that it uses women as a metaphor for what does not exist.

Thus we saw much in Hollywood romance that is reminiscent of Lacan's ' ... I love something in you that exceeds you ... I mutilate you', since the other side of idealization is the violence implicit in being called upon to be what no social being could ever be.[32] As a historically specific signifying economy within patriarchy, romance seemed to be a further example of socially instituted gender asymmetry. On this basis we interpreted the pleasure women experience from the genre as a function of their position within patriarchy. In watching *Pretty Woman* we hypothesized that the fantasy is that being what men demand will require no sacrifice on the part of the woman: like a latter-day Cinderella, Vivien is transformed into a princess, learning how to dress and behave in a way that commands universal admiration, while at the same time this entry into the symbolic makes apparent to everybody what she was all along, a wonderful person. In a sense, therefore, she is not transformed at all, unlike Edward who is transformed through his meeting her (and shows it by taking his shoes off in the park). As a human being she lacked nothing, the problem being with society that failed to appreciate her. Edward in his role of fairy godmother puts this to rights with his credit card; she in turn is then able to put Edward, as the representative of the society that saw her only as a prostitute, to rights with her innate decency. The episode described earlier where she is admired in her new dress is emblematic of the film's fantasy; her beauty is now manifest and she is thereby empowered to change Edward into someone with whom sexual rapport is possible. Thus castration is denied; in entering the symbolic she is not subjected to the gaze of the Other which is the ruin of all dreams of mastery, but is rather confirmed by it in being seen as she would wish to be seen. On this account, then, the fantasy that makes *Pretty Woman* (and other films within the genre) attractive to women is that it is possible both to be what patriarchal cultures demand without sacrifice and to transform men into beings with whom sexual rapport is possible.

However, the intense pleasure many women have experienced from this and similar films raises questions both of the adequacy of the above account and of the validity of the psychoanalysis on which it is based. It would seem that this enjoyment of romance is something that men by and large do not share: Cora Kaplan's comment that no man of her acquaintance had read *Gone with the Wind* except for professional reasons[33] tallies with the relative lack of pleasure most men appear to have experienced from *Pretty Woman* (whose structure is very close to the standard Mills and Boon formula as described by Ann Rosalind Jones[34]). The questions then would be: What is it about romance that engages women? What do they get out of it, and what do they put into it?

One possible answer would be that the fantasy of sexual rapport is an opiate, a way of making more endurable not only unsatisfactory relations with men but a whole panoply of subordinate social relations. As well as attempting to make good the lack in the Other, romance would thus be a compensatory fantasy for the relative absence of power in the social roles women are assigned. But as Tania Modleski suggests in her analysis of the American Harlequin series, this fantasy can 'induce' or 'intensify' women's problems, just as 'certain tranquillisers taken to relieve anxiety are, though temporarily helpful, ultimately anxiety producing'.[35] An alternative is to see romance as a way of negotiating (for Jones) or resolving (for Modleski) the problems faced by women by displacing them into the single one of finding sexual rapport. Another answer proposed by Modleski, drawing upon the work of Richard Dyer, is that romance is as much a challenge to as endorsement of the feminine condition.[36] Her emphasis here is upon the utopian dimension to romance, expressive of women's desire for community, transcendence, autonomy and honest sexual relations. In elaborating these various explanations of romance most commentators have agreed that it combines contradictory elements. Janice Radway, for example, argues that the oppositional (because non-self-denying) act of reading romance is at odds with the patriarchal ideology embodied within it[37] and Tania Modleski that, behind its seemingly innocuous escapism, romance 'simultaneously challenges and reaffirms traditional values, behaviour and attitudes'.[38]

In the light of which, the politics of romance are rather more difficult to determine than we assumed. One line of research as an alternative to psychoanalysis would be through an ethnographic approach, such as that adopted by Radway, where the emphasis is placed upon the responses of actual readers to particular texts. Such an approach suffers, however, from certain limitations, the most obvious of which is that (if psychoanalysis has any validity) readers can never know all that is feeding into their responses: there is always an unconscious. This is perhaps most evident in relation to symptoms: in Freud's classic case study, the Rat Man, the recounting of the rat torture that occasioned the patient so much distress was accompanied by signs of extreme pleasure. If, in other words, the symptom delivers *jouissance*, so arguably does art too. The formula for fantasy $\$ \Diamond$ a involves both the barred subject, that is never transparent to itself, and the *objet a*, which though unrepresentable is the very condition of the fantasy's functioning, since its absence provides the framework where alone the fantasy can appear. If the dialectic of the subject means anything, it is that the subject is present as, in Lacan's phrase, the response of the real; and the real can never be imaged or symbolized. Fantasy functions to bring together subject and object in a *jouissance* that eludes conscious thought; both the subject's implication and the object's operation are beyond reach. But if, because of this, ethnographic criticism can never pronounce a final word, neither can psychoanalysis. It too has its limitations; and worse, it has a tendency to forget them.

In saying 'there is no metalanguage'[39] psychoanalysis recognizes that because variously of the existence of the unconscious, the particularity of each analysand, and the temporality of truth, it too can never pronounce a final word.[40] But equally the statement makes it clear that recourse to a metalanguage is unavoidable, since it is itself metalinguistic; and the practice of psychoanalysis (like other social practices) requires that it do so – even terminating the analytic session involves the analyst in an interpretation of some kind. But the risk is that such necessary local intervention becomes a totalizing discourse, reducing all other discourses to the status of object languages whose truth it knows. Yet on its own account psychoanalysis has no claim to any such status.

We conclude, therefore, on a note of caution concerning psychoanalysis, all the more so since from its beginnings it has been incapable of providing a convincing account of female subjectivity. Psychoanalysis for the moment may be seen as exemplifying what Jean-François Lyotard calls the 'differend', where 'something which ought to be able to be phrased cannot yet be phrased'.[41] In such a situation there can be no question of assigning psychoanalysis a privileged or, worse, monopolistic position in relation to discussions of femininity and romance. Different discourses must be allowed to develop in all their possible incommensurability; psychoanalysis must never become a totalizing theory, silencing that which is other to it. In conclusion, then, we would register our concurrence with Lyotard's call, in his paper 'What is Postmodernism?', for discursive heterogeneity: 'Let us wage war on totality; let us be witnesses to the unrepresentable; let us activate the difference and save the honour of the name.'[42]

Notes

1. Quoted by CHARLES JENCKS, *What is Post-Modernism?* (London: Academy Editions, 1966), p. 18.

2. JACQUES LACAN, 'God and the *Jouissance* of The Woman' in *Feminine Sexuality*, ed. Juliet Mitchell and Jacqueline Rose (London: Macmillan, 1982), p. 138.

3. LACAN, 'Kant avec Sade', *October*, **51** (1989): 62.

4. LACAN, 'A Love Letter' in *Feminine Sexuality*, p. 158.

5. ROSINE and ROBERT LEFORT, '*Les Demoiselles d'Avignon*', *Ornicar?*, **48** (1988): 81–92.

6. LACAN, 'L'étourdit', *Scilicet*, vol. 4 (Paris: du Seuil, 1973), p. 11.

7. STUART SCHNEIDERMAN, 'Art as symptom: a psychoanalytic study of art' in *Lacan and Criticism*, ed. Patrick Hogan and Lalita Pandi (Athens and London: Georgia University Press, 1990), p. 209.

8. JACQUES-ALAIN MILLER , 'Montre à prémontré', *Analytica*, **37** (1984): 28–9.

9. MICHEL SYLVESTRE, 'A la recontre du réel' in his *Demain la Psychanalyse* (Paris: Navarin, 1987), p. 307.

10. LACAN, 'A Love Letter', p. 158.

11. SYLVESTRE, 'A la recontre du réel', p. 312.

12. MIREILLE ANDRÈS, *Lacan et la Question du Metalanguage* (Paris: Point Hors Ligne, 1987), p. 76.

13. LACAN, 'The meaning of the phallus' in *Feminine Sexuality*, p. 84.

14. BERNARD BAAS, 'Le désir pur', *Ornicar?*, **83** (1987): 71.

15. ALAIN JURANVILLE, *Lacan et la Philosophie* (Paris: Presses Universitaires de France, 1984), p. 133.

16. GEOFFREY HAWTHORN speaking on *Analysis*, BBC Radio 4, 23 December 1990.

17. LACAN, 'The function and field of speech and language in psychoanalysis', *Écrits* (London: Tavistock, 1977), p. 54.

18. Quoted in SLAVOJ ZIZEK, *The Sublime Object of Ideology* (London: Verso, 1989), p. 172.

19. LACAN, 'Kant avec Sade', p. 63.

20. SERGE ANDRÉ, *Que Veut Une Femme* (Paris: Navarin, 1986), p. 200.

21. RAYMOND BELLOUR, 'Hitchock the enunciator', *Camera Obscura*, **2** (1977): 69–91.

22. ZDENKO URDLOUEC, 'Pas de printemps pour Marnie' in *Tous de que vous avez toujours voulue savoir sur Lacan sans jamais oser le demande à Hitchcock*, ed. Slavoj Zizek (Paris: Navarin, 1988), p. 210.

23. DAVID RODOWICK, 'The Difficulty of Difference', *Wide Angle*, **5**:1 (1981): 4–15; ELIZABETH COWIE, 'Fantasia' (see above, pp. 147–61); CORA KAPLAN, '*The Thorn Birds*: Fiction, Fantasy, Femininity' in *Sea Changes* (London: Verso, 1986).

24. DAVID BORDWELL, JANET STAIGER and KRISTIN THOMPSON, *The Classical Hollywood Cinema* (London: Routledge and Kegan Paul, 1985), p. 16.

25. ROBERT LAPSLEY and MICHAEL WESTLAKE, *Film Theory: An Introduction* (Manchester: Manchester University Press, 1988), pp. 53–4.

26. Juranville, *Lacan et la Philosophie*, p. 84.

27. Ibid., p. 85.

28. Jacques-Alain Miller, 'Microscopie', *Ornicar?*, **47** (1988): 57.

29. Raymond Bellour, 'Alternation, Segmentation, Hypnosis', interview by Janet Bergstrom, *Camera Obscura*, **3–4** (1979): 93.

30. Quoted in Juranville, *Lacan et la Philosophie*, p 199.

31. Andrès, *Lacan et la Question du Metalanguage*, p. 61.

32. Quoted in L. Casenave, 'Un fils naturel' in *Traits de Perversion dans les Structures Cliniques* (Paris: Navarin, 1990), p. 96.

33. Kaplan, '*The Thorn Birds*: Fiction, Fantasy, Femininity', p. 120.

34. Ann Rosalind Jones, 'Mills and Boon Meet Feminism' in *The Progress of Romance*, ed. Jean Radford (London: Routledge and Kegan Paul, 1986).

35. Tania Modleski, *Loving with a Vengeance* (London: Methuen, 1982), p. 57.

36. Richard Dyer, 'Entertainment and Utopia' in *Genre, The Musical: A Reader*, ed. Rick Altman (London: Routledge and Kegan Paul, 1981).

37. Janice Radaway, *Reading the Romance*, 2nd edn. (London: Verso, 1987), p. 210.

38. Modleski, op. cit., p. 112.

39. Lacan, 'L'étourdit', p. 6.

40. For a discussion of this concept, see Jacques-Alain Miller, 'Les réponses du réel' in *Aspects du Malaise dans la Civilisation* (Paris: Navarin, 1987).

41. Jean-François Lyotard, *The Differend* (Manchester: Manchester University Press, 1983), p. 13.

42. Lyotard, 'What is Postmodernism?' in *The Postmodern Condition* (Manchester: Manchester University Press, 1983), p. 82.

Glossary

CAMERA OBSCURA (Latin: 'dark room') Apparatus consisting of a darkened enclosure with a small aperture through which light enters to form an inverted image on the opposite surface.

CREATIONISTS Theorists of cinema (such as Rudolf Arnheim and Sergei Eisenstein) who stress that film creates an effect rather than reproduces a reality can be referred to as **creationists** or **formalists** in contrast to **realists.**

DIACHRONIC One of a pair of terms introduced by Ferdinand de Saussure to refer to the two basic perspectives for the study of language. So **diachronic** specifies the historical dimension in which a phenomenon changes across time in opposition to **synchronic.**

DIEGESIS Originating as a term from classical rhetoric, **diegesis** in film theory refers to the whole 'world' or character and events represented 'in' a film, the signified or represented content of a narrative.

ENOUNCED or ENUNCIATED As **signifier** is to **signified** with reference to a single term, so in terms of discourse **enounced**, what is represented or narrated within a discourse, is to **enunciation**, the process of signification by which the **enounced** is produced and on which it depends.

FETISHISM In psychoanalysis the fetish is an object placed as a substitute for the phallus the mother is imagined to lack. Some film theory argues that the **diegesis** of a film can be understood as a fetished substitute for the absent reality, the **profilmic** from which it is derived.

FILM NOIR So called 'black film' is a term introduced by French film critics to refer to Hollywood genre productions (as distinct from major features) between 1940 and 1955, especially thrillers, films characterised by (1) a pessimistic narrative and (2) photographic techniques dependent on a single light source and so giving strong black-and-white contrasts.

FORMALISTS Theorists of cinema (such as Rudolf Arnheim and Sergei

Eisenstein) who stress that film creates an effect rather than reproduces a reality can be referred to as **formalists** or **creationists**, in contrast to **realists.**

ICON/ICONIC In **semiotics** and particularly in the work of Peirce (1839–1914) an **iconic** sign is one of three types, that which resembles in its form the object it stands for, as a photograph of a tree does the tree it reproduces; see also **indexical** and **symbolic.**

INDEXICAL In **semiotics** and particularly in the work of Peirce (1839–1914) an **indexical** sign is one of three types, that which is related to its object by relations of contiguity or proximity or causality, as for example smoke to a fire; see also **iconic** and **symbolic**.

INTERPELLATION Borrowing from French legal terminology (where it refers to the process in which someone is summonsed to appear in court) Louis Althusser introduces **interpellation** to refer to the process in which ideology produces subjects who apparently 'work by themselves'. Ideology 'hails' the subject to recognise/misrecognise their identity as a free individual, overlooking the social structures and practices which actually interpellate them. Applied to film the term names the way a text addresses its reader, hailing them into an identity, providing them with a position.

JOUISSANCE (French) Noun from the verb *jouir* meaning to enjoy the rights of property, to experience ecstasy, including sexual ecstasy (orgasm). Roland Barthes in *The Pleasure of the Text* (1973) contrasted texts a reader can enjoy and master in a comfortable fashion, 'texts of pleasure', with those which leave the reader at a loss, 'texts of bliss' (*jouissance*).

LANGUE (French) Language considered **synchronically** as a system with specific rules (such as in Modern English the syntactical rule according to which word order governs meaning, 'dog bites man' means something different from 'man bites dog'. **Langue** is contrasted with **parole**.

METALANGUAGE When one discourse refers to or describes another discourse, the discourse which does the referring, the **metalanguage**, can be contrasted with the one referred to, the **object language**. For example, in an English book entitled *Teach Yourself French*, French is the **object language** and English the **metalanguage** in which it is discussed.

MISRECOGNITION According to Lacan's account of the mirror stage, human identity begins as the infant borrows from others a more perfect likeness or image of itself. Just as the face in the mirror can never be the same as the face which looks at its likeness in the mirror, so identity is always structured on the basis of a misreading or **misrecognition**.

OBJECT LANGUAGE   When one discourse refers to or describes another discourse, the discourse referred to, the **object language**, can be contrasted with the one which does the referring, the **metalanguage**.

PAROLE   An actual individual piece of speech or utterance performed according to the rules (**langue**) of a given language.

PROFILMIC   This consists of the elements, the physical reality, placed in front of the camera for filming.

QUATTROCENTO   (Italian: 'Four hundred') Term used to refer to the 1400s, or fifteenth century, and so to the development then of the perspective tradition in Italian painting.

REALISTS, REALIST THEORY   Theorists of cinema (such as André Bazin and Siegfried Kracauer) who stress that film reproduces a reality rather than creates an effect can be referred to as **realists** in contrast to **creationists**.

SCOPOPHILIA   Although 'visual pleasure' is a literal translation of the German *Schaulust*, Freud's English editor did not feel it sounded serious enough so translated the word as **scopophilia**. Freud explained how the gaze could provide visual pleasure by becoming erotically charged, even leading to perversion in the form of a pair of opposites, exhibitionism and voyeurism.

SEMIOTICS, SEMIOLOGY   The terms are virtually synonymous and refer to the theory or analysis of signs and sign systems.

SIGNIFIED   This refers to the meaning or concept produced from a **signifier**.

SIGNIFIER   In language **signifier** refers to the sequence of organised sounds able to yield a meaning or **signified**.

SYMBOLIC   In **semiotics** and particularly in the work of Peirce (1839–1914) a **symbolic** sign is one of three types, whose relation to its object is arbitrary rather than **iconic** or **indexical**, as for example the relation between **signifier** and **signified** in language.

SYNCHRONIC   This is one of two terms introduced by Saussure to refer to the two basic perspectives for the study of language; so **synchronic** is the state of a phenomenon as it exists at a given time in contrast to **diachronic**.

Further Reading

(1) General theory

ALTHUSSER, LOUIS *For Marx* (London: New Left Books, 1977).

— — *Lenin and Philosophy*, 2nd edn (London: New Left Books, 1977).

— — and ÉTIENNE BALIBAR *Reading Capital* (London: New Left Books, 1975).

BARTHES, ROLAND *Writing Degree Zero* (London: Cape, 1967)

— — *Mythologies* (London: Cape, 1972).

— — *S/Z* (London: Cape, 1975).

— — *Image-Music-Text* (London: Fontana/Collins, 1977).

BENVENISTE, EMILE *Problems in General Linguistics* (Coral Gables: University of Miami Press, 1971).

BENJAMIN, WALTER 'The Work of Art in the Age of Mechanical Reproduction' in *Illuminations* (London: Fontana/Collins, 1973).

BRECHT, BERTOLT *Brecht on Theatre*, ed. John Willett (London: Methuen, 1964).

BRYSON, NORMAN *Vision and Painting: the Logic of the Gaze* (London: Macmillan, 1983).

DERRIDA, JACQUES *Of Grammatology* (Baltimore: Johns Hopkins University Press, 1976).

ECO, UMBERTO *A Theory of Semiotics* (London: Macmillan, 1977).

FOUCAULT, MICHEL *The History of Sexuality 1 : 'An Introduction'* (Harmondworth: Penguin, 1981).

HIRST, PAUL 'Althusser and the Theory of Ideology' in *Law and Ideology* (London: Macmillan, 1979), pp. 40–74.

JAMESON, FREDRIC *The Political Unconscious: Narrative as Socially Symbolic Act* (Ithaca: Cornell University Press, 1981).

KRISTEVA, JULIA *Revolution in Poetic Language* (New York: Columbia University Press, 1984).

— — 'Signifying Practice and Mode of Production', *Edinburgh '76 Magazine* (1976): 60–76.

LACAN, JACQUES *Écrits: A Selection*, trans. Alan Sheridan (London: Tavistock, 1977).

— — *The Four Fundamental Concepts of Psycho-Analysis* (London: Hogarth Press, 1977).

— — *Feminine Sexuality: Jacques Lacan and the École Freudienne* (London: Macmillan, 1982).

MACHEREY, PIERRE *A Theory of Literary Production* (London: Routledge and Kegan Paul, 1978).

MITCHELL, JULIET *Psychoanalysis and Feminism* (London: Allen Lane, 1974).

SAUSSURE, FERDINAND DE *Course in General Linguistics* (New York: Philosophical Library, 1959).

(2) Classic film theory

ARNHEIM, RUDOLF *Film as Art* (*Film*, 1933) (London: Faber, 1958).

BALAZS, BÉLA *Theory of the Film: Character and Growth of a New Art* (London: Dobson, 1952).

BAZIN, ANDRÉ *What is Cinema?* 2 vols (Berkeley: University of California Press, 1967 and 1971).

EISENSTEIN, SERGEI *Film Form: Essays in Film Theory* (London: Dobson, 1963).

KRACAUER, SIEGFRIED *From Caligari to Hitler: A Psychological History of the German Film* (Princeton: Princeton University Press, 1947).

(3) Film theory (general)

ALVARADO, MANUEL and JOHN O. THOMPSON *The Media Reader* (London: BFI, 1990).

ANDREW, DUDLEY *The Major Film Theories: An Introduction* (New York: Oxford University Press, 1976).

— — *Concepts in Film Theory* (New York: Oxford University Press, 1984).

BENNETT, TONY, SUSAN BOYD-BOWMAN, COLIN MERCER and JANET WOOLLACOTT (eds) *Popular Film and Television* (London: BFI/Open University Press, 1981).

BORDWELL, DAVID *Narration in the Fiction Film* (London: Methuen, 1985).

BORDWELL, DAVID, JANET STAIGER and KRISTIN THOMPSON *The Classical Hollywood Cinema: Film Style and Mode of Production to 1960* (London: Routledge and Kegan Paul, 1985).

BRANIGAN, EDWARD *Narrative Comprehension and Film* (London and New York: Routledge, 1992).

BURCH, NOEL *Theory of Film Practice* (New York: Praeger, 1973).

BURGOYNE, ROBERT, SANDY FLITTERMAN -LEWIS and ROBERT STAM *New Vocabularies in Film Semiotics: Structuralism, Post-Structuralism and Beyond* (London and New York: Routledge, 1992).

CAVELL, STANLEY *The World Viewed: Reflections on the Ontology of Film* (Cambridge, Mass.: Harvard University Press, 1979).

COOK, PAM (ed.), *The Cinema Book* (London: BFI, 1985).

COWARD, ROSALIND and JOHN ELLIS *Language and Materialism: Developments in Semiology and the Theory of the Signifier* (London: Routledge and Kegan Paul, 1977).

EASTHOPE, ANTONY 'Film Theory' in *British Post-Structuralism: Since 1968* (London: Routledge, 1988), pp. 34–70.

ELLIS, JOHN *Visible Fictions: Cinema, Television, Video* (London: Routledge and Kegan Paul, 1982).

GIDAL, PETER *Materialist Film* (London: Routledge, 1989).

HARVEY, SYLVIA *May '68 and Film Culture* (London: BFI, 1978).

HEATH, STEPHEN *Questions of Cinema* (London: Macmillan, 1981).

JAMESON, FREDRIC *Signatures of the Visible* (London: Routledge, 1991).

KAPLAN, ANN E. (ed.) *Psychoanalysis and Cinema* (London: Routledge, 1990).

LAPSLEY, ROB and MICHAEL WESTLAKE *Film Theory: An Introduction* (Manchester: Manchester University Press, 1988).

MACCABE, COLIN *Theoretical Essays* (Manchester: Manchester University Press, 1985).

METZ, CHRISTIAN *Language and Cinema* (The Hague: Mouton, 1974).

– – *Film Language: A Semiotics of Cinema* (New York: Oxford University Press, 1974).

– – *Psychoanalysis and Cinema: The Imaginary Signifier* (London: Macmillan, 1982).

NICHOLS, BILL (ed.) *Movies and Methods: An Anthology II* (Berkeley: University of California Press, 1985).

PENLEY, CONSTANCE *The Future of an Illusion: Film, Feminism and Psychoanalysis* (Minneapolis: University of Minnesota Press, 1989).

RODOWICK, DAVID *The Difficulty of Difference: Psychoanalysis, Sexual Difference and Film Theory* (London: Routledge, 1991).

Screen Reader I: Cinema/Idealogy/Politics (London: Society for Education in Film and Television, 1977).

Screen Reader II: Cinema and Semiotics (London: BFI, 1982).

WOLLEN, PETER *Signs and Meaning in the Cinema*, 3rd edn (London: Secker and Warburg/BFI, 1972).

(4) Film theory and gender

ADAMS, PARVEEN and ELIZABETH COWIE (eds) *The Woman in Question* (London: Verso, 1990).

COWIE, ELIZABETH 'Fantasia' in *The Woman in Question* (ed. Parveen Adams and Elizabeth Cowie) (London: Verso, 1990), pp. 149–96.

DE LAURETIS, TERESA *Alice Doesn't: Feminism, Semiotics, Cinema* (London: Macmillan, 1984).

DOANE, MARY A. *The Desire to Desire: The Woman's Film of the 1940s* (Bloomington: Indiana University Press, 1987).

— —, PATRICIA MELLENCAMP AND LINDA WILLAMS (eds) *Re-Vision: Essay in Feminist Criticism* (Los Angeles: American Film Institute, 1984).

DYER, RICHARD *Gays and Film* (London: BFI, 1979).

FLITTERMAN, SANDY 'Women, Desire, and the Look: Feminism and the Enunciative Apparatus in Cinema', *Ciné-Tracts*, **2**: 1 (1978): 63–8.

HEATH, STEPHEN 'Difference', *Screen*, **19**: 3 (Autumn 1978): 50–112.

JOHNSTON, CLAIRE, *Notes on Women's Cinema, Screen*, Pamphlet 2 (London: Society for Education in Film and Television, 1973).

— — 'The Subject of Feminist Film Theory/Practice', *Screen*, **21**: 2 (Summer 1980): 27–34.

KAPLAN, ANN E. (ed.) *Women in Film Noir* (London: BFI, 1978).

— — *Women and Film: Both Sides of the Camera* (London: Methuen, 1983).

KUHN, ANNETTE *Women's Pictures: Feminism and Cinema* (London: Routledge and Kegan Paul, 1982).

MODLESKI, TANIA *The Women Who Knew Too Much: Hitchcock and Feminist Theory* (London: Routledge, 1988).

MULVEY, LAURA *Visual and Other Pleasures* (London: Macmillan, 1989).

PENLEY, CONSTANCE (ed.) *Feminism and Film Theory* (London: BFI, 1988).

ROSE, JACQUELINE *Sexuality in the Field of Vision* (London: Verso, 1986).

SILVERMAN, KAJA *The Subject of Semiotics* (New York: Oxford University Press, 1983).

(5) Specific studies

BENNETT, TONY and JANET WOOLLACOTT *Bond and Beyond* (London: Macmillan, 1987).

CAUGHIE, JOHN (ed.) *Theories of Authorship* (London: Routledge and Kegan Paul, 1981).

DYER, RICHARD *Stars* (London: BFI, 1978).

EDITORS of *Cahiers du Cinema 'Young Mr Lincoln'*, *Screen*, **13**: 3 (Autumn 1972): 5–44.

HEATH, STEPHEN 'The Work of Christian Metz', *Screen*, **14**: 3 (Autumn 1973): 5–28.

— — 'Welles's *Touch of Evil*', *Screen*, **16**: 1 (Spring 1975): 7–77.

NEALE, STEPHEN *Genre* (London: BFI, 1980).

MACCABE, COLIN *Godard: Images, Sounds, Politics* (London: BFI, 1980).

THOMPSON, JOHN O. 'Screen Acting and the Commutation Test', *Screen*, **19**: 2 (Summer 1978): 55–69.

WILLIAMS, CHRISTOPHER (ed.) *Realism and the Cinema: A Reader* (London: Routledge and Kegan Paul, 1980).

WOLLEN, PETER 'Counter-Cinema: *Vent d'Est'* in *Readings and Writings: Semiotic Counter Strategies* (London: Verso, 1982).

(6) Counter-currents

BRITTON, ANDREW 'The Ideology of *Screen*: Althusser, Lacan, Barthes', *Movie*, **26** (Winter 1978/79): 2–28.

CADBURY, WILLIAM and LELAND POAGUE *Film Criticism: A Counter Theory* (Ames: Iowa State University Press, 1983).

CARROLL, NOEL *Philosophical Problems of Classical Film Theory* (Princeton: Princeton University Press, 1988).

— — 'Address to the Heathen', *October*, **23** (Winter 1982): 89–163.

HALL, STUART 'Recent Developments in Theories of Language and Ideology: A Critical Note' in S. Hall, D. Hobson, A. Lowe and P. Willis (eds) *Culture, Media, Language* (London: Hutchinson, 1980).

HENDERSON, BRIAN *A Critique of Film Theory* (New York: Dutton, 1980).

LOVELL, TERRY *Pictures of Reality: Aesthetics, Politics, and Pleasure* (London: BFI, 1980).

McDONNELL, KEVIN and KEVIN ROBINS 'Marxist Cultural Theory: the Althusserian Smokescreen' in S. Clarke, T. Lovell, K. McDonnell, K. Robins and V.J. Seidler (eds) *One-Dimensional Marxism: Althusser and the Politics of Culture* (London: Allison and Busby, 1980).

WILLEMEN, PAUL 'Notes on Subjectivity', *Screen* **19**: 1 (Spring 1978): 41–69.

— — 'Remarks on *Screen*', *Southern Review* (Adelaide), **16**: 2 (July 1983): 292–311.

(7) Journals

After Image

Cahiers du Cinema

Camera Obscura

Ciné-Tracts

Jump Cut

Film Comment

Film Criticism

Film Reader

Framework
m/f
Movie
Screen
Screen Education
The Velvet Light Trap
Wide Angle

Index

List of Films